THE NEW
EQUALITY

NAT HENTOFF

THE VIKING PRESS

NEW YORK

ORIGINALLY PUBLISHED IN 1964
NEW EDITION WITH ADDITIONAL MATERIAL ISSUED IN 1965 IN A
VIKING COMPASS EDITION
BY THE VIKING PRESS, INC., 625 MADISON AVENUE, NEW YORK, N.Y. 10022
FOURTH PRINTING AUGUST 1968
PUBLISHED SIMULTANEOUSLY IN CANADA BY
THE MACMILLAN COMPANY OF CANADA LIMITED

LIBRARY OF CONGRESS CATALOG CARD NUMBER: 64-20500
FOR THIS NEW EDITION THE AUTHOR HAS SUPPLIED ENDNOTES TO THE PRO-
LOGUE AND TO CHAPTERS 3, 5, 7, 8, 9, AND 12, AND A NEW EPILOGUE.

FOR BAYARD RUSTIN

Contents

THE NEW
EQUALITY

Prologue

In early February 1964 the first session of a unique Leadership Training Institute for Civil Rights Activists took place in Nyack, New York. The student body consisted of twenty-five of the most militant members of CORE (the Congress of Racial Equality) in New York and four equally committed youngsters from HARYOU (Harlem Youth Opportunities Unlimited). Nearly all were in their late teens or early twenties, and twenty-two were Negro.

The Leadership Training Institute was under the auspices of the League for Industrial Democracy, a fifty-nine-year-old educational organization composed of civil libertarians, labor officials, academicians, churchmen, and free-lance intellectuals. The league describes itself as "dedicated to increasing democracy in our economic, political and cultural life."

The idea of the institute itself, however, had come partly from Bayard Rustin, for many years a leading behind-the-scenes strategist for civil rights organizations and only recently a public figure on his own—first as deputy director of the March on Washington for Jobs and Freedom in August 1963, and later as the actual organizer of the successful February 3 boycott of the New York City public schools, an action to protest *de facto* segregation in those schools.

Rustin had been increasingly concerned with a major deficiency in "the movement," as the thrust for full equality is called by its participants. While there had been no lack of courage to demonstrate and to engage in other forms of nonviolent direct action, "the movement" had yet to formulate a clear set of goals—and means of achieving them—beyond civil rights.

In November 1963 Rustin had spoken at the fourth annual conference in Washington of the Student Nonviolent Coordinating Committee. He told those battle-seasoned activists, "Heroism and the ability to go to jail should not be substituted for an over-all social and political reform program that will not only help the Negroes but will help all Americans. Only then can we win." Rustin's advice to the SNCC field workers, therefore, was, "Study. Read. Understand the social changes which must take place if there are to be integrated schools and jobs."

The students involved in the training institute at Nyack were to be in the vanguard of this new genre of post-civil-rights activity, although they also fully intended to continue using direct action techniques between classes to cope with the sizable body of unfinished work in the civil rights field itself.

The Leadership Training Institute was scheduled for five nonconsecutive weekends through mid-April, after which other such institutes were to be started elsewhere in the country. While a general curriculum plan had been coordinated by Martin Fleisher, a thirty-eight-year-old Assistant Professor of Political Science at Brooklyn College, the faculty realized that the plan might have to be changed, depending on the students' reactions and needs as these were made known during the experiment.

At eight o'clock on Saturday morning, February 8, I met the student body and several faculty members in front of the Hotel Theresa in Harlem to wait for a bus which would take us to the site of the institute—Shadowcliff, the national headquarters and conference center of the Fellowship of Reconciliation, a nondenominational pacifist organization which has long been active in civil rights work. (Both Bayard Rustin and James Farmer, national director of CORE, are former staff members of the FOR, and Dr. Martin Luther King is on its National Advisory Council.)

Although a few of the weekend students were attending college in New York, most were either unemployed or in routine jobs which were secondary to what they considered to be their primary work in the movement. As they found places in the bus one of them, a somber young man, immediately became absorbed in a book, *The Ruins of Empire*. "Omar," a friend across the aisle asked him, "what did you think of Kenyatta and all them cats calling in the British troops to keep things in order?"

"I'll tell you later," said Omar, returning to his book.

"Okay, my man, but I tell you, I didn't dig it."

"I didn't either," Omar answered grimly.

We were passing a dreary row of tenements at 138th Street and Lenox Avenue when a voice boomed from the back of the bus, "We'll be arriving in Jackson, Mississippi, in one hour!"

Amid the laughter, one of the young recruits muttered as he looked out the window, "Back to the old block."

"It takes a lot of guts to go down to Mississippi," said a Negro girl beside him.

"It takes more to live here," he answered.

Soon the inevitable freedom songs began, accompanied by hand-clapping, shouts, and laughter, as when one huge Negro, whose name I later learned to be Joe Louis, began to sing "Nobody Knows the Trouble I've Seen" and interpolated, "It ain't over yet."

Encouraged, Louis began to improvise a blues while the others punctuated his lines with, "Yes, Lord!"

> "Every morning finds me moaning,
> I'm tired of singing these blues.
> It's a losing gamble for me,
> I'm tired of this moaning."

"What key are you in, Joe?" a girl asked.

"Key?" Louis laughed. "Baby, that's natural singing. I don't know any keys."

Louis moved into a harsh, preacher-like chant, his sermon focusing on the state of the blacks in South Africa. It spiraled to a roaring climax:

> "One of these days *we* will have a
> revolutionary army and ride across
> the water and take back our land.
> Are you with me, brethren?"

There were scattered shouts of "Yes!" and more laughing as Joe Louis and two colleagues rushed down the aisle, mimicking church members taking up a collection.

Back in his seat, Louis called out, "Anybody want to go to Angola? We can get our revolutionary training there."

Another youth picked up the idea, singing, "Angola, here we come," and others responded, "Right back where we started from."

In an hour we had arrived at Shadowcliff, a large rambling house set on spacious grounds overlooking the Hudson River. Joe Louis got off the bus, paused to survey the scene, and said as he swaggered into the house, "Yes, I've got seven hundred darkies out there."

The morning was to begin with a lecture, followed by questions, and then the students were to be divided into four workshops, each headed by a member of the faculty. As the youngsters were being shown their rooms, I talked with Vera Rony, national secretary of the Workers Defense League, a civil libertarian group which is informally allied with the League for Industrial Democracy.

Miss Rony, an energetic, irrepressibly optimistic woman in her late thirties, was restless with expectancy. "A lot can come of this," she said. "It's amazing that it's taken so long to start something like it. We've been meeting with some of these kids to get their ideas of how the institute should work, and basic tools are what they fundamentally want. One of them, for example, asked me, 'Where does Bayard Rustin get all those *facts* he uses in his arguments?' Well, that's one of the things we can do here. We can show them where they can find the facts; we can show them how to use journals and how to read an article without accepting it all just because it's in print. These kids are very bright, but so far many of them have gone by ear. They don't read enough. They don't think their opinions through."

Martin Fleisher, an ebullient man who is quick with laughter and argument, joined the conversation. "We have to get them into the habit of making scientific observations of what the problems are," he said, "but it's very hard to persuade them to do that when they're so involved and so militant. Today we're going to start with a history of the civil rights movement —all the way back—so that we can begin with something in which we know they're interested."

At eleven-thirty all the students assembled in Shadowcliff's sunny first-floor conference room. Norman Hill, national program director of CORE, rose to start the institute. Hill, a slight Negro in his early thirties, had obviously long since won the youngsters' respect. Many had worked with him in demonstrations and they knew of the extraordinarily long hours he puts into the movement. During the past two years, in fact, weariness has become an integral part of Hill's bearing. This morning too his face was slack with fatigue. He had come to Shadowcliff after a lengthy meeting in New York the previous night to decide whether a second school boycott should be called, and he was due back in the city at midnight for another meeting on the same subject.

"I've been given," Hill began softly, "the peculiar task of introducing you to your own institute. This is something *you* wanted and helped us put together to make the movement more effective. The movement is making demands on us to be more disciplined, to be able to anticipate, not just react.

"Our problem," he said with the beginning of a smile, "is that we've not had enough people who were both angry *and* smart. Here we hope you'll get an understanding of the tools which can help you make the decisions we now have to make in the movement. Not only is the society in trouble but the movement is too. And we don't have much time."

Hill turned the chair over to Preston Wilcox, an assistant professor at the Columbia University School of Social Work. A tall, wiry Negro with an easy air of command, Wilcox is an expert at organizing low-income communities to act for themselves to bring about social change, and he formerly headed a project in that vein in East Harlem. Wilcox emphasized the seriousness of the occasion and then introduced August Meier, a white professor of history at Morgan State College, a Negro school in Baltimore.

Meier, brisk, cool, and authoritative, rattled through a history of Negro protest movements from slavery to the New Deal. The students listened intently, some taking notes, some formulating questions for Meier, and others simply staring at him. At one point Meier asked, "Do I have to explain sharecropping?" One of the youngest in the class said, "I'd like it if you would," and Meier described the system.

At a later stage of his lecture Meier asked how many knew of William Du Bois. Half the students raised their hands. "You're better informed than my classes are," Meier observed.

"He teach in a Negro school?" a youngster from Harlem whispered.

"Yeah," said another. "Surprising, isn't it?"

"I'm not surprised," the first boy noted impassively.

The question period following Professor Meier's formal talk turned into an impasse between him and several of the students, who insisted that economics was at the root of race prejudice. "You can't explain segregation," said a CORE member from East Harlem, "unless you point out that a 'nigger' is needed to keep up the capitalistic system."

Meier replied that he was not an economic determinist and that other factors besides economics were involved in prejudice. "There are people," he pointed out, "who need someone to feel superior to in order to hide their own feelings of inadequacy, and once these attitudes are engendered, they may exist when there is no external reason—economic or otherwise—for prejudice. Their kids get trained that way. Members of minority groups, for one example, because they do feel inadequate, are apt to be more prejudiced against other minorities than the majority is."

"Yeah," said Joe Louis, slouched in a chair in the last row, "like the Puerto Ricans and us."

"I can see," Vera Rony was whispering to Martin Fleisher,

"that we really ought to have a psychologist on the faculty." Fleisher nodded in agreement.

The questioning over, a list was read—accompanied by an obbligato of mock groans—of those who were assigned to kitchen detail for lunch and dinner. The four workshops then began to form in separate rooms. In charge of them were Fleisher; Wilcox; Robert Koblitz, a Professor of Political Science at Bard College; and Harry Fleischman, Director of the American Jewish Committee's National Labor Service and Chairman of the League for Industrial Democracy's Executive Committee.

As I circulated among the workshops, it was evident that the students were less interested in the pre-Civil-War history of Negro protest ("We knew all that before we came here," Joe Louis asserted) than in the implications to the movement of the events of the past few decades. Professor Koblitz's group began to explore the difficulties labor had in organizing workers in the South following the Second World War.

Vera Rony, who was sitting in at that session and had formerly worked in the labor movement, explained the ways in which Southern employers had played on the anti-Negro feelings of white workers to block the unions.

"I understand that," Joe Louis interrupted, "but it comes down to the fact that *economic* conditions were so bad for the white workers to start with that they had to feel superior to someone. You see, it *is* economic at base."

"Economics is a prime factor," said a bearded Negro leader of East River CORE, "but there are others. There ain't anything that easy."

In another workshop a slim, intense, soft-voiced member of HARYOU was trying to explain his objections to capitalism. "What I'm saying"—he spoke very slowly—"is that the ghetto is there because there's an economic need for it to be there. Capitalism is based on having a group you can exploit, and so long as you keep that lower class stabilized, you can go on exploiting the white as well as the black poor by encouraging the whites to use up their energies to keep the 'niggers' down.

"The way they keep *us* down," he continued, "is the way they educate us. It's no accident that Negro kids don't learn to read and write well. We're being directed to the lowest kind of work. That's why I'm not so much concerned with integrating the schools as I am with changing the curriculum and the teachers we get in the ghetto. We need teachers who can help us find out who *we* are and what we're capable of doing."

"I know what you're saying, Roy," Preston Wilcox broke in. "When I was in high school I did everything. I made the honor roll and the football and basketball teams. But not *one* teacher encouraged me to go to college. As I think back on it, they were friendly enough toward me personally. Some even lent me money when I needed it. But they never thought of me as college material. A couple of weeks ago I got a letter from one of those teachers, congratulating me on having been made a professor at the Columbia School of Social Work; but that woman doesn't know yet that I achieved it in spite of her. She's still unaware of what *she* failed to do."

"Right," said Roy. "I want my child *educated*. If integration means putting whites and blacks together but still teaching the blacks as if they can't learn what the whites can, I don't need that kind of integration. Sure, social experience between white and black is a wonderful thing to learn, but by itself integration doesn't fill my child's basic needs. The way it is now, black kids, whether they're in integrated schools or not, are being drained of their motivating forces. They become the 'niggers' the whites tell them they are."

"But," said a white girl who teaches school in New York and had participated in the February 3 boycott, "even if you do give a black child a sense of himself, he still has to cope with the white world outside the ghetto. If the society isn't changed, he'll still get frustrated out there and maybe fall apart."

Roy shook his head. "He'll fall apart twice as fast if he doesn't get that strength while he's still in school. That's what I'm talking about."

"But what if you had integration *and* the kind of curriculum and teachers you want?" the teacher asked.

"Oh, sure," said Roy. "That would make the most sense. All I'm saying is that if I have to choose just between physical integration and real education for my child as to who *he* is, I want the education. You suppose they're going to put up the money to do *both*?"

In a third workshop Harry Fleischman, a stocky, amiable man, was trying to counter the thesis that economics was the only cause of prejudice. His chief opponent was Blyden Jackson, who was one of the least formally educated of the students. A vigorous, handsome Negro in his late twenties, Jackson had dropped out of school in the eighth grade and now worked as a messenger when he wasn't involved in civil rights activities. Jackson, I had been told by an executive of CORE, has proved to be one of the most charismatic natural leaders among the lower-class Negroes who have been coming into civil rights work in increasing numbers during recent years. "He's got it," the CORE official had said, "if he can discipline himself and learn to organize as well as fight."

"Look at the unions," Fleischman was saying, "in which apprenticeship training programs are closed to everyone but the children and relatives of those already in the union. That's prejudice against other whites as well as against Negroes."

"Wait," said Jackson. "That kind of closed circle comes from having a system in which we go from boom to depression in fairly regular cycles. So you get unions afraid of unemployment, and therefore they want to keep as much of the pie to themselves as they can. If we had full employment and if that full employment was permanent, they wouldn't be afraid and they'd open up the apprenticeships."

"Nah." A Negro in blue denim shirt and pants spoke out. "The guys on the left are always talking about economics and getting together and we'll all walk into the valley of success. I can't hear that noise any more. There's something *more* than economics. I've fought whites too long to have any faith that if all of us are working, they're going to be any less of a drag."

I moved on to Martin Fleisher's workshop. The subject there was how to develop leaders among the masses in Harlem. "Now Malcolm X," said a boy from central Harlem, "showed one way to get a movement going. But how else can you do it—besides using hatred?"

"First of all," a friend of his from the same neighborhood answered, "that's no movement. A movement is something that moves. A restaurant, a factory, and some mosques ain't a movement. To do it the right way you've got to get an intellectual group working in the ghetto to show the people how they can organize and use their power."

"Yeah, but how does that intellectual group get recognized as leaders by the black community?"

"You can't stand on a pedestal," his friend emphasized. "You have to show results. Now Jesse Gray, now that he's got that rent strike moving, people know him and they'll work with him if he goes on to other bread-and-butter issues."

"But all this is inside the ghetto," a Negro girl from East River CORE objected. "We have to break out by forming alliances with whites."

"Look," said the admirer of Jesse Gray, "we're in the ghetto now, and the ghetto is increasing. Before you can break out, you've got to use the power that being crowded together in the ghetto gives you. That's where the strongest potential for action *now* is."

"It sure is only a potential," said the girl. "We got all those numbers in New York, but look at the jobs we get."

At lunch a white civil rights worker who had helped set up the institute was telling of the seven weeks she had recently spent in Jackson, Mississippi, working with CORE, the Student Non-violent Coordinating Committee and other actionists. "The kids down there need something like this too," she said. "For three years they've been going all over the country there like cowboys, dodging bullets. Sure, they're brave, but they have to learn how to be an organization, how to plan.

"I tell you"—her voice sharpened—"aside from the disorganization, I found out how hard it is for a white to work in Mississippi. Those kids don't want you if you're competent. They're learning to be men and to be competent by themselves, and they resent a white person who can get things done."

Norman Hill, who was sitting opposite her, smiled wryly. "There is a place for a white actionist in Mississippi," he said, "if he's inadequate." Hill was silent for a few moments. He looked around the room. "I hope this works. We need leaders badly, all down the line. The masses are ready to move, but the movement is fragmentized. We need people to give it cohesion, to formulate plans. And there's not all that much time."

At another table Harry Fleischman was telling Vera Rony, "They have done some reading, but it all comes out in an odd combination of jargon and idiom. Freud and cats in the same sentence."

"No," Robert Koblitz, the professor from Bard College, said to Joe Louis as they walked into the dining room, "I don't want you to change your ideas. I simply want you to sharpen them."

Koblitz sat down alongside Fleischman. "They need to know so much more," he said. "Economics to them is making a living. Power structure is a slogan, a phrase. They don't understand the complexity of how power actually operates. But they *are* in contact with reality. The ground under their feet is firm. I only wish I had classes like this all the time. They have a real sense of themselves. They're not neurotic and they're not insular."

After lunch Professor Meier continued his history of Negro protest movements, bringing it up to the present. Toward the end of his lecture he disturbed his audience by counseling the movement not to enter partisan politics. "Political action," Meier warned, "is very dangerous. In order to stay elected, you have to compromise."

The girl who had worked in Mississippi had difficulty containing her anger as she rose to challenge Meier. "The danger of compromise," she said bitingly, "is already present in the civil rights movement—partisan politics aside. Furthermore, at some point you *have* to get into politics. In the South, Snick [the Student Nonviolent Coordinating Committee] has found out that you can integrate just so many restaurants before you have to start thinking of how to change the sheriff, the state representatives and senators, and so on. Already, in the best organized Snick areas, they're running or planning to run candidates. The possibilities of compromise exist all over. The primary question now is how you build power."

Professor Meier had also emphasized that the current lack of unity among civil rights groups was to be encouraged rather than deplored, since competition has beneficial effects.

"That"—the white girl continued her attack—"sounds like a fund-raiser's device. Disunity is one of the most horrifying factors in the movement today. CORE wants to pull out of Mississippi because Snick is getting all the credit there. We compromised our March on Washington program because Snick, CORE, and the Southern Christian Leadership Conference had to give in partially to the more conservative NAACP and Urban League. And look at what disunity is doing in New York now to the coalition that made the school boycott work! It's unity we need, not competition."

In Preston Wilcox's workshop that afternoon, Velma Hill, Norman Hill's wife, herself on CORE's staff, was explaining the differences of philosophy within that organization. "Some feel the Negro can be integrated into the present society as it is, and others say you have to change that society for the Negro to really have opportunity to be equal. Those who feel the second way claim it doesn't matter whether Eisenhower or Kennedy or Johnson is in, so long as the structure of our institutions remains the same."

"I'm just marking time, baby," the Negro youngster in the blue denim shirt and pants drawled. "I'll use them all until we can get power of our own."

"It has nothing to do with personality." Blyden Jackson got to his feet. "You could have Jesus Christ in office and if you left the social and economic system the way it is—you know, everyone competing for status and for profit—he couldn't help us. You've got to change the basic values of society. And in the movement we've got to have leaders who know this."

"Who is such a leader today?" Wilcox asked.

"Wilkins isn't and Whitney Young isn't," Jackson answered. "James Farmer tends to be, but it's his secondary leadership in CORE that really knows what's happening. I'd say the kinds of leaders I mean are A. Philip Randolph, Bayard Rustin, and Norm Hill. They understand what has to be done.

"Look." Jackson began to speak more slowly. "Velma said there were two choices. There are three if you're a black man who wants to do something. You can be a reformist within the existing social order—you know, like the NAACP and the white liberal. You can get frustrated and say let's go back to Africa or join some black nationalist movement. Or you can try to create a new social order. Take automation. You can't stop it, but you can try to figure out a way of social planning by the government so that people thrown out of work by automation have a chance to make a decent living. The government *has* to take a much more active role in planning the national economy."

"Yeah," said Richard, one of the youngest of the students and one of the quietest so far, "and our job is to convince all those twenty million black men out there that the present system can't work."

"Just a minute." Preston Wilcox held up his hand. "Velma, what specifically is CORE's strategy beyond civil rights?"

"There is no CORE program in that sense," she answered. "That's why we're here. There are varying opinions, but that's as far as we've gotten."

"So at least we can agree on that." Wilcox smiled. "You have no position."

"We can also agree," Jackson said tartly, "that we *need* one. How can you rally people without a program?"

"But," Wilcox suggested, "you may need a different strategy in Mississippi, let's say, from in New York."

"Different tactics, yes," Jackson answered impatiently, "but not a different philosophy. Look, I'm not talking about overthrowing the government, but I am against the usual reformist approach. All along the white liberals talk about changing things a little bit here and a little bit there to keep us from storming out of Harlem and out of the South Side in Chicago. So long as they can get away with reformist answers, they'll do it. The role of CORE—and of the movement as a whole—is to get at basic problems, and that means a program for basic change. Of course we need white allies, but we can't let any allies we do get force us to accept reformist solutions. And above all, CORE has *got* to get into politics—as soon and as strongly as possible."

"What do you mean exactly by reformist solutions?" Wilcox asked.

"Well," said Blyden, "increasing unemployment benefits, for example, instead of having a massive federal public works program."

Richard sighed heavily. "I still say there is that whole other problem of how you're going to reach the black masses. Me being black, a lot of us being black, we get to know that life is a little precarious. So we get in a certain groove. People find a little thing they can hang on to, and they *hang*, baby. They say, 'I've got a little hustle, a job, and I'*m* all right, baby.' So we're all at sea, each by himself, and all them sharks are out there. All them white sharks. Me, I'm not content with just hanging on. I'm selfish. I want a lot more. But how am I going to convince those others to get together because there's a better way to survive?"

"That's also why we're here," said Velma Hill, "to find out what power is, how it works, how to organize people to get it."

A discussion of "reformist" as contrasted with "radical" solutions was also taking place in Martin Fleisher's workshop.

"What you want"—Fleisher was addressing Roy, the youngster from HARYOU who had been emphasizing to Wilcox during the morning that physical integration of the schools was not enough, "is a truly integrated society in which every human being is respected for himself."

"But," a CORE member interrupted, "that won't happen. That's not human nature."

Fleisher struck the side of his head with his right hand. "What a supreme irony! You complain about stereotypes of the Negro, and you use a stereotype like this—that there's a constant 'human nature' that is fixed for all time."

Omar, the unsmiling young man who had been reading *The Ruins of Empire* on the way to Shadowcliff, boomed out in a Paul Robeson-like voice, "Maybe not for all time, but you cannot underestimate how long it's going to take to change something like the division between the races. I'm in a room here with three white people, but I'm not *really* in a room with three white people."

"You're implying, then," the white schoolteacher said, "that the division is so great that hardly anything can be done. You're too negative. Why, just a couple of months ago we received a bulletin about bringing Negro history into the curriculum."

"Sure," Roy said sardonically, "Booker T. Washington."

"No." The teacher was exasperated. "It wasn't a bad plan at all."

Omar looked at her coldly. "Whether it's bad or not depends on the viewpoint of the person looking at it. I'm sure you don't have the same viewpoint of Negro history as I do."

"I'm not so sure," said the teacher.

"I am," Omar replied.

"Yeah," Roy said with a smile, "yours is Negro superiority."

Omar frowned. "No, it is not."

"I was just kidding," Roy said hastily. "What this is really about is that so *much* education is needed on both sides. Do you think all the black kids who stayed out for the boycott knew what it was all about? My little sister came in the house and said, 'Mommy, we had a boycott today. When we gonna have a girlcott?'"

There was some laughter, but Omar was not amused.

Fleisher turned to Roy. "I'd like to know more specifically how you define the kind of integration that makes sense to you."

"Economics," Roy started, "is such a tremendous part of it. I can't be equal to you if you're making a hundred thousand dollars a year and I'm making only five thousand. Even the right kind of education in the schools isn't enough. We've got to have a redistribution of income."

"You're recommending socialism, then," said Fleisher.

There was a pause, and Roy leaned forward. "I don't know anything about socialism."

"But you said capitalism doesn't work."

"Look, I don't know a damn thing about capitalism and less about socialism. I think there are things wrong with the capitalistic system and I think there are assets in the socialist system, but for me to say I *understand* either would be idiotic. Right now I'm in the process of learning. I have to be honest with myself and say I don't know when I don't know. I don't know in theory and I don't know the consequences of any action I might recommend."

"The truth of the damn matter," said Fleisher, "is you *never* know all the factors in any situation. You can never predict the consequences of any action you take. You start the ball rolling, but you never know what all the results are going to be. Now, that's not an excuse for ignorance. You're here to gather as much information and as much ability to analyze that information as you can. I just want to point out there are no utterly predictable solutions."

"I know." Roy suddenly seemed tired. "Suppose I was in a position of influence right now. I'd hate it. I wouldn't want to be able to control the destinies of people, because I don't really know what should be done. But if my doing nothing would be more harmful than doing something, then I'd sit down and try."

"You'll always be in that position, Roy," said Fleisher.

In a corner a Negro girl and a white girl were still talking about the division between the races. "I've been in the movement in North Carolina," said the Negro, "and there were whites in it too. We got arrested together and we were beaten together, but we were still divided because there was no real understanding between us."

"Are you for black nationalism, then?" asked the white girl.

"No, I'm not. I'm just telling you how things are. Even in the cell, the whites were at one end of the cell and we were at the other end."

Roy had come over and was listening. "What," he asked the white girl, "motivates whites to identify with the Negro?"

"Well, I mean, we're all human beings."

"My feeling," said the Negro girl, "is that most who try to come with us are outcasts from their own society."

"I don't really know the answer to my question," Roy said. "But for whatever reasons they come, I'm not optimistic that there'll be enough of them for a long time. You know one real answer to what must be done? We've got to make change by ourselves, in our own communities. That's what HARYOU is doing—getting the community itself organized to make social change. We're even getting Muslims into it. In that direction, I do see good things ahead. And we'll also go into politics from that base. I don't know but what the NAACP and CORE aren't already obsolete."

"Is there no place for white people?" the white girl asked.

"No," said Roy. "Not unless you live in Harlem. Look, the kids I'm working with, they're only going to identify with people who live in the same ghetto they do, who have the same problems they have. Only people like us can organize them. We've already divided Harlem into ten basic districts, with a coordinator for each. And then each block has its indigenous captain. He contacts his friends in the various apartments, and then we have house captains. When we really establish this kind of organization throughout the community, can you conceive of the things we can do? But to do this, to get everyone involved"—he looked at the white girl—"you have to get these people to appreciate their blackness."

In Preston Wilcox's workshop the talk had returned to the recent New York school boycott. "It's unfortunate," said

Velma Hill, "that we didn't have more whites on the streets with us. If more of the white liberals had been out there, we could have caused more damage and we could have gotten the Mayor to act."

"I agree," Blyden Jackson countered, "that we could have won a bigger victory with them, but there was an advantage to *not* having them. We set a precedent for what we could do *without* them. If they can't go along with our terms, to hell with them."

"Who is 'they'?" a Negro girl asked as she walked into the room.

Richard turned around and grinned. "Who is always they, dear? The white liberals."

The girl grimaced. "Can't you find another topic?"

"Let's be realistic," Velma Hill said to Jackson. "We have to operate with the knowledge that we need allies. That means whenever we present demands they should be demands which ought to be able to get us allies. Then, if we still don't get them, we move anyway, because most people won't get off the fence until you push them."

"Would you be more specific?" Wilcox asked.

"In the boycott," Velma Hill answered, "CORE had a very specific list of demands—even if they didn't get into the papers. We didn't ask *only* for integration. We asked for quality education for everyone. We asked for smaller classes for everyone. That's what I mean by broadening the base of our demands."

It was time for dinner, and the workshops broke up. In the evening there was dancing to jazz records and a highly informal reappraisal by the students of the day's events. The consensus was that, so far, the workshops had been more stimulating than the formal lectures.

On Sunday, Shadowcliff was not available in the morning, the conference room having been promised previously to a group of Quakers. A woman with a large house half a mile down the road had offered her living room, and the institute moved there. It was a cold morning, and Joe Louis, as he walked into the house, shook himself. "Mighty kind of the white folks," he bellowed. "They let the field hands in the house today."

The morning's lecturer, Martin Fleisher, was to talk on the theory and practice of capitalism. "Before I begin," he announced, "I can't resist telling you something I heard on the radio this morning. Bayard Rustin made a speech to an ADA group in New Jersey last night, and he said the Negro movement is over—as a Negro movement." Fleisher paused for effect. "He said it's now going to have to be a broad social movement, an alliance of all the poor, and organized labor, as well as the civil rights groups."

The students looked at him without expression. No one commented.

"Okay," said Fleisher, "as someone said in a workshop yesterday, you have to decide whether you're going to assimilate into the society as it now is or whether you're going to have to change that society. However, you can't do either until you understand how the society functions and what changes in it are possible."

For the next hour Fleisher delivered an exceptionally lucid analysis of the theory of liberal capitalism along with the changes in capitalism in practice as industrialization increased during the nineteenth and twentieth centuries. His was a much more successful lecture than Meier's. Most of the students were unfamiliar with the precise definitions and implications of such terms as "division of labor," "the means of production," "free labor market" and "private property."

As Fleisher traced the development of capitalism and the rise of organized labor within the system, the students listened with mounting absorption. "Eventually," Fleisher concluded, "as more and more power was concentrated in fewer hands by capitalism, there were increasing demands by workers, small farmers, and other groups to modify the system; and that's what led to minimum-wage legislation, old-age compensation, and the like. These modifications were accomplished through political means, and in future sessions of the institute we'll discuss

—with historical examples—the nature of political power, how it's organized, and how it operates."

"Very good, very good," Joe Louis whispered. "We're finally hearing something."

At the end of the lecture Blyden Jackson raised his hand. "Marty, what you said today seems to me to prove that, whatever psychological reasons there are for race prejudice, it all comes down to who owns the means of production—and who doesn't. And yet you didn't support those of us who were saying that yesterday."

"I'm not here," Fleisher answered, "to give you any neat solutions like that. Maybe by the fifth weekend we can have a more fruitful discussion about the relationship among economic, social, and psychological forces, but we ought not discuss this on an oversimplified level. The structure of society is too complex, as you'll see, for instance, when we get a lecture from a psychologist about the authoritarian personality."

"Yes," Omar proclaimed in his deep voice, "even if the state ran everything and made sure everybody had jobs, we still wouldn't solve the problem of race relations. Look at Russia. It's still black against white there. How do we get above *this*?"

"Here we go again," Joe Louis muttered.

"I've got to say it again." Preston Wilcox intervened. "By the end of the institute, whatever answers you find, if any, will be your own. All we're trying to do is stimulate you to look at things in a creative, questioning way."

Before the students prepared for the trip back to New York, each was handed a paperback edition of Richard Hofstadter's *The American Political Tradition*. "I want you to read the first five chapters by next time," Fleisher instructed them. "And I want answers of between seven hundred and fifty and a thousand words to two of the following three questions: 1) What is liberal capitalism? 2) What is the theory of states' rights? 3) What was Jefferson's idea of democracy?"

As the faculty gathered to discuss plans for the next institute, the CORE members among the students remained in the living room to hear Blyden Jackson outline the details of a project to tie up traffic in a key section of New York City as a protest against the inferior education in East Harlem schools.

"Man," said Joe Louis appreciatively, "this is going to inconvenience a hell of a lot of people."

"Well," Blyden Jackson commented dryly, "living where we have, we've been inconvenienced all our lives. It's time for some of those whites to share our inconvenience."

Outside the living room, Martin Fleisher was telling the other faculty members, "This is the way it looks from here on. A. Philip Randolph will talk on the Reconstruction period, and then we'll have to get a specialist on the whole period of radical discontent and reform in the eighteen-eighties and nineties. Mike Harrington has said he'll give an analysis of the New Deal, and Vera is going to get someone from the labor movement to discuss the dynamics of *that* development. Now we have to figure out the lecturers we'll recruit on psychology, on automation, on urban politics, and, for the final institute, on the theory and practice of socialism, communism, and democracy. That should do it."

"Yes," Miss Rony said. "The question at the moment, however, is how many of them will come back."

A few days later, while walking along a street on the lower East Side, I met Joe Louis. I asked him how many of the students planned to return. "We'll all be back," Louis said. "We asked Vera if we could bring six or seven more, and she's working on finding the extra space up there. You know, we were hesitant to go up there for five weekends. We have a lot to do here. But Marty got to us with that lecture on capitalism. We need more basic things like that."

"For instance?" I asked.

"Like what happened to the union movement. We know labor once had an outlook like we have—you know, making basic changes in the society. But they lost it. They got all their members fat and they didn't care any more about all of the rest of us who weren't making it. I want to know how that happened. Could it have been prevented? How can the movement avoid going that way? Another thing I want to know is the real political situation in Harlem. I mean where the power is, how it's connected downtown. If we're going into politics, we have to have that kind of information."

"So all in all," I said, "you figure the institute is a good idea."

"Sure," said Louis. "But damn, it's such a small beginning. People talk about 'the movement' and we haven't hardly gotten started, not only with educating ourselves, but even in direct action. It's a hell of a thing that we're only just beginning to set up a working alliance with the movement in the South. Damn, there's so much to do."

Joe started to leave. "By the way," he said, "I've been reading that Hofstadter book. That's good stuff. We've got some questions on it for Marty, though. In fact, we've got a lot of questions for next time. I still think they don't really know who we are."

On March 6, 1964, during the early-evening rush hour in New York City, Joe Louis and six other members of East River CORE—three of them white—caused a major traffic jam on the Manhattan approach to the Triborough Bridge. They had arrived in three cars, parked them abreast across three out-of-Manhattan lanes, and had then dumped empty cans, bottles, and other garbage—to symbolize living conditions in East Harlem. The stage thus set, the seven linked arms and spread themselves across the lanes.

Some of the angrier motorists left their cars to curse the demonstrators. A number grabbed handfuls of the garbage on the ground and threw it at the seven. Meanwhile, other members of East River CORE handed out leaflets to the enraged commuters. Their message was in part:

East River CORE is engaging in civil disobedience today to protest the unsafe and overcrowded schools in East Harlem. We regret to inconvenience people passing through our neighborhood on their way home to better sections of the city, but we are both very sorry and very angry about the way Negro and Puerto Rican children are treated in the richest city and the wealthiest country in the world. . . .

East River CORE works in a community where the schools

are immensely overcrowded. Schools built to hold 500 children now hold over 1,000. Many have no auditoriums, few toilets, cracked plaster and overcrowded lunchrooms. When the children eat, they smell the garbage close by. . . .

We are asking that New York commuters stop for a moment to look at Harlem and the people they leave behind, and that they do something about this problem that is not only Harlem's but all America's.

CORE has participated in many great marches and boycotts—all useful in their time and in their way for pushing the movement for freedom and equality forward. But now it is necessary to go to the root of this problem, to organize in local communities to help make the poor visible and vocal in defense of their rights so they can no longer be ignored by America's commuters.

After traffic had been delayed for twenty minutes, the demonstrators—including Joe Louis—were arrested.

———————————

In the more than a year that has passed since the Leadership Training Institute described here, no consistent, systematic plan to continue this series or to establish similar institutes has been put into operation. The need for them, of course, is increasingly acute. Since foundation aid is unlikely, it is to be hoped that such organizations as SNCC, CORE, NAACP, the Southern Christian Leadership Conference, the Southern Student Organizing Committee, the A. Philip Randolph Institute (directed by Bayard Rustin), Students for a Democratic Society, and the Northern Student Movement will fuse resources to set up Leadership Training Institutes for ghetto youngsters, black and white, throughout the country.

ONE

1

A White Problem in America

> To hell with your love for us! To hell with your pity for us! To hell with your anger at us! We don't want nothing from you but a chance to live better than the rats that share our homes!
>
> —A Negro woman at a Harlem rally, quoted by Gordon Parks in *Life*, August 16, 1963

In the summer of 1963, as "the movement"—or "the unfinished revolution," as A. Philip Randolph calls it—spread into Northern streets, James Finn in *Commonweal* spoke for an awakening group of whites. He was discussing James Baldwin, and he complained that "Baldwin has turned the white person into the invisible man; he is not really seen as he is."

From hysterically rigid segregationists to the increasingly anxious liberals who feel they are misunderstood and undervalued by Negroes, whites in America are experiencing a double dislocation of their self-image. First came the realization that they had known practically nothing about Negroes. Most whites had never come close to imagining the complexly diverse capacities of Negroes for rage and hurt and pride. Now, gradually and bewilderedly, more and more whites are coming to feel that Negroes do not know *them*.

There are Negroes, Lorraine Hansberry for one, who deny that "the alienation is equal on both sides." Miss Hansberry has mordantly pointed out that "the employer doesn't go into the maid's house. . . . We have been washing everybody's underwear for three hundred years. We know when you're not clean." Yet whites differ in their ability to accept Miss Hansberry's précis of American race "relations." Some would protest: "However much you have seen and overheard while you yourself were invisible to us, you cannot know us as individuals because you seem to be marching indiscriminately against all of us."

A deeper level of self-dislocation has been reached by only a comparatively few whites. That stage is the realization that they themselves do not yet know how they fundamentally *feel* about Negroes; and they are beginning, with what capacities for emotional honesty they possess, to explore in pain and convoluted guilt the degree to which they have used their image of the Negro to obscure and falsify their understanding of themselves.

A basic theme in James Baldwin's writing is that whites do not know themselves, and, until they do, they cannot know Negroes. If, therefore, there are white Americans who are beginning to recognize that they all look alike to the majority of Negroes, these suddenly faceless whites are further exacerbated by being told that, essentially, they are only partly visible to themselves.

In any case, for most of us, Baldwin's challenge is exceedingly difficult to accept. We have made a settlement with life; and while we sometimes vaguely wonder what we may have missed by building constricting defenses of self, family, and class, our anxieties and frustrations are at least familiar. We mute our joy; we mute our grief at what we might have become; and we exist.

But we are no longer, in this country, being allowed to exist comfortably. In the forced confrontation with the Negro, we *are* being forced to confront ourselves, and the resistance is huge.

The same question is insistently thrust at every white. As Baldwin put it in a television interview: "I'm not a nigger. I'm a man, but if you think I'm a nigger, it means you need it. . . . If I'm not the nigger here and you, the white people, invented him, then you've got to find out why."

Although "the movement" has provided those whites who will hear with this dangerous initial stimulus to self-exploration, its function is not and cannot be to provide mass group therapy for whites. When Baldwin speaks of the Negro's possibly "saving" the white man and when Martin Luther King talks of the power of "redemptive love," they obviously do not mean, as *The New York Times* and General Eisenhower used to harmonize, that a basic change in the condition of the Negro in America will have to wait on change "in the hearts" of whites. The core of their message, as Baldwin put it, is: "I don't care if I live to be a thousand years old and you don't love me. I just want you to let my children go!"

Most of the Negroes actively involved in various phases of the unfinished revolution do not have the time or energy at this point to worry long about how quickly each of us whites gets to know why he needed a "nigger." They are not primarily depending on a heightened sense of morality to move whites but are rather concentrating on ways to alter the sources and distribution of power—economic and political. Among other formidable challenges, this aim involves the organization of a vastly greater number of the Negro masses than has yet been directly involved in the struggle.

The majority of the Negro militants do recognize that they must also recruit as much white support as possible because numerically Negroes alone cannot finish the "revolution" they have begun. They cannot be expected, however, to focus a major part of their attention on each white's personal battle of self-liberation in relation to Negroes. On this score, each white is on his own.

"What am I to do to prove my sincerity?" a young woman in New York asked a Negro friend a few months ago. She is far freer than most whites of delusions about Negroes and about herself, but she cannot convince all the Negroes she knows, of that. "It is *such* a difficult situation," she continued. "If I demonstrate, I'm not trusted. If I don't, then I'm not doing anything. What can I do that isn't suspect, aside from be myself and be as honest as I can about how I feel?" Her friend told her she had answered her own question as well as she, or any white in America now, could.

To most Negroes we are all suspect, even when we seem most virtuous to ourselves. In the Greenwich Village weekly, *The Village Voice*, Marlene Nadle, describing an integrated bus trip to the March on Washington in August 1963, told of a young white member of the Peace Corps who was soon to leave for Nigeria:

> Frank Harman was asked why, since he was white, he wanted to go to Nigeria. He replied, "I want to go to help those people because they are human beings."
>
> Suddenly Wayne [a Negro] shouted, "If this thing comes to violence, yours will be the first throat we slit. We don't need your kind. Get out of our organization."
>
> Completely baffled by the outburst, Frank kept repeating the questions, "What's he talking about? What did I say?"
>
> Wayne, straining forward tensely, screamed, "We don't need your kind. Get out of our organization."
>
> Other Negroes joined in. "We don't trust you." "We don't believe you're sincere." "You'll have to prove yourself."
>
> Frank shouted back, "I don't have to prove myself to anyone except myself."
>
> "We've been stabbed in the back too many times."
>
> "The reason white girls come down to civil rights meetings is because they've heard of the black man's reputation of sex."
>
> "The reason white guys come down is because they want to rebel against their parents."

Pain and confusion will be the "dues" of many whites who try to bridge the racial chasm in the years ahead. But for authentic communication to begin between whites and Negroes, more and more of the compressed accumulation of Negro anguish must first be released.

Ready or not, whites are going to experience new dimensions of irony—with themselves as targets. Leslie Fiedler, for instance, tells of what happened to one of his children some seven years ago in a newly integrated first grade in Princeton, New Jersey. Suddenly, inexplicably, the boy was pushed by several Negro children, and they shouted at him, "You're a nigger." In Birmingham, in early 1963, when police threatened to disperse a group of demonstrating youngsters working for the Student Nonviolent Coordinating Committee, the Negroes looked at the white cops and taunted them, "All right, *niggers*, come on."

2

The Chicken and the Eagle

I like [the word] black. I like to use it. It's an attempt to have some identity. It . . . [tells] the white man, "What you used to call me is no longer a symbol of inferiority." To do this is to have an inner security.

—James Forman, executive secretary of the Student Nonviolent Coordinating Committee

Today, in America as elsewhere, the Negro has made us forcefully aware that the rights and privileges of an individual rest upon the status attained by the group to which he belongs—that is to say, by the power it controls and can use.

—David Danzig, Commentary, February 1964

A young woman on the staff of the Student Nonviolent Coordinating Committee was addressing a meeting of Negroes in a small, deteriorating church in a Mississippi town. She was urging them to register to vote, and, as she spoke, cars full of white men drove slowly and menacingly by the church. She told her audience a fable. It was about an eagle which for a long time had been told it was a chicken and had believed it.

Clearly, a primary stimulus for "the movement" has been the decision of more and more Negroes to reject white men's images of them and to shape and define their identities by themselves. It is among the young, of course, that a swifter and deeper change from chicken to eagle is taking place. Not all of the young. The growing numbers of undereducated, unemployed, and unorganized youths in the Negro ghettos have been affected by the ferment; but with no ways of channeling their anger and no meaningful place in the society now or in the foreseeable future, they, like many of their fathers, sink into apathy and despair and occasionally release some tension in bombastic fantasies. And some become criminals.

In so far as it is possible to measure degrees of hopelessness, the young Negro who now feels he is sentenced to the ghetto for life is going to be even more alienated from the rest of society than were his predecessors. Unless he is motivated to join it actively, the very existence now of a Negro-led "revolution" serves to deepen his frustration because, despite all the tumult and all the slogans, *his* life has not been changed and *his* expectations remain bleak. A Negro drug addict in his early thirties says of some of the teen-age users he has come to know in central Harlem, "There's a new breed of cat out there now. They don't even have a dream."

Here, however, I am concerned with those Negroes in whom the spell *is* broken, those who do have a "dream." The majority, including, I expect, many young demonstrators, North and South, would agree with Negro actor Godfrey Cambridge: "I want my piece of the American dream. None of this beat philosophy for me. I want my apartment with a terrace. I like to live well, and eat well." Or, as Whitney Young, executive director of the National Urban League, puts it: "The Negro is in revolt today, not to change the fabric of our society or to seek a special place in it, but to enter into partnership in that society."

On the other hand, a minority—a growing number of Negro intellectuals, the more radical workers for the Student Non-violent Coordinating Committee, CORE, the NAACP, and militant local groups led by Negroes—is not only working for an end to all forms of segregation but also intent on changing the society as a whole.

In an essay, "The New Negro in the North," in the volume

The New Negro (1961), Dr. Kenneth Clark asserts that "the new image of the Negro and the responsibilities associated with this new image involve him in the role of social critic. . . . He cannot be content to demand integration and personal acceptance into a decaying moral structure." He cannot, Dr. Clark continues, be willing "to share equally in a tottering structure of moral hypocrisy, social insensitivity, personal despair. . . ."

Until 1963, however, there had been small evidence that a broader and deeper social criticism than an attack on race prejudice and its results had become a pervasive preoccupation in "the movement." But gradually, as the goals widened and more emphasis was placed on radically improved housing, education, and employment opportunities—as well as on the attainment of those civil rights toward which the first waves of sit-ins and "freedom rides" were directed—the objective situation has been leading more Negro activists to explore the basic structure of the society as a whole.

I do not mean that there has been a growth of any doctrinaire political or economic ideology, nor do I mean that Thoreaus or Paul Goodmans abound among the leaders or among the rank and file. What *is* inexorably happening, even among the majority who want to "enter into partnership" rather than "change the fabric of our society," is a recognition that partnership cannot be achieved without also altering that fabric.

In order to get more Negroes *inside* the society, it will be necessary to combat not only the moral hypocrisy or plain insensitivity that has allowed the constriction of the Negro, but it will also be essential to deal with the conditions and attitudes which explain why we permit the huge "other America" of the poor to exist.

For the Negro to get inside, many others will also have to find ways to enter. It will be impossible to make full citizens of what Gunnar Myrdal calls "the underclass" of all colors without a degree of political and economic change which goes far beyond the past scope of civil rights campaigns. And as the root failures of this society are analyzed and attacked, more and more of us may then be forced to look, in James Farmer's words, at "the reasons that we all, North and South, have allowed so much power to accrue to so many dubious institutions . . . and so many mediocre men."

There is also, however, a quite different attitude being taken by some Negroes who claim to be concerned only with "making it" by themselves. They do not want to be part of the necessary alliances with whites—or, for that matter, with blacks—which have to precede extensive political and economic changes.

Whatever their criticisms of the foundations of this society, these Negroes insist they are not interested in engaging in organized social and political activity in the years ahead. Shaped in the chill and bitterness of the daily struggle first to acquire and then to retain their self-respect, they have become "separatists" of an order different from the Muslims or from those non-Muslim radical Negro intellectuals who are convinced, as the Muslims are, that action for change in Negro living and working conditions must be conducted on an all-black basis but who regard the Muslims as lacking a realistic program.

The non-organizational "separatists," however, profess to have no faith that any *collective* alteration of the Negro condition can take place in the foreseeable future. These are Negroes who do want—and in some cases have already acquired—their material piece of the "dream," but they have hardened into an individualistic defensiveness. One of them, a successful photographer, says: "I've never wanted integration. In any case, I don't think it's going to happen within my lifetime or within my children's lifetime. I'll be conscious of being black all my life, and I'm going to be suspicious of whites all my life. More to the point, I don't need social relationships with whites in order for me to prove anything about myself to myself. Nor do I need to be part of any all-black 'movement' to get self-respect.

"I know," he continued, "few whites who have the same breadth of interests I have. There are very few I'd want to spend an evening with. I don't need the company of whites in order to continue growing. I can cook in wine and I can cook in fatback, and whatever else I want to learn, I can do without whites.

I just want to be left alone to do what I can do best. I *don't* want to be hampered any more by Jim Crow, and so I'm for getting the laws passed which will end all public forms of segregation. That much is going to be accomplished, but once we do have all those laws, let me go as far as I can by myself. I'll be all right."

It is impossible to determine how many of this genre of "separatists" exist. They are certainly small in number so far, but I mention them because they too are among those who have, in their own way, reshaped their sense of themselves. They differ from what E. Franklin Frazier called "the black bourgeoisie" in that they are not trying to "whiten" their way of life. They are not ashamed of being Negro. What they no longer have is the hope—and, they say, the desire—ever to be part of an entirely open society.

Except for the more assimilationist-minded of the Negro middle class and the majority of the black poor, a stronger affirmation of being black is the one element which is shared by all the varieties of nascent "eagles"—the Negroes engaged in civil rights activity and now also in organization for political and economic change, the Muslims, the radical intellectuals, and other kinds of "separatists."

A corollary effect of this pride in being black, in nearly all of its different manifestations, has been a growing realization among more and more Negroes that their past in this country is not exclusively a stigma, that they can draw strength from the heritage of the American Negro.

There have always been some Negroes who have learned on their own of the ancient cultures of Africa, the slave revolts in America, and the existence of American Negroes of widely diverse accomplishments. But unless they came from families which had already rejected the white man's and the white man's schools' definition of the Negro—and those families have been comparatively few—those Negroes have always had to *unlearn* the majority culture's image of them before they could begin to take pride in their past.

Now, largely as a result of the momentum begun by the

civil rights actionists, many more Negroes, particularly among the young, are seeing their history in this country in a new, re-energizing perspective. For one thing, they are beginning to comprehend more about the lives of those before them who did not appear to be achieving anything but simple survival. "I think," Miles Davis, the jazz trumpet-player, has said, "every Negro over fifty should get a medal for putting up with all that crap."

In several lectures to Negro students, James Baldwin has emphasized: "Negroes do not have to invent a reason to be proud. They have endured, achieved, and triumphed already over one of the cruelest oppressions in the history of mankind. We have every right to be proud that our mothers and fathers outwitted this civilization to the extent that they took the cross and made it into something which had more meaning than it ever had before. They are the only mothers who have produced children who could walk through mobs to go to school. When the chips are down, I've got to remember my mother carried white women's washing on her head and that my grandmother was a slave. For me to say that I come from a long line of African kings, which may or may not be true, is absolutely irrelevant."

Along with a new way of looking back, a deeper and stronger sense of black communality is building. In the past, to a greater or lesser extent, depending on particular times and places—and often excluding the more "whitened" of the Negro middle class —there has been a bond between Negroes, between "members," or, as Negro musicians put it, between "soul brothers." It has been a relationship of shared and dangerous high visibility as well as of shared frustration, outrage, and despair. Rarely, however, and not for long, has it been the resiliently affirmative and strengthening sense of "belonging" to one another which was expressed by a young Jewish emigrant to Israel in the summer of 1963. She had no relatives there, nor did she have any family to which she could return. "My heart," she said, "is happy to be here." "But," said an onlooker, "you are all alone." "How can I be alone," she answered, "in a country of two million Jews?"

In this decade a more durably positive sense of black kinship has been building. It is shown in a letter James Meredith received when he was agonizing as to whether he should finish out his year at the University of Mississippi. A former English teacher of his, Miss O. B. McLin of Saint Petersburg, Florida, wrote to Meredith: "You are no longer James Meredith. You have lost your identity. You are we Negroes and we are you. And we can't afford to give you up."

In this context it is instructive to read the reassessments by Negro intellectuals through the years of Marcus Garvey, the bombastic Negro nationalist and fantasist of the 1920s. At the time, as sociologist St. Clair Drake has pointed out, "Garvey was an embarrassment to Negro intellectuals. (It is significant that none has ever chosen to write a biography of him.)" Many fought him bitterly while he was accumulating mass support, but in 1963 Drake was able to say that now "all of them concede that black folks were given a sense of pride and worth as a result of his efforts." Even twenty-five years ago, for example, Benjamin Mays, a Negro educator and minister who himself has never been identified with black nationalism, observed that Garvey had focused on the idea of a black God "to arouse the Negro to a sense of deep appreciation for his race" and "to stimulate the Negro to work to improve his social and economic conditions."

The more recent surge of race pride in the 1960s operates in many different ways. It can, and does sometimes, become angrily imperious. The same James Meredith was bitterly attacked at a July 1963 convention of the NAACP in Chicago because he did not appear to the younger Negroes there to have enough pride in what they were most interested in—the spiraling growth of mass direct demonstrations. His critics in Chicago quickly characterized him as a "moderate," and because he used the word "burr-head" in admonishing his audience not to expend all their energies on demonstrations instead of on self-achievement, they lacked any patience to hear him out and try to understand his point, whether they agreed with it or not.

On that painful day ("I wept my first tears since I was a child") Meredith learned that race pride, submerged for so long, is going to propel many Negroes for some time to come to an intolerance of any attempts, real or fancied, to diminish or question that pride.

Another manifestation of it is the concept among some Negroes of black superiority. This conviction does not exist only among the Black Muslims with their diagnosis of the white man as fatally corrupt and their vision of the black man as the luminous ruler of the future. There are other Negroes, both active and inactive in "the movement," who consider themselves morally superior to the vast majority of American whites because the latter have at best condoned and have at worst directly participated in the compression of the black man. "Some of us turn bad," a young Negro once told me, "but we haven't sat on and choked a whole people."

Increasingly there are American versions of the often amorphous idea of *negritude,* most widely proclaimed for blacks everywhere by Léopold Senghor, a poet and political leader in Senegal. Although Senghor asserts that "today our negritude no longer expresses itself in opposition to European values, but as a complement to them," the essence of his writings on the subject is that negritude has elements of superiority to white values in several of the most vital areas of existence. He speaks of the "active abandon of the African Negro toward the object," and then goes on to claim that "European reason is analytic through utilization; Negro reason is intuition through participation." Senghor also describes as basic components of negritude "the sense of communion, the gift of myth-making, the gift of rhythm," as well as a "softness, spirituality," and a more direct and more richly symbolic appreciation of sexuality.

Among those American Negroes and white romanticists who are trying to develop native definitions of "special" Negro qualities, the general tendency is to claim that Negroes are more emotionally spontaneous and direct and that they taste more of the "salt" of life than do most whites.

Examples of some of the varieties of American Senghors would include Negro jazzmen who say only Negroes can swing, off as well as on the bandstand; such white naïfs as Jack Kerouac and Robert Gover; the more complexly disoriented Norman Mailer; and, if read out of the context of his writings as a whole, James Baldwin in certain moods.

In addition to his exposure of the wounds of being black in America, Baldwin has also written in *The Fire Next Time* (1963) of:

> . . . rent and waistline parties where rage and sorrow sat in the darkness and did not stir, and we ate and drank and talked and laughed and danced and forgot all about "the man." We had the liquor, the chicken, the music, and each other, and had no need to pretend to be what we were not. This is the freedom that one hears in some gospel songs, for example, and in jazz. In all jazz, and especially in the blues, there is something tart and ironic, authoritative and double-edged. . . . White Americans do not understand the depths out of which such an ironic tenacity comes, but they suspect that the force is sensual, and they are terrified of sensuality and do not any longer understand it. The word "sensual" is not intended to bring to mind quivering dusky maidens or priapic black studs. I am referring to something much simpler and much less fanciful. To be sensual, I think, is to re-spect and rejoice in the force of life, of life itself, and to be *present* in all that ones does, from the effort of loving to the breaking of bread.

Baldwin's definition of Negro "sensuality" in this passage is, as a matter of fact, similar to many descriptions by anthropologists and sociologists of life styles in sections of the culture of all the poor, white as well as black. What is particularly Negro in the kind and quality of transient release which Baldwin describes is a result of the fact that survival requires more "force of life" when one is *both* black and poor in this country. Or, as a Negro in Charles Wright's novel *The Messenger* (1963) puts it: "I know damned well I learned something from being born black that I could never have learned being born white."

In whatever form it bristles—from an apotheosis of black "intuition" to an appreciation of existential "tenacity" and "sensuality"—there is a rise in pride of black, often involving a feeling of some kind of superiority, which may or may not be consciously acknowledged.

Shortly after the March on Washington in August 1963, Ike Reynolds, a field secretary in the South for CORE, said: "I think that if you look all through history, you find that no enslaved nation or group of people have ever freed themselves without some nationalism within the group. I think it's necessary. I don't think it's reached the danger point here in this country. I'm not talking about organized nationalist groups. I'm talking about the nationalism within individual Negroes. I think this is why we're having demonstrations all over the country, why the civil rights movement has started to move at a rapid pace. I think without this, we'd still be in a low position. I say this: I'm not a black nationalist, I am not defending it, but I do think it's necessary to have black nationalism. It implies a person has some type of pride in himself, in his race. I think our job would be to replace black nationalism with American nationalism by winning real freedom and equality."

Without, then, defending black nationalism or, I might add, American nationalism, I think it is possible to appraise this growing affirmation of blackness with more than the automatic warning by some white liberals that aggressive expressions of racial or group pride are divisive and therefore ought to be criticized as "reverse racism."

It may even be that for some Negroes, as a writer to *Life* pointed out after that magazine had printed an unusually sensitive and understanding study of the Muslims by Gordon Parks, "the black man must go further than merely demanding acknowledgment of his equality. Only by going on to the far-out concept of superiority can the Negro people level off to a healthy reality."

Among Negroes breaking through the racial looking glass, there are certainly those who do not need the spur to self-confidence which a belief in "superiority" can bring, however distortedly, but there are others who may overreact to the momentum of being released from a self-image of inferiority, and it will indeed take "real freedom and equality" for them to "level off." I make a point of this phenomenon because it *is* happening and those whites who are concerned with understanding the complexities of "the movement" have to recognize its full range of results, however disturbing some of them may be.

There is a change, for instance, in the criteria of beauty among those Negro women who are wearing their hair "natural," and who have foregone the devices which would allow them to approximate certain white standards of attractiveness. With this change there often comes such an assertion as that of a Negro actress who told me that "the black woman is the most beautiful woman in the world." This is a form of nationalism, but I think it preferable to the way many American Negro women used to try to see themselves. "The girl-child's hair," Margaret Burroughs has said, describing the spiritually disfiguring process, "is washed, pressed, curled or waved. At an early age, one is made aware of the temporary quality of this transformation. One learns to guard against moisture of any type, perspiration or rain, for fear that one's hair will go 'back.' One develops a mind-set against swimming, unless it is just before one is to go to the beauty parlor. . . . Perhaps now you understand the reasons for my revolution and why I am wearing my hair the way God made it. . . . We women who now wear our hair natural are being our own true selves. We have ceased to look for the key to unlock the spiral in our hair."

The "leveling-off" point in this context, of course, would be a recognition by Negro women that there is no single immutable criterion of beauty and that it is possible to be one's "true self" without also claiming that "the black woman is the most beautiful woman in the world." But until that stage is reached, even if she considers her image "superior," the Negro woman who no longer has the need to look as white as she can possesses a stronger and more resourceful sense of self than those who have anguished through the years over hair-straighteners and creams which could not perform miracles.

Unlike many American Negroes before this decade, Jews, for example, have had a continuum of pride in a distinctive heritage and body of accomplishments. Yet many Jews in "the old country" and in the initial decades of their families' adjustment to America, have helped themselves transcend ghettos and vocational restrictions by cultivating a certain sense of "superiority." Except among the dwindling group of Orthodox Jews, this has not been a claim to be "the chosen people" of God so much as a pride in intellect, in the *Yiddishe kop*. Certainly this kind of defensive "superiority" can breed damaging distortions of reality, but it has not been an entirely negative influence. Growing up in a Boston neighborhood in which I could expect to be beaten up at any time by invading gangs simply because I was Jewish, I took strength as a boy from the legend of the *Yiddishe kop*. It was a slippery way to shape self-respect, but at the time it was *a* way—when there appeared to be few other immediate possibilities—of keeping myself from feeling that my role in life was to be a victim.

In view of the particular history of the American Negro, it is not surprising that, as long-delayed race pride multiplies, there will be Negroes who will use some form of nationalistic feeling as a support until they can achieve that degree of inner balance and impregnably *personal* identity which allows Julian "Cannonball" Adderley, the jazz musician, to tell an interviewer for the Negro weekly *The Pittsburgh Courier* why he appreciated the manner in which *Time* magazine a couple of years ago described conditions in Haiti. The reason for his pleasure in that account, he pointed out, was:

> They just printed the fact that what was wrong with Haiti was caused by corruption in high offices. They didn't say Haiti was in a mess because it was run by black men. It was not a case of black corruption and white money.
>
> I'm kinda glad, not happy, though, that it happened this way. It proved to the white man that Negroes can be just as corrupt as they can be. Now I just want the Ellenders to realize that we also can be just as pious, sanctimonious and talented as the white man.
>
> The story of John Thomas, the great high-jumper, amused me. When he broke the world's high-jump record, they called him the greatest colored high-jump champ. As soon as

the Russian Valerie Brumel beat Thomas, they referred to the Negro star as an "also ran." I was glad because I want them to know that we are human too. We can be also-rans just like they (whites) can be. We can be champions just like they can. We don't claim any super-superiority nor do we admit to being super-inferior, just human, like they are.

Adderley, then, has "leveled off," if indeed he was ever out of balance to begin with. But many have not. Wally Nottage, a psychologist who is also a Negro, has been director of a New York State project known as START (Short-Term Adolescent Resident Training). He works with sixteen- and seventeen-year-olds who have broken the law, are on probation, and appear headed for more trouble. One of the youngsters (and Nottage's charges are both Negro and white) told Nottage during a group psychotherapy session, "Man, you really loused me up. You asked me: Who am I? Nobody ever asked me that before. And ever since, I can't sleep nights."

Few whites can begin to answer that question in depth without being engulfed by anxiety. Considering how much has been done to strip the Negro of a fundamentally positive sense of self, it is probably going to be inevitable that for the next decade or more there will be an increasing number of Negroes who will use prideful, sometimes exaggerated racial identification as an initial stage in regaining a feeling of worth. Throughout this book I am trying to indicate what *is* happening as well as what *should* happen in American race relations. Clearly it is the responsibility of the schools and of other elements of the community to stimulate each Negro to a realization of his own unique worth and capacities, but when this function is not performed with nearly enough skill and sensitivity, I do not think that even an overblown pride of race is worse than lack of any pride.

The Muslims, after all, do possess a strong feeling of dignity. They do keep their families together. They do not seek release from despair in alcohol, drugs, and violence. To be sure, they are also, in many ways, building their self-reliance on a fragmented, contorted, and essentially irrational view of reality.

But is the damage wrought by illusory separatism and inculcating in oneself hate and distrust of all whites worse than the effects of the utter lack of self-confidence which can be found in so many among the black masses? Both alternatives are dismaying, but until Negroes in this country are given sufficient reason to feel that equality of opportunity exists and is meaningful to them, in many the vacuum of self-respect will either remain unfilled or be occupied by different degrees and concepts of protective racial unity and sometimes of racial superiority.

When a twenty-two-year-old Muslim, Ralph Davis, was indicted a couple of years ago in Elizabeth, New Jersey, for two murders he had allegedly committed, he rejected a court-appointed white defense attorney and said he would defend himself unless he was assigned "a black lawyer like myself who understands me." If whites were to try role-reversal and could begin to imagine themselves to be Ralph Davis with *his* experience with whites, what color attorney would they have demanded? Toward the end of 1963, when Adam Clayton Powell urged his Harlem congregation to boycott that part of the celebration of Christmas which involved the giving of gifts—as a memorial to and a protest against the deaths by bombing of four Negro girls in Birmingham, Alabama—he also asked his audience, "Have you ever seen a black Santa Claus?" Forget, if you can, Powell's own opaque character and consider what emotions that question, peripheral as it may appear on the surface, must evoke in terms of the Negro's experience in America.

A frequent white complaint is that "Negroes are getting so damn hypersensitive." Consider why. At Mobilization for Youth, a massive project on the lower East Side of New York, one of whose goals is to train "disadvantaged" youngsters to be ready for the challenge of equality of opportunity, as and when it comes, two teen-age apprentice carpenters were asked to sweep the floor one day. The white youngster took a broom and started. His Negro colleague refused absolutely. The Negro was close to being suspended from the project until he finally revealed why he had not cooperated. "My mother," he said, "told me never ever to pick up a broom for any white man. She told me that if I did, that broom would always be in my hand."

Another illustration of the rise of race-assertion has been the decision of CORE, SNCC, and other Negro groups to have black leadership at the very top as well as in many other policy-making positions. Whites have responsible roles in both CORE and SNCC, but in making certain that the apex of the leader-ship is Negro these groups are responding to a powerful emo-tional need in those Negroes they want to recruit. In writing about this situation in the summer 1963 issue of *New Politics*, August Meier has noted: "It is natural that Negroes should want to discard paternalistic white leadership. But the ironic result is that a movement for racial equality operates ideologi-cally with the notion that whites should be subordinate in it to Negroes. Undoubtedly this is a passing phase; as we approach genuine full citizenship for American Negroes, this sort of anomaly will disappear."

This will have been a passing phase if that "genuine full citizenship" is reached; but my point is that this decision for black leadership, however ironic from an egalitarian perspective, came out of a powerful present need among militant Negroes to redress the balance of power wherever they can.

As Negroes, in and out of civil rights groups, begin to feel they are finally becoming the eagle of the fable, an indetermi-nate number are going to keep testing their new-found size. Some may treat whites as "niggers." Others, like the youngster with a violent aversion to being told to pick up a broom by a white man, may take a great deal of convincing before they fully believe that any white with whom they are dealing does not still see all Negroes as menials. And how many whites *do* see Negroes as individuals?

A young Negro woman experienced in civil rights work in New York City was invited by a group of white women in Scars-dale in early 1962 to advise them on the steps they could take to integrate their community. When she arrived at the house where the meeting was to take place, the hostess's seven-year-old daughter called down the stairs, "Mommy, is that the new maid?" The child's mother apparently was able to see Negroes as having more than one "place," but the process of instantly assuming that all Negroes were of lower status had already begun in her small daughter. The child can be educated out of this narrowness of perspective, but what of those children in other Scarsdale homes whose parents' conceptions of Negroes are still exceedingly limited? They are going to be as unprepared for the further stages of the unfinished revolution as their parents are.

3

"I've Been Down So Long
Till Down Don't Bother Me."

For the next inevitable objective is full-scale participation, on easy and equal terms, in the ordinary operations of American society. It will be won only when the average Negro (not just the brilliant exception) is willingly accepted by the average white (not just the self-conscious "liberal") as a reliable neighbor, a good colleague to have in the office or plant, a welcome addition to the local political club, bowling league, trade association and PTA. This obviously will mean the erosion of a lot of white prejudices; but it also demands some big changes in the habits, character and ambitions of a lot of Negroes. —John Fischer, editor of Harper's

At the bottom of the social heap is the black man in the big-city ghetto. He lives night and day with the rats and cockroaches. That Negro has given up all hope. He's the hardest one for us to reach, because he's the deepest in the mud. But when you get him, you've got the best kind of Muslim. Because he makes the most drastic change. He's the most fearless. He will stand the longest. He has nothing to lose, even his life, because he didn't have that in the first place. —Malcolm X

As pride in being black rises among both integrationist and separatist Negroes, there remain all those others whose quality of existence has been described by Douglas Ferrell, a Los Angeles minister, state assemblyman, and Negro. In an interview with Theodore White for *Life*, Ferrell explained: "A man says to himself, 'I've been down so long till down don't bother me.' Something happens to him. Defeat sets in like a disease. It's like a cancer. It eats away his will power. He gives up. He wants to be with other people like himself, no matter what level he lives on. He's got no design for living, no pride, no courage, no ambition."

He does, however, have rage. James Baldwin's "Letter from a Region in My Mind" first appeared in *The New Yorker* of November 17, 1962. The book *The Fire Next Time*, in which it was included, became a national best-seller. The most remarkable aspect of the reaction to the book among many whites, including liberals, was the extent to which Baldwin shocked them. "Is this really true?" an editor asked me. "Implicit in what Baldwin is saying is that every Negro hates every white."

A labor-union official, a man I'd thought particularly sophisticated in terms of the realities of race relations, was deeply troubled by the Baldwin book. "I hadn't realized," he said, "that this is the way they really feel. Anger, yes. I know the anger. But so much contempt beneath the anger."

After Baldwin and after the increasingly sharp-edged thrust of Negro demonstrations in the North, more whites are beginning to realize some of the depth of Negro anger. It is astonishing that any white can doubt the existence of some rage in every Negro. How could it be otherwise? There are Negroes who have largely transcended their hostility and have hurled most of their energy and conscious aggressions into working for integration or building a career or creating music or literature. Yet, just as Jews who experienced pogroms in "the old country" never became entirely free of some hatred of *goyim*, though the rage was often suppressed, no Negro who has grown up in America can be entirely free of hostility to whites.

Martin Luther King, on his way to a New York civil rights rally a couple of years ago, told a friend, "I just saw Malcolm X on television. I can't deny it. When he starts talking about all that's been done to us, I get a twinge of hate, of identification with him." Roy Wilkins, a disciplined, uncommonly reasonable man, heard the news on a Sunday in 1963 of the death by bombing of four children in a Birmingham church. "After that," he told a *New York Herald Tribune* reporter the next day, "I don't know. I don't know how I felt. I wanted to grab somebody. Just grab somebody."

King, Wilkins, James Farmer of CORE, and other Negro spokesmen—except for the Muslims and some of the black nationalists—would agree with James Baldwin that nothing of worth to Negroes can be built on hate. When Baldwin returned to Harlem in June 1963, to talk to the graduating class of the Frederick Douglass Junior High School, a school from which he had graduated in 1938, he said: "We are not after a reversal of this long nightmare with the shoe on the other foot. What one seeks is not revenge. Revenge is a cold, cold plate. We are trying to build a new Jerusalem, to make the world a more human place to live in."

Baldwin, as he says, is not yet speaking for the mass of Negroes. Nor is Martin Luther King. Among the "underclass" there are those who would like revenge, if revenge were possible without the simultaneous destruction of the avenger. And some say that, even if resistance is suicidal, they are no longer going to be nonresistant to provocation beyond a certain point.

Much of the talk in the ghettos about "next time I'm going to take one of them with me" is bombast, but not all. I know a Negro cab driver who enjoys his family and gets considerable satisfaction from his work and friends. For several years he had been harassed by white police in Harlem. One afternoon, while he was protesting what he considered a grossly unfair police reprimand, a nervous rookie cop slugged him on the head with the side of his gun. The cab driver beat the policeman to the ground and stopped only when the cop's partner drew his own gun.

"It wasn't blind rage," the Negro told me. "I knew what was happening and the dues I was going to pay. But I couldn't take it any more. And if it happens again, I'll probably do the same thing. I'm past being nonviolent with whites who are on my back. Because of my family, I'm not going to look for trouble, but if there were a race riot, where do you think I'd be?"

On an evening in May 1963 I stood at 125th Street and Seventh Avenue in Harlem during a rally to protest what was happening in Birmingham. A group of speakers—ranging from Malcolm X to the Reverend A. D. King, brother of Martin Luther King—was addressing some two thousand Negroes and perhaps a dozen whites.

The response to Malcolm X was more intense and more ragingly enthusiastic than was that to any other speaker. A goodly number of Muslims, to be sure, were there, but not all of the two thousand were Muslims. When one minister began his talk, "I did not come here to inflame you," a shout rose from within the crowd, "We *want* to be inflamed!" The shout was followed by a chorus of "That's right!" A Negro I didn't know stopped in front of me, shook his fist in my face, and said, "You better watch out. All of you better watch out. I'd rather get shot through the heart than get beat up on any more." When another speaker told of Negroes who had fought for their country, there was another shout, "Hell, we ain't got no damn country."

Yet Robert Kennedy was shocked when, at a 1963 meeting with Negro intellectuals, one youngster, active in integration work in the South, where he had often been beaten and jailed, said he would not fight for "his" country until that country did indeed become his. One of that Negro's worst beatings had taken place while two FBI men watched. The president of the Oakland, California, school board was similarly surprised and disturbed in the fall of 1963 when the East Bay NAACP supported a threat by some Negro students in Oakland to stop reciting the pledge of allegiance. He apparently could not really understand what Horatius Perry, president of the Oakland Youth Council, meant when he said that for a Negro the pledge of "liberty and justice for all is so naïve that it is almost facetious."

After centuries during which the majority of Negroes did not dare admit to whites, nor fully to themselves, how much they hated, the feelings being released now do indeed startle whites by their fierceness. In itself, this long-delayed rush of rage can be therapeutic. The high incidence of hypertension among Southern Negroes for decades was not unconnected with buried anger. An index of the residue still suppressed is the contention of Dr. John Caldwell, an expert on hypertension, that twice as many Negroes as whites die from high blood pressure and other diseases caused in large part by the damming of the emotions.

"If I reacted as strongly as I felt each time I run into the white wall," a Negro professor once told me, "I'd be burned out. I'd be dead. Not that it does me any good to keep it all in. You have to try to learn how to strike a balance between exploding outside and exploding inside."

Just as whites in general do not *know* the tensions of staying sane though Negro (to use the phrase of semanticist S. I. Hayakawa) they also do not know, or they underestimate, other afflictions of blackness in this society. In the July 1962 *Harper's*, John Fischer, the magazine's editor, wrote an article, "What The Negro Needs Most: A First Class Citizens' Council" (later reprinted in *Reader's Digest*). I focus on the piece, not in a desire to engage in *ad hominem* conflict with Mr. Fischer, but rather because I am convinced his article does speak for many whites who consider themselves well intentioned toward Negroes and well informed about their "problems."

Fischer admitted the validity of the claim that "frustration crimes—dope addiction, drunkenness, sexual assaults, sometimes murder" are statistically "closely correlated with overcrowding, slums, and—perhaps most important—the sense of hopelessness that afflicts so many Negroes." Nonetheless, the gravamen of his article was that "so long as the Negro blames his plight entirely on circumstances, history, and the white man, he is going to stay in that plight. He will get out of it only when he begins to change his circumstances, makes new history, and shoulders a bigger share of the responsibility for the fix he is in."

Accordingly, Fischer advocated the formation of a new Negro organization, a First Class Citizens' Council, with the slogan, "Let's Make Every Negro a First Class Citizen." The basic flaw

in Fischer's homily—along with a series of major misunder-
standings—is caused by the distance from which he, a white
man, sees the Negro condition. There is small evidence in his
article that he knows the depth of the lack of motivation among
many black poor to "improve" themselves.

Fischer's naïveté is unwittingly underscored in this passage:
"At last the law, the full force of the federal government, and
the overwhelming weight of public opinion have all come over
to the side of racial justice. No matter how stubbornly pockets
of resistance in the Deep South (and some Northern cities) may
hold out, the result is no longer in question. The rest is a
mopping-up operation, like the war in Europe after Bastogne."

On the contrary, the result is very much in question. Unless
there are vast breakthroughs in education, housing, and job opportunities, the racial chasm is going to become deeper. Nor,
two years after Fischer's article appeared, is there evidence that
"racial justice" means the same to Negroes as it does to those
who form "the overwhelming weight of public opinion."

Crime is one of Fischer's specific concerns. "As the proportion of Negroes in a community increases," he writes, "the
crime rate usually rises sharply." First of all, as Robert C.
Weaver noted in his contribution to *The Negro as an American*,
a paper published in 1963 by the Center for the Study of Democratic Institutions, there is not a one-to-one ratio between crimes
and criminals: "When people read that more than half the
crime in a given community is committed by Negroes, they unconsciously translate this into an equally high proportion of Negroes who are criminals. The fact is that the proportion is extremely small."

The wonder of the history of the Negro in America is that
many more Negroes have not become criminals. There is no
denying, however, that proportionately the crime *rate* is often
higher in Negro neighborhoods and proportionately more Negroes are jailed than whites. But in this, as in other areas, statistics alone are not all they seem. In an answer to Fischer, Henry
Lee Moon of the NAACP protested: "Hundreds of unknown
Negroes are arrested every day on charges which would never

be brought against white persons. This is true in the North as well as in the South. Every week scores of poor, inadequately defended Negroes are convicted on evidence which would be promptly thrown out of court if the defendants were white. . . . This unequal law enforcement swells the statistics on Negro arrests, convictions, and prison population."

Justice is less likely to be done you if you are poor, and it is in worse imbalance if you are Negro and poor. A study by the United States Department of Justice reveals that in some areas guilty pleas are three times as frequent among prisoners who have to be assigned court-appointed attorneys as among those who can afford to retain their own lawyers. As for capital cases, Norman Redlich, a professor of law at New York University and a close student of capital punishment, claims that hardly anyone is executed in this country who has money or influential friends. Clarence T. Duffy, former warden of San Quentin, adds: "Negroes are more likely to die than white men—and for less serious crimes."

Admittedly, even when crime statistics are put into perspective on the basis of unequal justice because of poverty and color, there still is a high Negro crime rate. But, as Fischer seems to realize only imperfectly, there has always been more crime among the dispossessed, of whatever color. In this country at this time, the most dispossessed of all are black.

As one of many examples of how poverty's concentric circles of failure accelerate crime, there is the effect of deficient slum schools. The New York Citizens' Council of the National Council on Crime and Delinquency reported in July 1963 that 90 per cent of all criminal offenders in that city had been school dropouts. And 50 per cent had never completed grammar school.

In the particular history of the American Negro there has been another reason—in addition to the effects of poverty—why it is remarkable there has not been much more Negro crime. As Roy Wilkins observes, "most of the Negroes in the North are end products of the system in the South." The system of justice in the South—and in some sections of the North as well—has often been based on yet another kind of different standard for the Negro.

As was indicated, Negroes, in some circumstances, have been arrested and sentenced on charges for which whites would either be warned or given a shorter jail term. At other times, however, the reverse has been true. Roy Wilkins has described how exponents of this element of vintage Southern jurisprudence think: " 'Negroes will steal. If they steal just a little, we won't punish them. If a Negro steals from another Negro, that's no crime. If he kills another Negro, why, that's just a misdemeanor. But, if he kills a white man, why, that means electrocution.' " As Wilkins adds, "that type of justice—which is slowly changing—doesn't breed respect for the law."

Wilkins no more excuses criminality than does John Fischer. He has often emphasized that deprivation ought not be used as "a blanket excuse, because I think people ought to have some restraints on their conduct, regardless of how much they suffer." Where Fischer and Wilkins separate, however, is in Fischer's inability to recognize how much more it takes than an admonition to make a desperate or a hopeless man care about the law.

Fischer's ingenuousness concerning one aspect of this challenge is illustrated when he writes: "In many Negro neighborhoods (and a few white ones, too) the bystanders not only refuse to help the police; they help the criminals." Fischer cannot project himself into the mind of a Negro who all his life has witnessed how police operate in Negro neighborhoods.

In 1962, radio station WCBS in New York broadcast an indignant editorial because police moving in for an arrest in predominantly Negro or Puerto Rican neighborhoods were being attacked themselves, while bystanders made no effort to help them. In answer, the station received this letter:

> I am a black woman who was born in New York and have lived here all my life. Why anyone should be surprised over attacks on police officers is beyond me. I have seen streetwalkers plying their trade so openly that the police would have to be blind not to see it. The drug peddlers have their field day in Harlem. Recently a columnist for the *New York*

Amsterdam News named the streets where the traffic flour-
ishes, in detail. There were no mass arrests. What conclusion
can be drawn from this? It must mean that certain parties can
be tolerated but when some individual commits a crime he
is subject to arrest.

The police have lost their right to respect from the community. The people you think are apathetic are neither deaf
nor blind. The man with the badge has deteriorated in their
eyes. I am just another black face in the crowd . . . just one
more "face of apathy." I know the person who attacks a
policeman is wrong in the narrow sense, but I also realize that
that person is inflicting on that unfortunate policeman a
pressure built up for years, nay, for generations. I am not a
dam to hold back Niagara.

Nor can support of the police be expected when, as in many
ghetto neighborhoods, police brutality is so common that a fair
cop is regarded as an exotic. In the summer of 1963, after listing
a chilling series of incidents of police viciousness against Negroes in Washington, D.C., Chuck Stone, then editor of the
weekly *Afro-American,* warned: "The day is coming in Washington, D.C. when it will be worth a white policeman's life to
walk in the colored community just as it has happened in
Harlem, Bedford-Stuyvesant and the South Side [of Chicago]."

In his anxiety about Negro crime, Fischer fails to emphasize
or to recognize the full significance of the fact that most of
that crime is directed against other Negroes. During the past
couple of years, for instance, there has been considerable national publicity about the Negro crime rate in Washington,
D.C. In April 1963 Robert Murray, the District's police chief,
disclosed that, of all crimes committed in the District of
Columbia, 80 to 85 per cent were by Negroes. In cases of
aggravated assault, rape, and homicide, 85 per cent of the
victims were also Negroes. Of those robbed, 70 per cent were
Negro. In every ghetto throughout the country, it is Negroes
who suffer most from assault by Negroes. During a period in
the winter of 1964, the morgue in Chicago, where Negroes
comprise 25 per cent of the population, received 158 Negro

murder victims as contrasted with 82 whites who had been murdered.

More than the propinquity of segregation is involved in intraracial violence. Added to frustration and to hatred of whites, which sometimes rise until there has to be some release —whether boisterous ("I *am* here"), drink, gambling, or criminal behavior—there is self-loathing. It is the white man who has kept him down, but a desperate member of the black "underclass" hardly thinks well of himself for having submitted to his "fate." Since it is much more dangerous to express direct aggression against whites, he is likely to release both inner and outer rage at someone like himself.

Significantly, again and again in recent years, when a large section of a Negro community has been caught up in a movement against discrimination, the crime rate in that community has gone down and remained down so long as mass action continues. Mrs. Gloria Richardson, Chairman of the Cambridge, Maryland, Non-Violent Action Committee, told Murray Kempton of *The New Republic* in November 1963: "It's funny, but during the whole time we were demonstrating actively there were almost no fights in this ward and almost no crime. . . . Now they've gone back to fighting each other again. They've been thrown back to carrying a chip on their shoulder."

In the fall of the same year, in Americus, Georgia, after many Negroes had been mobilized through the efforts of CORE and SNCC, a boycott was set up against the town jail. The local Sumter County movement announced: "Don't forget that our fines and court costs every morning are helping to pay for new police cars and extra policemen who are just here to intimidate Negroes." Obey the laws, the Negroes of Americus were told, and make the cops poorer. Before the boycott, the weekly total of bail bonds and fines had averaged from $2000 to $3000. For weeks afterward, it was $500.

Another point in John Fischer's bill of particulars against Negroes is the charge that when Negroes move into a neighborhood in large numbers it tends to deteriorate. He admits there is also evidence to the contrary throughout the country, and that when deterioration does exist it can be due "in part . . . to overcrowding and to income so low that the owners can't afford to keep their places up properly." But, adds Fischer, "it is also partly due to plain old don't care. . . . Moreover the same families that can't find money for a bucket of paint or a pane of glass somehow manage, surprisingly often, to drive fancy cars and buy a fifth of whisky every weekend."

How "plain" is "old don't care"? It is difficult to muster incentive to "keep up" one's place when living conditions are so appalling that nothing short of dynamite will help "clean up" a neighborhood. I remember the exacerbation of a Puerto Rican woman, living with six children in two rooms, when a social worker asked her why some of the children weren't yet toilet trained. "You try it," said the woman. "Try handling six at once with the bathroom out in the hall. And broken."

A "fifth of whisky" at least provides some immediate, if transitory, release, and it's surprising that a great deal more whisky is not consumed among the poor. As for conspicuous consumption, when there is money for it to happen, the purchase of a resplendent car or an expensive set of furniture is a demand, as Kenneth Clark points out, "for the attention and recognition he [the Negro] has been denied because of his race and which he believes he deserves as a human being."

Of course these are hardly optimum compensatory techniques, nor are they universal among the Negro poor. Clean apartments in the Negro slums are not uncommon, and Negroes do save for their children's education or for a home outside the ghetto; but for many of those who have been crushed all their lives the future is as damned and damnable as the present, and the overriding hunger is for some form of instant gratification.

Here too, as in the consideration of other counts in his indictment, Fischer would have been wise to try role-reversal. Doctors Abram Kardiner and Lionel Oversey, after the intensive study of the psychodynamics of Negro life which resulted in *The Mark of Oppression* (1951), concluded: "The authors have been amazed at the remarkable ingenuity and stamina that most of the subjects showed, and each of the authors has privately thought that under similar circumstances, neither could have done as well."

Mr. Fischer is also concerned about the "civic apathy" of many Negroes. So many, he charges, do not register and vote. Why, he might have asked, do so many of the poor, of whatever color, not bother to register and vote?

"I wonder now and then," writes Robert Smith, a columnist for the York, Pennsylvania, *Gazette and Daily*, "just who is the smartest—the man who persuades himself that his daily lot will be different if we have a different millionaire in the White House, or the man who knows that the people who really run his life—the owner of the plant, the landlord, the cop on the beat, and the wealthy folk who supply the muscle to keep him in his place—that these guys never run for office and so can't be voted in or out."

When and if the poor are given a chance to choose political programs and candidates with whom *they* can identify, it may be possible to convince them that voting makes a difference. Until then, as Smith adds, many are likely to continue to "figure that riddling out the difference each four years between Tweedledum and Tweedledee is a silly business, best left to those who are amused by it."

"White people," John Fischer's brotherly advice continues, "also are bothered by the casual attitude of many Negroes about sex, and about their family responsibilities." He cites the high illegitimacy rate among urban Negroes (ignoring the rising rate of abortions among those whites who can afford them). And, he claims, "even when they are married, Negro fathers tend to abandon their families with lighthearted frequency."

The presumptuousness of the term "lighthearted" is astonishing. Aside from the history of the Negro family—the emasculation of generations of Negro men who had to rely on their wives to support the household because there were no adequate jobs for them—Fischer gravely underestimates the economic realities of Negro life *now*. When income rises, family stability increases. It is in the lowest economic class that the largest numbers of Negro men "abandon" their families. And it is in *this* class in which unemployment is currently not only more than double the national average but, in more and more cases among Negroes, has become permanent.

Nor is this "abandonment" always what it seems to be. "You have no idea," Bayard Rustin has pointed out, "of the number of black men in Chicago, Detroit, St. Louis, Pittsburgh who purposely move out on their families because they cannot support them on $35, $40, $50 a week. And it is because they leave home, because they desert their families, that the $400 or $500 a month necessary for the family to survive can come in from relief. And they sneak in every other night or so to kiss the children or go to bed with their wives, and slip out before dawn."

Others never return, but to assume that their self-imposed exile is usually "lighthearted" reveals ignorance of the ways the poor are sometimes forced to take in order to survive.

For many American Negro males in the past hundred years —and into the present—"abandonment" of their families has resembled the pattern in South Africa described by Peter Ritner in *The Death of Africa* (1960): "Many of the finest and most vital young urbanized Africans desert their wives and children in their early twenties as a matter of course. It is not that they do not love their families enough to want to work to support them—this is the *Afrikaner* view—but they *cannot*. Therefore they elect to let them die out of sight if not of mind."

Fischer asks: "Can a man who won't support his children call himself a first-class citizen?" Does a man who is *unable* to support his children have any reason to *consider* himself a first-class citizen?

Broken families, Fischer continues, increase the burden on relief rolls, thereby causing "a growing resentment among white taxpayers; nobody likes to support somebody else's bastards." The answer to that is Dick Gregory's point: "When the white man gives us all the things we're due, we'll relieve him of paying us all of those relief checks. But, until he relieves us, let him keep on paying his dues."

As for illegitimacy in the ghetto, it too is allied to the results of poverty—overcrowding; the seizure of present pleasure, such as it is, when there is so little incentive to defer gratification; and the lack of birth-control information among the poor, a lack which is frequently reinforced by state and municipal regulations forbidding social workers and clinic personnel to instruct their clients in birth-control techniques.

As I noted, John Fischer does have some general—though quite surface—awareness of the societal causes of civic apathy, illegitimacy, and the like among the Negro poor. He claims, however, that this sort of explanation can be too easily used as "an excuse for despair" and that it offers no solutions. The Negro, he insists, must begin to rehabilitate himself. And in more and more cities, under the direction of local ministers, action-oriented social workers, and other Negroes with leadership capacity, this is exactly what has been happening in recent years. What Fischer does not recognize, however, is that there remain many who cannot be reached until there is much greater economic and social change than can be accomplished on a local level. They are what Roy Wilkins calls "the casualties of systematic oppression, the walking wounded."

North and South, at the bottom of the ghetto are Negroes, Wilkins adds, who "are scarred by hundreds of years of the vilest indignities and humiliations." If they have lived long in the North, many become chronic cynics. With regard to the more recent emigrants to the urban centers, Wilkins has spoken in a *New York World-Telegram* interview of those Negroes who come "from little crossroads towns and small cities, and they find it very different—big and fast and bewildering. They have no preparation, no education, no skills. They have no citizenship training. They weren't citizens where they came from. They know nothing of government, except that it usually meant trouble for them. They see themselves as outsiders, aliens who may get by if they are lucky and shrewd and manage to stay out of trouble."

But Fischer, listing the shortcomings of Negro parents, asked: "How many attend the meetings of their Parent-Teachers Association? How many help collect for the Community Chest or offer to lead a Girl Scout troop?"

Fischer's is the kind of middle-class myopia that led Marcella Whalen, a former English teacher of James Baldwin, to write a letter to the *National Review* in which she wondered why Baldwin had called New York the most hostile city he knew. She cited Baldwin's success on the high-school literary magazine and the recognition he had received from several of his teachers. Miss Whalen added that she is still literary adviser to that magazine, where "color or racial background" remains no obstacle to those who can qualify, as did Baldwin, for editorial positions. "Come now, Jimmy," she ended her letter, "New York is not completely hostile!"

"Apparently," Baldwin said when I asked him about Miss Whalen's letter, "she never really knew where I had to go and where I had to live when I wasn't in school." For those Negroes, like Baldwin, who have changed their images of themselves, the process has been much more complex and painful than Miss Whalen or Mr. Fischer apparently realizes.

Toward the end of his *Harper's* article John Fischer provided yet another illustration of how little he knows about the black dispossessed. "Curiously enough," he writes, "the Black Muslims seem to be more effective than any other Negro organization so far in stimulating a sense of pride and self-reliance. Their doctrine springs from race hatred and their political program is sheer fantasy; nevertheless, in teaching thrift, hard work, business enterprise, decorous conduct and self-discipline, they can claim some notable accomplishments."

As I've shown earlier, there is nothing at all "curious" about whatever success the Muslims have had in "stimulating a sense of pride and self-reliance." However twisted their credo, they have made their converts feel that blackness is reason for pride. Having been convinced thereby that they are of worth, the new Muslims can *then* be motivated toward some of those qualities of "first-class citizenship" which Fischer urges all Negroes to acquire. That the Muslims can "claim some notable accomplishments" despite their "fantasy" is a measure of how unconvincing other present alternatives to apathy and self-destruction have been to their converts.

Those in the ghetto who are not Muslims and do not lead Girl Scout troops and are resistant to even local Negro-led social actionists have not yet been convinced there is any meaningful alternative to the way they live now. James Baldwin describes their present condition as clearly as is possible: "There is nothing they can do for themselves so long as they don't think there is."

Since the original writing of this book, it has become clear that the Muslims—at least those under the leadership of Elijah Muhammad—are becoming an increasingly narrow and nonviable sect. However, it is also clear that black-led organizations of blacks (or Afro-Americans, as more and more black intellectuals prefer to call American Negroes) have a decisive role to play in creating and sustaining an initial organized dynamism for basic change in the ghettos. So far no such group is powerful enough because no such group has sufficient mass support. In addition, some are not yet coherent enough as to program and means of implementing a program. The murder, moreover, of the evolving Malcolm X leaves a vacuum of potential charismatic leadership. But more and more movements in this direction are taking place in the black ghettos, and some will take hold. Their subsequent direction depends, of course, both on how much more desperate the situation in the ghettos will have become and on the readiness for real, radical social and economic change among putative white allies outside the ghetto.

4

The Mystery of Black

In a way, if the Negro were not here, we might be forced to deal within ourselves and our own personalities with all those vices, all those conundrums, and all those mysteries with which we have invested the Negro race.
         —James Baldwin

JOHN FISCHER's concern over the "casual attitude of many Negroes about sex" is part of the pyramid of white sexual beliefs about the Negro which are reflected in fears of Negroes' getting "too close" in housing and in schools. The foundation of the pyramid is dread of miscegenation.

The more sophisticated whites recognize, at least consciously, that differences in sexual behavior and attitudes are class rather than racial differences. The average middle-class Negro is no more casual about sex than the average middle-class white. Among Negro middle-class girls, as a matter of fact, there appears to be a greater degree of sexual "morality" than among their white counterparts. These girls, as Kenneth Clark notes in *Prejudice and Your Child* (1955), react "against the stereotyped concept of the Negro by rigidly controlling their own behavior and at times maintaining almost unrealistically high standards of personal and sexual conduct."

It is the lower-class Negro, then, who creates sexual anxiety in the largest number of whites. And the anxiety is often highly ambivalent. Edgar Z. Friedenberg describes the problem of many white middle-class teachers in the slums. They are confronted by children "inconveniently aware of their own sexuality and inconveniently skilled at bringing it to the attention of others. They live, their teachers sometimes say, like animals; and as they say it, a ghost sobs, harshly."

Distorted white conceptions of Negro "sensuality" will die hard. For many whites, their own sexual guilts, unconsciously projected onto the Negro stereotype, cannot be admitted. Without seeing Negro sex life as it actually is, they will continue to fear and condemn in Negroes what they fear in themselves. In other whites there is a related form of distortion—the idealization of the greater instinctual "gratification" among Negroes; and that idealization obscures reality as much as does moral condemnation of "the casual attitude of many Negroes about sex."

Both the moralists and the romanticists are often remarkably ignorant about sex in the slums. They *do* know about those places described by Anne Petry in her novel *The Street* (1946), "where people were so damn poor they didn't have time to do anything but work, and their bodies were the only sources of relief from the pressure under which they lived; and where the crowding together made the young girls wise beyond their years." And the young boys too.

But what of the quality of that relief from pressure? And how unalloyed is the "wisdom" of the young? In their study of New Haven, *Social Class and Mental Illness* (1958), August B. Hollingshead and F. C. Redlich proved again, as Michael Harrington notes in *The Other America* (1962), that the poor "are never really that informed." Commenting on that study, Harrington continued: "Along with a cynical version of the facts of life, there went an enormous amount of misinformation. For instance, young girls were given systematic misinformation on the menstrual period. They were often frightened and guilt-ridden about sex at the same time they were sophisticated."

Similarly the moralists and the romanticists seldom mention the frequent incidence of impotence in the Negro male. There is more sexual freedom among adolescents in the ghetto, but as they grow older this "freedom" often changes into yet another affliction of being poor and black.

When, as in many lower-class Negro families, the male cannot feel himself a man, the sexual roles become confused. Men dominated first by mothers who were their central support as children often find that their wives too are economically the "heads" of the household. In this context masculine potency can be as maddeningly elusive in bed as it is everywhere else.

As for lower-class Negro women, Kardiner and Oversey in *The Mark of Oppression* concluded that:

> The most prevalent complaints of the females in this group about their marriages are: the marriages are loveless; there is no companionship; the women are only bed mates; the husbands do not support them. The entire relationship is more often than not taken up with a power struggle between husband and wife, with the former usually in a submissive role, and the female holding dominance by virtue of her actual or potential capacity as a provider. The absence of affectionate relatedness is the predominant feature of these marriages.

Dr. Kermit T. Mehlinger, a Chicago psychiatrist who specializes in marriage counseling, also contrasts reality with "these general myths about the sexual potency of Negro males and the desirability of Negro women." Actually, says Dr. Mehlinger, "there is great sexual disturbance among the Negro population. Repressions and inhibitions utilize psychic energy. With so much energy tied up in hostilities and conflicts, it is only natural that there would be disturbances in the sexual sphere. The unconscious knows no color bar."

What of the sensuality in the music of the black ghetto? Listen to it again. There is anguish as well as the irony of the blues in Ray Charles, the prototypical musical spokesman for the Negro masses. Listen to the aggressiveness of the tenor saxophone-organ combos which proliferate in Negro neighborhoods. There is some joy in this music, but there is also much rage and often a chilling sense of loss.

Whites, moreover, who admire and envy the sensual "grace" of Negro athletes and dancers seem, first of all, to be amazingly oblivious to how many awkward Negro athletes and dancers there are. And they do not recognize *all* the elements in the gracefulness they do see. Take that "natural" rhythm, for example. A Negro aware of being invisible when he works downtown for "the man" may well try to show in his dancing how remarkable and unavoidably visible an instrument he can make of his body. In the process he can also release some of his aggression against "the man" in the very pyrotechnics of the dance.

In his essay "My Negro Problem—and Ours," in the February 1963 issue of *Commentary*, Norman Podhoretz admitted to the persistence in him of "twisted feelings about Negroes." Among them were "twinges of fear . . . and resentment," but there was also envy: ". . . just as in childhood I envied Negroes for what seemed to me their superior masculinity, so I envy them today for what seems to me their superior physical grace and beauty. I have come to value physical grace very highly, and I am now capable of aching with all my being when I watch a Negro couple on the dance floor, or a Negro playing baseball or basketball. They are on the kind of terms with their own bodies that I should like to be on with mine, and for that precious quality they seem blessed to me."

Podhoretz speaks of "they." Middle-class Negro secretaries? Certainly not the middle-aged maids listlessly walking to the subway for the ride uptown? And does he ache only when he sees a Negro dancer or athlete? There are, after all, lithe young whites who dance with grace. It is a highly selective view of the physical appearance of Negroes which focuses on the young and graceful among them. Reading Podhoretz's tribute to "their superior physical grace and beauty" is like watching an MGM all-Negro musical in the 1930s. All God's chillun in the ghetto are lissome swingers. Where *do* they put the old and the ugly, the fat and the scrawny?

Another form of idealization is Norman Mailer's attempt in "The White Negro" and other works to construct an action philosophy of the "hip" out of what he considers to be the attitudes of those Negroes who have not already turned gray in their desire to become part of the majority culture.

"If," Mailer writes in "The White Negro," "the fate of twentieth-century man is to live with death from adolescence to premature senescence, why then the only life-giving answer is to accept the terms of death, to live with death as immediate danger, to divorce oneself from society, to exist without roots, to set out on that uncharted journey into the rebellious imperatives of the self . . . where security is boredom and therefore sickness, and one exists in the present."

A source of this life-giving prescription, Mailer adds, is the Negro. "Knowing in the cells of his existence that life was war, nothing but war, the Negro (all exceptions admitted) could rarely afford the sophisticated inhibitions of civilization, and so kept for his survival the art of the primitive, he lived in the enormous present, he subsisted for his Saturday night kicks, relinquishing the pleasures of the mind for the more obligatory pleasures of the body, and in his music he gave voice to the character and quality of his existence, to his rage and the infinite variations of joy, lust, languor, growl, cramp, pinch, scream and despair of his orgasm."

As I have tried to indicate, those Negroes who more or less fit Mailer's description of the "hip" prototype live in a present that is far from enormous. And how much knowledge of themselves—Mailer's goal of hipsterdom—do they gain in their existentialist immersion in "the more obligatory pleasures of the body"? To what extent do they thereby "open the limits of the possible" for themselves?

I cannot answer with any exactitude, nor can Mailer. It is one thing for him, a white man of the middle class, to seek danger and violence as a means of self-liberation, but I do not believe he can begin to equate whatever he thinks he has discovered in his own raids into himself with the way the "authentic" Negro hipster lives and feels. And here I am talking of the Negro hipster in the ghetto, not the more recent "beat" Negro in Greenwich Village, New York, and similar integrated enclaves of disaffiliation in other cities.

Through the years I have known a considerable number of Negroes who have "liberated" themselves "from the Super-Ego of society." I first met them through my interest in jazz and the men who made it; and then, as, for various reasons, I spent more and more time in Negro neighborhoods in Boston and New York, my acquaintanceship with them broadened outside the jazz life. As a white, I was not "accepted," but I hung out with many Negro hipsters long and closely enough to be extremely skeptical of Mailer's conceptions of how they live.

I write, I should point out, with no more admiration for the way most Americans exist than Mailer has. I have not, however, seen an existential Elysium in the black slums. The Negro hipsters, with all the reservations about Negro "sensuality" I've noted, do *use* their senses more than the "squares," and in that respect theirs is a more intense way of life. There is also among them, however, a pervasive sense of rootlessness, the price of which is much higher than Mailer acknowledges.

I am not even speaking primarily of the constant anxiety about money. Nor do I mean, if one has found a way of making money in an illegal or extralegal manner, the anxiety of constantly staying ahead of the cops or of other predators in the ghetto. This kind of floating dread can ultimately wear a man down as effectively as can the acquisitive struggle for upward mobility in the middle-class world. What I do mean essentially is the feeling of being lost, of coming to that inevitable point at which the kicks lose strength and have to be greatly intensified in order to match the gratification less powerful stimuli used to bring.

Speaking in another context, Lenny Bruce once said, "There's nothing sadder than an aging hipster." The Negro hipster in the slums gets old quickly, and he is sad more and more often as he does grow old. In terms of survival, he does learn a great deal about himself and others. There is a cunning and a nakedly real knowledge of interpersonal relations and motivations which a man on the edge of society has to acquire if he is to survive. But using Mailer's criteria—the expansion of the potentiality of self—this knowledge is limited, because once you do learn it, it is basically repetitive.

You learn to be cynical and manipulative and resilient. But

how much can you learn of pleasure that is more durable than quick kicks, or of satisfactions more lasting than having conned somebody in order to survive? It is instructive that Mailer, who knows the satisfactions of work one feels is worth doing, does not mention this absence of meaningful work in the lives of the prototypical Negro hipsters. Yet this absence is felt, all the more gnawingly as the hipster gets older.

Fundamentally Mailer appears to be unaware of the depth of anxiety, desperation, and sheer physical discomfort which ghetto living imposes on all the poor, hip and square. In an exchange with Lorraine Hansberry in the *Village Voice*, Mailer wrote: "For fact, dear lady, you have lived no doubt in as many cold-water pads as any of us. Or known the people who did. Did we suffer so much? Did the cockroaches crow worse than the transistor radios in the thin swindle walls of the New Barracks?"

For a middle-class writer, this assessment of comparative suffering is posturing. Setting up the hollow values of "upward mobility" as an alternative to slum living evades the question of what is most acutely relevant to those who live in the slums. Miss Hansberry was much closer to reality than Mailer when she wrote in the same exchange:

> . . . blues or no blues, life roots or no life roots, Negroes of *all* classes have made it clear that they want the hell out of the ghetto just as fast as . . . anything . . . can thrust them. Worse, they have a distinct tendency to be astonished and/or furious that *everyone* doesn't know it. Misery may be theatrical to the onlooker but it hurts him who is miserable.

Mailer proclaims in *The Presidential Papers* (1963), that "what is at stake in the twentieth century is not the economic security of man—every bureaucrat in the world lusts to give him this—it is, on the contrary, the peril that they will extinguish the animal in us." Before worrying about the health of the animal in them, millions of Negroes in the slums would like to find that lusting bureaucrat.

It is not that Mailer's essential point is irrelevant. He, along with Paul Goodman and other critics of middle-class unlife, is concerned that the rise out of the ghettos, if it ever happens, may well mean that the Negro will become like the rest of us and will, as Mailer wistfully puts it, lose "his salt." However, it is possible that the social and economic changes necessary to enable the Negro to get a *chance* to escape from the slums may alter the values of the society as a whole. But even if a basic revision in American values does not take place as "the movement" increasingly focuses on institutional change, the solution Mailer provides as to how all of us, Negro and white, can save our souls ("explore that domain of experience where security is boredom and therefore sickness") is meaningless to those in poverty, particularly the black poor. They want to "make it," not in Mailer's way, but out of where they are now.

Seymour Krim, who is no fonder of middle-class character-lessness than Mailer, is much more perceptive about hipsterdom in his book, *Views of a Nearsighted Cannoneer* (1961). Krim writes of the heightened pleasures and excitement he found in jazz and later in the streets and bedrooms of Harlem. But he has not deceived himself about life in the ghetto. In asking white jazz partisans to face the implications of the source of the music which attracts them, Krim points out: "Here is a life . . . that at home, in its intimate relationships, its man-woman relationships, is as sordid, as painful, as grotesque in its accumulation of miseries as anything in Maxim Gorki's auto-biography."

And in acknowledging the need for "chicks, color, barbecue, wild inventive humor with the stab of truth in it" which led him to Harlem, Krim also *saw* Harlem:

> I could never immunize myself to the garbage in the streets . . . the pawnshops, five to a block, the rat-infested tene-ments, the thousands of dollars spent on TVs and radio-phonographs at the sacrifice of medical aid and sanitation, the feverish traffic in drugs, the hordes of sullen-faced, corner-haunting hustlers . . . the wild red rage on the broken-beer-bottle 5 A.M. streets and the ceaseless stealing. . . . I will truly hate to see Harlem go—where will I seek then in my time of need, O merciless life?—and yet I would obviously help light the match that blows it out of existence.

In addition to Mailer, there are lesser writers who roman-
ticize the Negro as the present-day fount of "primitive," life-
giving passion. Jack Kerouac, for instance, writes: "At lilac
evening I walked with every muscle aching . . . wishing I were
a Negro, feeling that the best the white world has offered was
not enough ecstasy for me, not enough life, joy, kicks,
music . . ." To which James Baldwin has responded: "I would
hate to be in Kerouac's shoes if he should ever be mad enough
to read this aloud from the stage of Harlem's Apollo Theatre."

There has also been Kitten, the heroine of Robert Gover's
One Hundred Dollar Misunderstanding (1962). In the novel,
the fourteen-year-old Negro prostitute is the apotheosis of
mother wit. Condemnatory of white personal and public hypocrisy, Kitten is infinitely more vivid than the male pro-
tagonist, a puffy, unbelievably vacuous white college student.
Kitten's insights into the hollowness of the white middle class
are accurate enough, but the instinctual wisdom claimed for
this black child implies that, even at the cost of being a whore,
Kitten has grown up "natural" into a most enviable state of
being.

At the very end there is a faint indication that Kitten is
nonetheless not well enough equipped to fulfill her extraordinary
capacities—let alone to survive economically in any other profession—and so there is a passing reference to her saving her
fees to go to "readin college." Yet Kitten, "ol blackass Picka-
ninny me," is fundamentally a reverse Stepin Fetchit carica-
ture with a touch of the boy raised by wolves who goes on to
get a Ph.D. in natural history.

The wide appeal of *One Hundred Dollar Misunderstanding*
was due in large part to the fact that whites could accept
Kitten's biting criticism of them because it came from the kind
of person one could not take seriously. She was "advanced" for
her age and condition, but the moral impact of the novel was
glancing—somewhat like Smokey Bear telling us to watch what
we do with our cigarettes in the woods. What does a *bear* know?
Or, as Negro writer John Williams speculated, ". . . would
One Hundred Dollar Misunderstanding have been quite so well

received had Kitten been a Negro social worker instead of a whore, and the inability of man and woman, black and white, to communicate been put on an altogether different symbolic level?"

The romanticists, from Mailer to Gover, are of no use to the Negro who wants out of the ghetto. Neither are Norman Podhoretz and the other white liberals who are exploring their "twisted feelings" about Negroes—however necessary that exploration is now for *them*. Nor is John Fischer's "moral uplift" campaign of major use as motivation for the lowest of the dispossessed. But Fischer is more cogent than the others I have discussed in this chapter, and more cogent than he may himself realize, when he writes that the Negro will get out of his present plight "only when he begins to change his circumstances, make new history, and shoulder a bigger share of responsibility for the fix he is in."

Fischer is correct, but not in the sense he means—the establishment of First Class Citizens' Councils among Negroes. The "bigger share of responsibility" the Negro must shoulder as he makes "new history" is to be in the vanguard of those organized for change throughout the society.

Obviously, as has been emphasized, this change, which involves a much more massive assault on poverty than President Lyndon Johnson or any other political leader has yet suggested, cannot be accomplished by Negroes alone. But it will not be set in motion without Negro impetus. Accordingly, more of the Negro poor have to be enlisted in this campaign. For that to happen will require more Negro leaders who are aware of what has to be done and who can so explain specific programs to potential recruits that the latter are motivated to vote, to engage in direct action, and to apply pressure in any other manner which may be effective.

Although the over-all alliance and its leadership will have to be integrated, the next stage of organization among the Negro masses will be under black leadership because many of the Negro poor cannot now be moved to action by *anyone* with a white skin.

At a mass civil rights rally in Harlem in the spring of 1963, the organizer, a Negro, told those of his co-workers who were white that he could not allow them any longer to pass among the crowd with containers for contributions. "More and more often in recent weeks," he explained, "the containers have been snatched away from white hands. You can't expect them to see that *you're* pure in heart. From now on, all collectors will be Negro."

5

Moderation and Grace

. . . we urge that the term "moderate," within its true meaning, be restored to grace—not as any endorsement of a slow pace toward full freedom but as a recognition of how this struggle must finally be resolved. There has been too much emphasis on both sides upon the "uncontrollability" of the extremists, on the "inevitability" of bloodshed. This will prove to be a self-fulfilling prophecy unless it once more becomes respectable to advocate moderation and settlement. The sooner moderates talking to moderates begin to make the struggle their own, the less anguished the resolution is going to be.

—From a policy statement by the Public Affairs Committee of Freedom House, co-sponsored by the Commission on Religion and Race of the National Council of the Churches of Christ in the U.S.A., August 25, 1963

On the matter of race I am compelled to conclude that all over the world many of us who belong to the more civilized and polite society have been and continue to be more responsible for the perpetuation of racial discrimination than the out-and-out racists. And the damnable thing is that we do not know it nor do we want to know it.

—From an address to the U.S. Conference for the World Council of Churches by the Reverend Daisuke Kitagawa, Executive Secretary, Division of Domestic Missions of the National Council of the Protestant Episcopal Church, April 24, 1963

CAN the term "moderate" be restored to grace in American race relations? Not for a long time, as far as most Negroes are concerned. Writing of the South in *The New York Times* in June 1963, Claude Sitton said: "The inescapable conclusion is that the moderate has used an honorable term to screen dishonorable action." To make the indictment more comprehensive and to include moderates throughout the country, I would qualify Sitton's analysis by suggesting that the distrust of the word "moderate" among Negroes comes not only from "dishonorable" action by some white moderates but even more from the limited extent to which moderates act at all.

Admittedly there are many different kinds of moderates, a factor which increasingly blurs the meaning of the word. Some, such as the signers of the August 1963 Freedom House–National Council of Churches of Christ policy statement, approve certain kinds of demonstrations and even certain forms of civil disobedience, while they deplore others. Some are for the active recruitment and training of Negroes in all areas of employment but balk at attempts to end educational segregation by altering the "neighborhood school" concept of determining who attends which schools.

Essentially it has been the experience of Negroes that most whites who call themselves moderates do not move significantly enough toward ending inequality—even by their own criteria of permissible action—until they are pushed, and pushed hard, by Negro weight. It is probably true that most moderates are not consciously disingenuous. They believe they are being honest with themselves and with Negroes. They believe they are advocating the only possible route which can avoid stalemate, on the one hand, and violence on the other. The problem of communication comes from the fact that so few whites realize *emotionally* the urgency of the Negro's need for change. Harry Ashmore, one of the signers of the policy statement with which this chapter begins, has written: "There has emerged a set of Negro myths as dangerous and debilitating as their white Southern counterparts. The basic proposition here is that no white man can really understand how a Negro feels." But *do* most whites, including the moderates, understand how the Negro feels?

I think Robert Smith, the columnist for the York, Pennsylvania, *Gazette and Daily*, does, but he is no moderate. "No man," Smith points out, "who goes to a quiet . . . home at night . . . who feels no fret from landlord . . . or police, to whom courtesy and respect come as his daily due, can begin to share the burning unrest of men who know contempt and abuse all their waking hours. Nor can such a man presume to advise 'moderation' to men and women who have been strangled on false promises for three generations."

As Smith himself proves, some such men *are* able to begin to imagine "the burning unrest" of Negroes. Most whites, however, do not come at all close, figuratively and literally. Yet Smith's genre of accusation is often dismissed as being unduly "emotional," as not taking fully enough into account the difficulty of effecting changes after so many years during which whites have staked out and barricaded their "place" in American life. But emotions are precisely what whites are dealing with when they talk to Negroes—emotions which are continually exacerbated by the wide difference in the ways Negroes and whites define "progress" in race relations.

A few days before the March on Washington I was talking to a Negro minister in Harlem. He is one of the city's more prominent churchmen, and although he participates in conferences with liberal and moderate whites downtown, he spends most of his time helping his congregation—and as many others in Harlem as he can reach—organize themselves for action. He is also deeply involved in a series of projects concerned with upgrading the schools, the skills, and the egos of those in the ghetto.

"I am not against the March, mind you," he said with some asperity, "but it burns me that a lot of white liberals or moderates, or whatever they call themselves, will use the March as a salve for their consciences. They'll have their badge to show they've been there and that they're on the side of virtue. But what the hell are most of them going to do when they get back home, besides talk? Their apartment houses will still be all or mostly white, their union locals will still find reasons why Negroes have to wait and wait to get in.

"When you get there," he told me, "look at those noble white preachers in the March. How many of those bastards are going to look at a really integrated congregation the following Sunday? Oh, more and more of them say their churches welcome Negroes. There's one on the West Side, for example, in a neighborhood that's become more than forty per cent Negro and Puerto Rican, but only a small percentage of Negroes worship in that church because the church hasn't gone out to *get* them. You can't just *say* the door is open.

"I'll keep working as best I can with these liberals and moderates, but I'll tell you what I tell the kids here. Freedom is never voluntarily given up by the oppressor. We're going to have to be out on the streets a long time. First of all, compared to the white population as a whole, there aren't that many white moderates or liberals who actually have begun to know how we feel and what has to be done; and secondly, those who have started to learn don't *do* enough."

In March 1964 in New York a meeting of prominent white liberals and moderates was called in order to find ways of establishing closer contact between them and the increasingly militant Negro leadership in the city. The major white liberal organizations in New York had failed to support the Negro and Puerto Rican boycott of the schools the previous month, and the whites at this meeting were disturbed at the resultant growth in the distance between them and New York's Negroes. Most of the meeting was taken up with a debate on the precise wording of a statement by this new *ad hoc* organization—a statement which would put it on record as favoring "quality integrated education." As arguments intensified as to how "far" the group would go, the debaters began to list their own credits in the fight for Negro equality in the past.

Finally Cleveland Robinson, a labor official and one of the three Negroes present, rose and attacked the assemblage. "I gather from listening to you," he began, "that everybody here thinks he personally has done a great deal for us over the past twenty years. Everybody wants to pin a halo around his head. Well, with all you've done, we still have a stinking mess on our hands. You can be comfortable while you talk about what remains to be done, but most of the Negroes and Puerto Ricans in this city are living in misery as you talk. We're in New York, not Birmingham, but what the hell have you got to be proud of?

"You say," Robinson continued, "you're worried about some of those terrible extremist Negro leaders who are coming up. Let me tell you that there are going to be many more 'terrible' Negroes all over the lot and there will be rifts and crises like you've never seen before. Some of us have been dealing with you for years and we keep hearing how you're for decency. But when the time comes to make an actual commitment in your own neighborhood, your own city, you're suddenly paralyzed. We—the Negroes and Puerto Ricans—have no choice but to take the leadership into our own hands. You haven't even begun to learn who we really are."

"I speak," adds Negro humorist and social critic Dick Gregory, "at many of those hundred-dollars-a-plate dinners at which the good white people pay their dues once a year to the NAACP or CORE or the Urban League. They drop their money, listen to the speeches, but they leave without knowing any more about what's really going on than they did when they came."

Aside from attending meetings and fund-raising dinners and otherwise supporting civil rights groups, it would be highly instructive for an active moderate or liberal (and those words are becoming interchangeable to most Negroes) to live a day-to-day existence in a Negro neighborhood and to send his children to a school which is more than 90 per cent Negro. Exceedingly few middle-class whites, with the conditioning they have had concerning their due as Americans, would long endure that kind of life. They would become utterly scornful of the type of moderate's advice given by James Reston in *The New York Times* as late as June 1963: "To attack 'gradualism' and token integration, as some Negro leaders are now doing, is to attack law, for all law is gradual in a democratic society, and law is the Negro's only hope. He dare not give up on the slow processes of the law as if he were a Negro majority among a handful of white governors in a Portuguese colony, or invoke Federal law when it suits him and defy municipal or state law when it does not."

Reston was not in contact with Negro reality. For Negroes to depend only on the "slow processes of the law," without also organizing and demonstrating to speed up those processes and without moving for immediate changes by devices such as boycotts and rent strikes, is for them to acquiesce in the scarring and stunting of yet another generation or more of their children.

It is ironically instructive to many Negroes, for example, when some moderates object to the inclusion of Negro children in street demonstrations. These critics have no sense of what it means to a Negro child to be a direct participant in action intended to guarantee him his full manhood. They cannot understand, as George Gregory, a Negro and a New York Civil Service Commissioner, observes, that "any democracy which can produce six-year-olds who can turn around to their counterparts and say, 'Come on, Nellie, or you'll be late being arrested with this group,' has started on a maturity which you and I have never envisioned."

Herbert Hill, labor secretary of the NAACP, was in Jackson, Mississippi, during a demonstration in which children were involved. "There were kids," he said later, "who never used to be able to look you in the eye before. They shuffled and stuttered. Now, they stand straighter because they have a sense of their own power, their own sufficiency."

Nor is there an understanding among many white moderates of the spur to achieving a more positive sense of self among Negro adults who see their children muster the courage to confront "the system." Conversely, there is also the effect on the children when their parents take action directly concerned with them. All too often, in the North as well as in the South, an American Negro child has been able to receive little psychic sustenance from his parents. In terms of vocation, Negro fathers seldom were able to provide role models with incentive. And in many matriarchal families, while the Negro woman was a source of comfort, she could give her children small sense that she was able to help them cope with the threatening white world. Talking of his mother, James Baldwin has said, "She was the only person in the world we could turn to, yet she couldn't protect us."

As more Negro adults begin to protest actively, however, their children cannot but be changed. Negro attorney Paul Zuber has headed several school boycotts and sit-ins in the North—stratagems which outraged many white moderates and caused them to talk solicitously of the resultant breaks in Negro children's education. Zuber says: "I was criticized very strongly when the parents had their first boycott in Harlem, yet all those kids were promoted. Parents have said that the children's assurance within themselves was greatly increased because they felt they were an integral part of something that their parents were doing for them."

There are many other chasms between the varieties of white moderates and the diverse Negro actionists. In the following chapters on employment, housing, and education I examine specific difficulties in communication between white moderates in positions of power and the more radical Negro leaders (I use the term "radical" in the sense of "going to the center, foundation or source of something.")

At this point, however, it is also necessary to consider the majority of those whites who regard themselves as moderates but who are *not* leaders in their communities. Some, as will be shown, do engage in attempts to end segregation, but most simply sit and hope that change in *their* neighborhoods and in *their* schools will come with as little tension as possible. It is a vain hope.

In his speech during the March on Washington ceremonies on August 28, 1963, Rabbi Joachim Prinz, president of the American Jewish Congress, said: "When I was the rabbi of the Jewish community in Berlin under the Hitler regime, I learned many things. The most important thing I learned . . . under those tragic circumstances is that bigotry and hatred are not the most urgent problem. The most urgent, the most disgraceful, the most shameful, and the most tragic problem is silence."

Many Northern whites must have agreed when, after four Negro girls were killed in a Birmingham church bombing in September 1963, Charles Morgan, a white lawyer in that city, said to a meeting there of the Young Men's Business Club: "Who is guilty? The moderate Mayor who elected to change things in Birmingham and who moves so slowly and looks elsewhere for leadership? The business community which shrugs its shoulders and looks to the police?" He also included "the ministers of Birmingham who have done so little for Christianity," the press, and "every person in this community who has, in any way, contributed during the past several years to the popularity of hatred." And, he might have added, silence against the effects of hatred is also a "contribution" to its spread.

A week later Morgan went to New Haven, Connecticut, and before an audience at the Yale Law School auditorium he extended his definition of culpable moderates to a Northern species of that breed: "They are the Yale and Harvard men, the upper-middle-class-oriented respectable people. They are most concerned with golf, family cocktails at the club, money and respectability. Their lives are the antithesis of controversy." He added that the moderates he was describing move "when the business might of the community or nation moves." They speak "when, and only when, it's the thing to do; not sooner, not later."

Morgan, in sum, was addressing the white anywhere in the country who, as Martin Luther King has said, "is more devoted to 'order' than to justice; who prefers a negative peace which is the absence of tension to a positive peace which is the presence of justice."

Mr. and Mrs. Christopher McNair, parents of one of the girls killed in Birmingham, came to New York for a memorial meeting soon after the bombing. Mr. McNair was asked where *he* laid the guilt for his daughter's death. "I don't know who to blame," he answered. "I guess I blame America. You can't blame any one individual."

Fewer and fewer Negroes any longer believe that blaming white America is going to activate the kind of guilt which will move formidable numbers of whites to help Negroes basically alter the way in which they live. While more whites are admitting to uneasy consciences, guilt has so far proved an extremely minor stimulus for *fundamental* change. As for what has happened in the past, the vast majority of whites would claim that they cannot be held to account for what their ancestors did or did not do. Besides, the ancestors of so many were in other countries during slavery and during the century of incomplete emancipation.

With regard to the present, it is difficult to find many whites who are markedly troubled by James Baldwin's contention that white Americans share a collective guilt for what is happening *now* to Negroes in much the same way as guilt could be charged against the silent Germans during the years of the Nazis.

There are no Dachaus here, but the ghetto is a form of concentration camp. Furthermore, although a protester under Hitler put his life in danger, no American white—except in parts of the South—would run any risk to his personal safety by denouncing and working to change the practices of the real-estate interests, the mortgage-lending banks, the schools, the businesses, the police, and all the other institutions which keep the Negro down.

Another perspective is that of Bruno Bettelheim, who claims that the basic, chargeable guilt is "the guilt of the man who lives in comfort when others live in squalor." Bettelheim made this point in an article in the October 19, 1963, issue of the *Nation* which emphasized "the class basis of color prejudice." According to Bettelheim, whether we actually feel guilt or not, "what makes us uneasy in our relations to the Negro is exactly what makes us uneasy in our relations to the poor, and has precious little to do with skin color."

The equation, however, is *not* exact, and by turning the racial problem entirely into one of class division Bettelheim seriously underestimates the continuing effect of racial myths and stereotypes on white attitudes toward Negroes. But it is true that class hostilities and prejudices are vitally involved. Accordingly, a radical attack on poverty's perpetuation of so wide a split between classes is essential to any fundamental solution of *racial* divisions in this country.

Yet, just as most members of the middle class do not feel guilt that there are poor, most do not feel guilt of any acuteness at the generally more desperate state of those who are both *black* and poor. Of those white moderates who do feel some guilt, many tend to soften their discomfort by considering themselves free of personal prejudice and by not engaging in any direct, immediately *visible* exploitation or limiting of the Negro. Nor do white moderates usually understand why they too are going to have to pay in tension and conflict in their own communities for what "others" have done to the Negro.

There is, to be sure, a constantly growing number of exceptions, of whites whose consciences do ache. Some agonize over the compromises they make between what they believe and what they do. In the June 14, 1963, issue of *Commonweal*, John Cogley spoke for some of them:

> We talk bravely of integration but our lives are caught up, willy, nilly, in the evils of segregation. When we move in social or professional circles of compatible people, these circles usually turn out to be all-white or all-black. When the whites among us pick out the neighborhoods where we want to bring up our children, these neighborhoods turn out to be all-white. When we set our hearts on schools of a certain excellence, the schools usually turn out to be all-white. The impact of our anti-racism, then, becomes a verbal enterprise, a matter of proclamation and declamation, not of daily life.
> All of us . . . live more or less in accordance with the rigidities of segregation.

There are those who try to break through those rigidities. They join campaigns to desegregate their neighborhoods and schools, to investigate hiring practices of businesses with which they deal. What they do is important, but they are too few in number so far to bring about pervasive change. Moreover, the root remedies for Negro inequality in employment, housing, and education require a degree of massive governmental planning and funds which not enough voters, white and black, are thus far sufficiently oriented and organized to press for. I do not mean to underestimate the usefulness of those whites who are acting on their beliefs. They are vital because they form the vanguard of the "new white" who must multiply in the years ahead if communication (beyond debates on how to achieve black equality) is to take place between whites and Negroes. My point is that, essential as this vanguard is, it is not enough.

Similarly, it is valuable that the collective consciences of church leaders have belatedly awakened to the point at which churches are examining the racial hiring practices of corporations in which they invest funds; integrating their own staffs, schools, hospitals, and other institutions; and requiring fair employment practice clauses in contracts for church construction and various other services. Some are investing and making deposits only in savings and loan associations and banks that will make loans to Negroes buying homes in an integrated community or in one which is beginning to be integrated. Others have been heading or joining in protest demonstrations.

Those Negroes who have ceased to depend primarily on white moderates and liberals for the initial impetus to radical change regard these church decisions as welcome but also recognize that such church policy cannot alter the lives of the majority of the Negro masses soon or widely enough. In terms of the scope of the challenge, attempts so far to accelerate Negro equality on the part of individual whites, secular and church groups, and, increasingly, businesses, are only beginnings. The attempts are hopeful auguries; but as talks between whites and Negroes to achieve "settlements" increase, they are going to be preceded by much more organized black pressure on whites of all persuasions before the term "moderate" acquires the same meaning for both whites and blacks. Only then can it be restored to grace.

By that time, if it comes, moderate whites may well be surprised at how much their own definition of the word will have changed. What was moderate in race relations in 1943 is called tokenism and worse now. What was moderate, even according to the relatively "advanced" view of the National Council of Churches of Christ and Freedom House in 1963, will probably be seen in 1973 to have been quite conservative.

———

The fact that conditions in the black ghettos of the North have worsened since this book was first written makes it inevitable that "moderates" will have to be increasingly exacerbated and pressured if any significant change is to happen. For the Negro in the North, it is simply not true that the Far Right and racist Southern politicians are the primary "enemy." In the urban North, where Negroes do have the vote but little else, the "enemy" is precisely those "liberal" (some no longer call themselves "moderate") politicians, administrators, and wielders of power whose rhetoric is pious but whose actions are evasive and illusory. They are men like Mayor Robert Wagner of New York, under whose "liberal" administration poverty has broadened and deepened. They are the "liberal" congressmen who talk of the "real progress" the War on Poverty is making, ignoring its pyramid of hoaxes on the poor ("Community action" in which the poor are not involved in decision-making. Job training for what?). The cruel absurdity of much of the "liberal"-led War on Poverty has been distilled by Herbert Hill, Labor Secretary of the NAACP, who applies to it the vintage Talmudic saying, "If you don't know where you're going, any road will take you there."

6

Closing in on the Negro Middle Class

> *They [the black middle class] did not even want to be "accepted" as themselves, they wanted any self which the mainstream dictated, and the mainstream always dictated.*
>
> —LeRoi Jones, *Blues People: Negro Music in White America*

> *When I came to college, my goal was a big house in the suburbs. Then I joined SNCC and went to jail.*
>
> —A co-ed in a Negro college in the South

WHILE the division between Negroes and whites is more than a matter of class differences, class is one of the basic factors in the way the Negro poor are regarded by the middle class. And not only by the white middle class.

During an ABC-TV television documentary, *Walk in My Shoes*, in September 1961, a group of Los Angeles Negroes from various professions were shown in conversation. A young woman spoke of a recent sermon she had heard which focused on the accelerating migration of lower-class Negroes to the city. The minister had predicted there would be a million Negroes in Los Angeles by 1970. She saw, she added, Negro men of her class shudder during that sermon.

"We shudder," another Negro answered her, "because we are saying, in essence, the majority of those people are not like us and . . . maybe some of us felt we left the South because we were getting away from this problem but we are a little, maybe, embarrassed by the fact that here we are going to have a mass element come in that is going to create a tremendous social problem . . . to which we find a great deal of difficulty in relating."

Two years later, in *Esquire* for August 1963, William Melvin Kelley, in an article, *The Ivy League Negro*, expanded on the dilemma of the upwardly mobile black man. "As the Ivy League Negro becomes more learned, more refined, he develops," Kelley wrote, "certain feelings of superiority toward all uneducated people. . . . It is not so much real prejudice as it is that he has come to feel himself closer to the educated white than to the uneducated Negro. This has nothing to do with pomposity or snobbishness. It is that his interests are different."

It is not only, however, that many middle-class Negroes have found it increasingly difficult to identify with the mass of Negroes; they have also deliberately and sometimes desperately tried to disassociate themselves from the entire history of the Negro in America. Besides concentrating on acquiring the same emblems of status sought by the white American middle class, they have practiced what radical and nationalistic Negro intellectuals term "cultural opportunism."

The majority of the Negro middle class has tried to become absorbed into the mainstream of American society in so far as its visible appearance permitted. That appearance has been an insurmountable barrier for most Negroes. But if full acceptance by whites was not possible, the frustrated assimilationists could at least try to emulate their white models as closely as they could. One result, as such critics of the "black bourgeoisie" as E. Franklin Frazier insisted, was that much of the Negro middle class adopted as narrow and self-limiting a set of values as their white counterparts. Other critics would agree with Dr. Jeanne L. Noble, associate professor of education at New York University, that some became even *more* prototypical of the faceless bourgeois. "After all," Dr. Noble says, "when you make a carbon copy, sometimes it comes out a little clearer than the original."

So far as was possible, many of the black middle class abandoned whatever remnants of the Negro subculture they could. Negro blues and jazz, for example, were not "officially" accepted by the administrations and large sections of the faculty at most Negro colleges. When he was at Howard University, poet and jazz critic LeRoi Jones recalls, a professor of philosophy there told him, "It's fantastic how much bad taste the blues contain."

Langston Hughes adds:

In the great days of Ma Rainey, Mamie, Bessie and Clara Smith, many respectable Negroes looked down their noses at the blues. . . . The story of jazz is that of a hard road to go for many hard years. "That low-down music," said the better class Negroes. And today gospel singing is suffering similar condemnation in some quarters. While to many listeners gospel music seems "a joyful noise unto the Lord," to others it is merely noise—and an ignorant, uncultured noise, at that. Even the great Mahalia Jackson is outside the pale of appreciation for some colored listeners. . . .

Increasingly the Negro middle class is being lectured at by dissident young Negroes, many of whom come from that class, because of its attempts to forget or mute its black heritage. "It is high time," Elias Blake, Jr., has asserted in *The Negro History Bulletin*, "Negroes realized that their real identity is partly white and partly black and the black part is nothing of which to be ashamed." And James Baldwin tells his audiences of Negro high-school and college students that the only way to end what he calls the tyrannical power of one's past is to embrace that past so that "it no longer possesses you. You possess it."

Yet it appears to be difficult for middle-class Negroes fully to recognize that out of that past there emerged a Negro culture —or subculture, if you will—with some strongly positive elements. Not a "pure" black heritage, an impossibility in this country, but sufficiently Negro in its origins and evolution to fit a basic definition of the term, "culture," as suggested by W. D. Wallis in *Culture and Progress* (1930). "Culture,"

Wallis wrote, "is the life of a people as typified in contacts, institutions, and equipment. It includes characteristic concepts and behavior, customs and traditions."

Yet even Whitney Young, Jr., executive director of the Urban League, who is obviously not trying to evade his past, can still echo most white sociologists and claim: "Science now rejects the idea that there is a separate Negro culture." At the same time, Young deplores the fact that "the estrangement of the Negro elite from the Negro masses encourages the former to stop regarding themselves as Negro." Though denying that there is a distinctive black culture with which the "elite" can also identify, he does define culture as "the sum total of the individual's experience," and goes on to point out that poor Negroes do share "certain cultural patterns existing in lower-class culture." Among them he cites "codes of honor, family solidarity and responsibility for the care of relatives."

I would add that the Negro poor also have certain specific cultural expressions which come out of the sum total of their experiences—from the blues of Bessie Smith through ways of cooking, speech idioms and games, a particular flavor and thrust of humor, and various attitudes toward life that were formed in the course of learning how to survive at the very bottom of American society. At all its stages, the black subculture was influenced by other partially separate strains in the over-all American culture, and it affected them in turn. But it also sustained its own identity.

Inevitably, if integration increases rapidly and as American culture as a whole becomes more and more homogeneous, these distinctly Negro traditions will become as diluted as have those of Jews, Italians, Irish, and other minority groups. But some elements of this heritage are at least worth appreciating in retrospect, as they dissolve.

In any case, no matter what its attitude is to the Negro past, the Negro middle class is being pushed toward a feeling of responsibility to lower-class Negroes, if not to their "culture." As William Melvin Kelley notes, "The upper-class and educated white man can view, without guilt, the lower-class white man with a certain distaste and contempt. But an educated Negro carries on his back huge bundles of guilt. His Negro consciousness begins to work. He feels he has betrayed his race."

One of the women in the Los Angeles group of Negro professionals on *Walk in My Shoes* said of the rising influx of lower-class Negroes: "They will find their own level, and I do sound like a snob, but I don't mean it this way and they, too, might rise up above their origin and might one day be our associates. But I think it is up to us to help them."

Notwithstanding the patronizing tone, the woman does admit to a bond of color across the class line. Until the past few years, however, the "help" given by those of the Negro middle class who were impelled to act on their feeling of responsibility, whether or not it was laced with guilt, consisted largely of membership in and fund-raising for such organizations as the NAACP and the Urban League. Social clubs, sororities, fraternities, and organizations of Negroes in the professions also set up scholarships and other projects to aid those who had not yet risen. But there has been small sense among the Negro poor that the black middle class was directly concerned and involved with their most basic daily problems.

In much the same way as the white social worker, the middle-class Negro, including many of those on the staffs of the NAACP and the Urban League, did not until recently begin to acknowledge the need to achieve much more radical dislocation and reshaping of community institutions than they, as ameliorators rather than excavators of social decay, had in the past felt to be necessary.

Now Whitney Young of the Urban League presses for huge "crash programs" in education and housing and has made the league's image considerably more embattled than it was before this decade. The NAACP continues essential work in the courts, but it has greatly expanded its participation in direct-action demonstrations. Both groups have been responding to pressure from without (CORE, SNCC, Martin Luther King's Southern Christian Leadership Conference) and from young militants within the NAACP and the Urban League to get all elements in "the movement" to confront the white centers of power more directly, pervasively, and insistently.

Charges nonetheless grow that the NAACP, the Urban League, and sections of CORE have not reached more than a small percentage of the Negro masses in terms of drawing *them* into action by helping them organize themselves to cope with the specific problems in their own neighborhoods, schools, and labor markets. It is true that mobilization of the Northern masses has only just begun, but this is the direction in which the younger Negro leaders and potential leaders are moving. (Although the Urban League is primarily a social-work agency and also concentrates on relatively unpublicized negotiations with and education of business leaders, it is taking greater bargaining advantage of the momentum caused by the more aggressive mass actions of other groups. On occasion there have also been Urban League staff members on picket lines and at demonstrations. In New York City, moreover, in February 1964, the Urban League of Greater New York, after a long silence, surprised other Negro organizations by supporting a boycott of the public schools.

The past few years have been difficult ones for the middle-class Negro who either has been wholly detached from the struggle or has been appeasing his conscience by supporting "the cause" from a distance, through paying his annual dues to one or more groups and then cursorily watching the "progress" for the rest of the year. Increasingly, first in the South and inevitably in the North as more of the Negro masses are organized, the same kind of pressure is being directed against middle-class Negroes who are reluctant to join fully in direct-action campaigns and boycotts as is used against the white objects of these drives.

In April 1963 the Reverend Ralph Abernathy, treasurer of the Southern Christian Leadership Conference, told a large, highly appreciative audience of lower-class Negroes at a church in Ensley, a borough of Birmingham:

> You ought to threaten to cut the preachers' salaries if they don't stand up with you for freedom. They say this is the

wrong time and yet they've had 350 years. I want to know when the devil is the right time. There are a lot of Negro businessmen who are not with this movement. [There are] the elite, the bourgeois, the class of Birmingham, Alabama, who are now living on the hill, learning to talk proper. They've got their hair tinted various colors, trying to fool somebody. Year before last they lived like us across the railroad track, took baths in a tin tub and went to an outhouse. Now they're strutting around town proper. How did they get rich? We made them rich. Talk with your doctor, your lawyer, your insurance man, and if he's not with the movement, don't trade with him.

In Chicago, during their 1963 fight with school superintendent Benjamin Willis over *de facto* segregation in the schools, Negro activists picketed Mrs. Wendell Green, a Negro member of the school board and the widow of a circuit judge. Mrs. Green was not on their side, and accordingly, as reported by Hoyt Fuller in *The Nation*, she was the object of broadsides such as this one by a NAACP leader:

> You know, in the past, so many elite Negroes received appointments and honors—and considerable status and income —as representatives of the Negro community when they actually made every effort to cut themselves off from the true Negro community. They were too busy being like white people and trying to persuade white people they were different from the Negro masses. Literally carbon copies of white people, you know. It was self-degrading, and it is no wonder white people despise them. Well, it's not going to be like that any more, either outside the NAACP or inside it. The leaders must be with the people—or else.

In New Jersey, in September 1963, Robert H. Martin, president of the Oranges and Maplewood Chapter of the NAACP, tried to draw critical Negro attention to that unit by resigning in protest at the inactivity of much of its membership, which was largely composed of the middle class and of domestics. (Because of a different kind of conditioning, the latter are also difficult to move onto the street.) "We all can march on Washington," Martin said as he withdrew, "but how many of you find time to picket right here in our own bailiwick? Sometimes we can't get a dozen members out for a picket line."

In addition to public exposure aimed at making the Negro middle class feel guilty for not accepting its responsibilities toward the liberation of all Negroes, there is the further argument that it is in the economic self-interest of the Negro bourgeois to expend time, resources, and political power in working for the kind of changes in education, job training, and housing which will begin to raise more of the Negro masses.

Whitney Young, in the September 1963 issue of *Ebony*, after pointing out that "the Negro population has no upper class in the accepted sense of the term [since] upper-class Negroes are really middle class by conventional standards of income, education, housing, etc.," added that "available figures on Negro income levels reflect the growth of a new and vital middle class. Some 20 per cent of the Negro family population are in the $7000 a year or over income bracket." However, "some 60 per cent are in an income bracket of $3000 a year or under. While the Negro middle class is growing in numbers and influence, the large mass of unskilled, unemployable Negroes is growing at an even faster rate." (For more than a decade, the unemployment rate among Negroes has been more than twice as high as that among whites, and the gap is widening.)

If this pattern is not broken, Young warned, "we will soon see in America a large class of dependent permanently unemployed with Negroes contributing a disproportionate share. This holds alarming implications for the economic future of the Negro middle class because its income and wealth still derive preponderantly from the Negro community."

There are other directions from which force is being exerted on the Negro middle class to commit itself to "the movement." Formerly, and to a considerable extent currently, the children of the black middle class were even more intent on keeping and widening their distance from the Negro poor than their parents were. Now, however, pride of race and a sense of mission are characterizing a growing number of these children of the bourgeoisie.

The young leaders of the 1960 and 1961 sit-ins came primarily from the middle class, although August Meier, a close observer of the sit-ins and subsequent developments, has also pointed out that the rank and file were "chiefly of working-class origin . . . they tended to be upwardly mobile members of the Negro lower-middle and upper-lower classes." The key phrase for the future in his description is "upwardly mobile." And while more lower-class youths have since joined the activists, leadership among the young is still disproportionately middle-class in background. Far less concerned than their parents with the lack of "respectability" in the use of mass direct-action techniques, many of these militants, as they become adult members of the Negro middle class, may basically alter the attitude and behavior of that class toward the masses—unless, of course, their values change. It will be much more difficult, however, for an alumnus of a picket line to muffle his conscience than it is for a member of the middle class who has always been "protected" from involvement with the masses.

In addition, as more of the Negro poor begin to organize, there will be much fiercer pressure from below on the black middle class. More leaders will emerge from the lower class, and those of the black middle class who are still among the policy-makers will be constantly on trial. From now on, as Robert C. Weaver, Administrator of the United States Housing and Home Finance Agency, has emphasized, Negro leaders cannot provide models of "progress" to their followers "unless they can bring about social changes that will facilitate the emergence of these models from the *typical* environment of the Negro community."

Whether for reasons of guilt, a feeling of reawakened kinship with all blacks, multiple pressures from all sides and from below, or pragmatic self-interest, the strong likelihood is that the Negro middle class will intensify its involvement with the unfinished revolution. In both the black and the white middle class, there will be fewer and fewer who will be *able* to remain above the battle.

T W O

7

Reaching Equality by Special Treatment

> *. . . We are not judging individuals, but an en-*
> *tire community which has been disadvantaged by the*
> *society; and the problem for the trade unions, as well*
> *as for the entire nation, is how to make that group so*
> *truly equal in American society that we can then talk*
> *of individual merit.*
>
> —Daniel Bell, *The New Leader*, February 18, 1963

> *I'm ready to negotiate when the pickets are re-*
> *moved. I'm not going to have a gun at my head.*
> *They don't want equality, they want preference.*
>
> —Thomas J. Duggan, business manager of Steam-
> fitters Local 420, New York City, June 11, 1963

I<small>N</small> addition to the difficulty whites have had in recognizing the full scope and urgency of Negro demands for equality, the concept of "compensatory treatment" to make equality functional eludes and often appalls many of the most sympathetic.

To prevent the continued expansion of "the underclass," there will have to be extensive "compensatory treatment" for the poor and the unskilled of all colors. But since there has for so long been an *additional* disadvantage in being black, I wish in this chapter to examine the nature of and opposition to the idea of "special treatment" as it applies specifically to Negroes.

A characteristic illustration of resistance to this approach by whites with a long record of work for civil rights is Governor Nelson Rockefeller's reaction when asked about job quotas. "I have worked all my life for equal opportunities for all citizens," he began, and then added, "We can't go in for quotas. It's against the law and an unsound approach. We can't abandon equal opportunity by giving special privileges to some."

First of all, "special privileges" do not necessarily involve fixed quotas. Secondly, it is an ineluctable fact that, for many Negroes, the passing only of statutes to reaffirm everyone's "right" to equality is similar to proclaiming that a man with one leg has the "right" to enter a race with a man who has two.

Job quotas aside, I imagine that the following letter to the *New York Herald Tribune* on March 11, 1963, reflects the consensus of many whites concerning *any* form of "preferential treatment."

Frank G. Burke III, St. Thomas, Virgin Islands, wrote:

> I don't know how anyone can legislate or insist on personal or racial respect. Most of us have to learn respect. Many racial minorities have come to our shores—Irish, Germans, Swedes, etc. None was welcomed with open arms. All had to fight prejudice and carve their own niches in our social and economic structure. They commanded respect through intelligence and industry.
>
> Let the Negro follow this classical route. If he is equal, and many have proved their equality, let him prove it. Mere membership in a race entitles him to nothing.

The extent to which any white holds to the incredible assumption that the American history of immigrant groups can be set up as an incentive and model for the Negro is the extent to which he remains ignorant of what it has been to be a Negro in this country.

I will not conjugate the obvious at length, but will simply point out that no other group was enslaved and no other group had its families fragmentized, first during slavery and then by the spiraling incidence of matriarchy among the "free" Negroes when the mass of Negro males were denied all but crawling jobs, and, in the process, their manhood. No other group has been so persistently visible as a group and, therefore, so persistently ghettoized. In sum, the "classical route" of immigrants here has never been possible for the majority of American Negroes.

So concerned, though rather hurriedly, have we become with combating "special privilege" for any group that, when the Mayor of New York in early 1963 asked the heads of the various city departments to report the ethnic composition of their personnel, there were bursts of outrage from exceedingly respectable sources. "What counts on the job . . . is ability," *The New York Times* declared in an editorial titled "No Ethnic Surveys." "People," the *Times* added, "should be hired, retained and fired only on that basis. That is the way to break down prejudice. There must not be quotas—one way or another —on ability."

The *New York Herald Tribune* was equally disturbed by the ethnic survey: ". . . this strikes us as a piece of nonsense. It labels the employee where there should be no tag. Neither the civil servant nor anyone else should be thus identified. This is completely unnecessary. . . . When people stop identifying their fellow man by race, all of us will be better for it." And Theodore Kupferman, a city councilor and liberal Republican, joined the chorus of the righteous by asking: "Are we to return to a system of hyphenated Americans? We are and should be one people and not merely united on a percentage basis."

Such implacable obtuseness among the "advanced" citizenry of New York is a measure of white distance from reality. In simple logic, an ethnic survey is eminently sensible if we are concerned with discovering just what the Negro job situation is in various sectors of the economy. John C. McCabe, a member of the Mayor's Committee on Job Advancement, made this embarrassingly obvious point in a letter to *The New York Times*:

> Legitimate investigative processes, designated so as better to understand the results of past sins of commission and omission in employment practices, are necessary and legitimate. All involved—unions, employers and government—bear a responsibility. In the case of various levels of government, involvement includes not only their function as guardians of certain basic rights, but also the responsibilities that come in their capacity as employers.

Nonetheless, even when it is a matter of determining the extent of past injustice—let alone the establishing of present and future "special privileges"—there are those whites who seriously ask how Negroes can justify their having so long insisted that the law be color-blind if they now demand that their color be taken into account.

In answering exactly this question in an interview for *United States News and World Report*, Dr. Kenneth Clark couldn't have been more basic and more accurate:

> We can't tomorrow say: "All right, we're not going to have any more segregation, we're not going to have any more discrimination. We're going to treat all Americans as if they are Americans, and therefore everything will be all right." This is nonsense. During the transition period from injustice to justice, it is my personal opinion that we cannot pretend that there are no consequences of past injustices. We've got to face those consequences and do whatever is necessary to rectify them.

Clark was asked whether he, therefore, was advocating color-consciousness during the transition period.

> Absolutely, because the problems are problems that resulted from color-consciousness. It has to be resolved by color-consciousness until we get to that ideal state where we need no longer worry about a person's color.

Not only whites substitute pietism for analytical thought when confronted with the idea of "special privilege." The in-

domitably inconsistent Adam Clayton Powell has said, again in
United States News and World Report:

> I do not believe in preferential treatment for Negroes at all.
> All I'm asking for is that the doors of opportunity in every
> area be opened, and then let the Negro take his own chance
> on whether he will succeed or not.

But what of those Negroes who find a double lock on those
doors and cannot open the second because of inferior education
and inexperience in fields previously closed to Negroes? What
of them, moreover, in a period of growing structural unemployment?

An incisively pragmatic analysis of the long-range perspective
is that of Stanley Steinbaum, an economist on the staff of the
Center for the Study of Democratic Institutions:

> As long as the general unemployment remains acute, all talk
> about the race issue is as if in a vacuum. Equality in employ-
> ment will only be achieved in a full-employment situation; we
> all know how discriminatory the labor unions are, the more so
> the higher the level of unemployment. Both the union mem-
> bers and their officials will protect their own first, and to
> hell with the race problem. Therefore, as long as unemploy-
> ment remains high, the minorities are not going to be able
> to get a fair shake at jobs. The removal of unemployment is
> absolutely a necessary condition for the resolution of this
> aspect of the race issue.

But are Negroes to be expected to wait until then? As a
Negro picketer at a New York City construction site told me,
"We want to share what employment there is now. So far,
we've only been invited to share the unemployment."

Although, therefore, it is illogical for Negro militants to
focus *all* their energies on changing, for example, union apprenticeship programs, it is unrealistic to expect Negroes not to
continue pressing for an equitable proportion of both the apprenticeships and the jobs which *now* exist—even though the
available jobs can accommodate only a fraction of unemployed
Negroes in the indeterminate period before there is much
more employment for all. And in many cases an equitable

present proportion cannot be achieved without some form of "compensatory treatment."

An integral part of the pressure for a share of current employment is an exposure of white deceit, rationalizations, and other techniques of avoiding admission of what has been done in the past. The unavoidable result of this "speaking truth to power," to use a Quaker phrase, is exacerbated tensions because euphemism and evasion have become endemic to so much white discussion of "the race problem."

I would again suggest that white readers of this book try role-reversal. If you were Negro, consider Harry Van Arsdale, Jr., head of New York's Local 3, International Brotherhood of Electrical Workers, and president of that city's AFL–CIO Central Labor Council. In terms of its public image, Local 3 has become one of the more "open" of the building-trades locals in New York. Under NAACP pressure, the union agreed to admit a substantial number of nonwhites among the thousand additional apprentices it promised to take in as part of a 1962 settlement with employers which won nine thousand Local 3 members a twenty-five-hour week. The NAACP still has questions as to how thoroughly Negroes are integrated into all strata of the union, but to the city at large Van Arsdale is a "liberal."

Yet when Negro demonstrations against employers and unions began mounting in New York during 1963, Van Arsdale told a WCBS radio audience: "Some unions could possibly be criticized for not having given an equal opportunity, but that's a lot different from charging a person with discrimination whose life work has been trying to help workers of all kinds of backgrounds." As a Negro, would you be able to see the rather fine line Mr. Van Arsdale draws? The line is all the more dim in view of these statistics: in 1950, when Negroes were 13 per cent of New York City's population, they made up 1.5 per cent of the city's apprentices; and ten years later, when Negroes were 22 per cent of the population, they still constituted little more than 2 per cent of the total number of apprentices.

As in almost all other cities, the traditional craft unions in the building trades have been among those especially resistant to increased Negro apprenticeship in New York. Yet Van Arsdale was able to say on the same radio program that New York's Building and Construction Trades Council "historically has granted opportunities to all workers."

When Negro spokesmen deal with union officials who are not "liberals," the barriers to communication become impenetrable. As of mid-August 1963, Local 46, Metal Lathers Union, had between sixteen hundred and seventeen hundred members in New York City. Only two were Negro. John Mooney, a lawyer for Local 46, patiently explained to the City Commission on Human Rights that the local accepts as apprentices only those "sponsored" by other members. It is, in sum, a "family" union. In most cases fathers sponsored sons or other close relatives. White sponsored white. When asked if this custom could possibly be regarded as discriminatory against Negroes, Mr. Mooney answered, "Perhaps these methods are archaic, but they were never intended for racial discrimination."

Even if one were to accept the remarkable conclusion that the closing of the local to Negroes was never a factor in the continuance of these "archaic" methods, can a Negro be expected to care about the difference between the "intent" and the effect of the custom?

The pattern throughout the country has been drawn in the 1963 *Report of the United States Commission on Civil Rights*:

> In all sections of the country, the artisans of the skilled trades are overwhelmingly of the white race. Apprenticeship programs are maintained jointly by unions and employers to sustain the pool of skilled craftsmen; they contain almost no Negroes. The causes for lack of participation by Negroes in the advisory committee reports vary, but most important are: Traditional racial patterns of the skilled crafts; lack of encouragement and motivation of Negro youth to aspire to these occupations; discriminatory practices by unions and employers; and practices that have the effect of excluding Negroes, such as family preferences in selections by joint apprenticeship committees. . . . Consequently, Negroes are

forced to seek the dwindling opportunities for unskilled labor. The apprenticeship problem contributes to the Negro un-employment rate, which is over twice that of the white.

Herbert Hill underlines a legacy of this exclusion: "More than 50 per cent of all the unskilled Negro workers in the country were unemployed for substantial periods since 1958, and it is evident that the unskilled Negro, 45 years of age and over, who has lost his job will never again work at productive, gainful employment."

An end to discrimination within unions is not going to result from the voluntary pledges of the unions themselves. No matter what the national leaders of the AFL–CIO and of each international union promise, most local affiliates do not expect they will suffer any serious sanctions from within labor if they continue to bar Negroes, severely limit the number they accept, or discriminate against them once they're in. With the notable exception of the United Packinghouse Workers of America, exceedingly few international unions have put any degree of convincing pressure on those of their locals which practice bias against Negroes. In nearly all cases the local is subject only to "moral pressure" from the eyries in the "house of labor." Technically the AFL–CIO could expel a local which persistently discriminated, but it has never taken such an action and its present leadership gives no indication of changing that pattern, particularly with union membership decreasing.

Federal laws and regulations against discrimination in apprenticeship programs and in other union practices are of use only if administrators are given strong enforcement powers, including the right to initiate complaints, and only if those in charge are not vulnerable to the sizable political pressure against change which the construction unions in particular have been able to muster.

In the decade ahead there is sure to be an increase in such laws and rules and in their strength on paper. Excessive faith, however, cannot be placed in the potential effect of just promulgating laws and administrative rules—whether federal, state, or local. There are Northern cities with all manner of anti-discrimination ordinances, but the Negro in the ghetto has had little reason to be aware of them.

On January 3, 1964, a *New York Times* editorial noted:

> Thanks to progress made in 1963, every industrial state outside the South now has an enforceable fair employment law. More than 15 million Americans are protected by such a legal prohibition against racial or religious bias in job-hiring. More than 50 million Americans are covered by laws barring discrimination and more than 74 million by fair housing laws. Some 25 states strengthened their anti-discrimination laws in 1963—the largest number ever to take such action in a single year.
>
> The old year had its sunny side.

If the racial weather were that sunny and if all those laws were persistently *enforced*, there would be no reason for this and the next chapter in this book. I am not saying that all applicable laws should not be passed at every level of government, but I am emphasizing that the presence of a resounding law against discrimination can encourage whites in the delusion that the law is *working*.

(I have, incidentally, cited *The New York Times* here and in other sections of the book because, more than any other communications medium in the country, the *Times* editorially represents the thinking of whites of good will who consider themselves well informed on race "relations" and capable of suggesting responsible solutions to the multiple aspects of the "Negro problem." Yet, because the *Times*, for all its conscientiousness, is so often at a great distance from Negro reality, it—and those for whom the *Times* speaks—contributes greatly to further confusion, rather than clarification, of the basic issues.)

With regard to making it possible for Negroes to get a fairer share of jobs *now*, one of the more practical ways of insuring that union locals enroll Negro apprentices in meaningful numbers is—besides passing any new laws required—reshaping the boards which actually administer apprenticeship programs. Depending on the local situation, along with union and management representatives, a board could also consist of "public members" appointed by city or state governments; personnel from a state or local agency which has been specifically charged with eliminating bias in apprenticeship; and representatives of minority groups, civil rights organizations, and local human rights commissions.

In many communities any such eventuality will require mass pressure in the form of demonstrations at construction sites and businesses as well as other forms of dramatized protest. Most effective, of course, is the acquisition of enough unified power —including political force—to make it exceedingly uncomfortable for unions not to reappraise their "customs."

In Detroit, for example, the Trade Union Leadership Council, an affiliate of the Negro American Labor Council, was instrumental in electing the city's Mayor in 1962 against a candidate endorsed by the United Auto Workers. While demonstrating that degree of power, the TULC, with a membership of over ten thousand, has also opened the rolls of eighteen out of nineteen construction unions in Detroit to *all* qualified applicants. In addition, the TULC set up its own program for training Negro youngsters for skilled work—to assure that there will be enough qualified Negroes for apprenticeship openings.

The root solution in particularly refractory cases would be the National Labor Relations Board's readiness to implement the NAACP demand for the decertification as a bargaining agent of a union barring or otherwise discriminating against Negroes. Despite the roar that would rise from all sections of organized labor if the NLRB were to proceed actively along this line, I expect that in the years ahead the threat of decertification may become an increasingly effective way of bringing unions to the first stage of conversion.

As unions do start admitting apprentices without discrimination, there are ways of making it easier for Negroes to take advantage of the end of bias. These are methods which are likely to face less white resistance because, while "preferential," they apply to the disadvantaged of all colors. But since there are proportionately more Negro than white poor, the methods could increase the percentage of Negroes in those trades based on the apprenticeship system. In an analysis in the *New York Herald Tribune,* June 16, 1963, labor reporter Joel Seldin noted that when a Negro becomes an apprentice in, for example, one of the building trades, he has to face the fact that:

> Even an accepted apprentice is subject to the sporadic employment in the building trades, and must be able to bridge periods of no work. Government officials who report a Negro drop-out rate of 30 to 50 per cent in apprentice programs, also point out that a white employed craftsman can afford to support his son through apprenticeship, while an unskilled, unemployed Negro father cannot. . . . One suggestion being considered as a labor proposal is that the government underwrite the slack periods in apprenticeship training, and possibly the wage differentials to make the programs economically possible for Negroes [and for the white poor].

Furthermore, there are many Negroes and dispossessed whites who, because of inferior education, are not eligible for apprenticeship programs as they are presently constituted. In this context Walter Reuther suggests "special consideration" in the form of special training classes for such applicants. It is an idea some unions could accept before a civil rights siege begins.

Even, however, if all bars were down in all unions, another basic dilemma would remain in many. Once on the list as an apprentice, how—without some form of "special privilege"—does a Negro transcend the results of past discrimination to get a "fair share" of current work? In New York, officials of Pipefitters Union Local 638 admitted in 1963 that there were no Negro or Puerto Rican members among the 4000 in the local who were engaged in construction work. There were, moreover, some 431 whites and six nonwhites already on a waiting list to participate in the pipefitters' five-year apprentice training program. Any Negro or Puerto Rican accepted by the local at that time could not become an apprentice until 1972.

Concerning the apprenticeship system as a whole in New York—and his analysis applies for much of the rest of the country—Roy Wilkins of the NAACP estimated in May 1963 that "given a continuance of the present rate of advance, it will take

Negroes . . . until 2098 to secure equal participation in skilled craft training or employment."

Although, as I have noted, much more than opening present apprenticeship rosters is necessary to provide work for the mass of Negroes, I am discussing this aspect in detail to indicate what happens at this point in our history if color is forgotten and each man is judged on his own. A man who could not have been admitted to a union because of his color before, let us say, 1963, and is then told he has to wait his turn "democratically" is not likely to consider that he is being given equality of opportunity.

As for increasing the number of apprenticeships so that at least more Negroes can begin the ascent sooner, few craft unions are going to abandon voluntarily their tradition of planned scarcity of apprentices—a practice which is meant to assure a maximum amount of available work for current members. It may be that, as campaigns for short work weeks become more successful, there will be a corollary rise in apprentices, but this is all too speculative so far as those Negroes are concerned who want more than prognoses. Another longer-range possibility is that many kinds of seniority—from apprenticeship lists to priority on the job—are going to become obsolete. A. Philip Randolph suggests that one benefit to minority groups from automation may be that it will obliterate more and more historic craft lines. Special new skills are necessary for the proliferating range of new jobs, and this continually changing alignment of job qualifications could bring about the breakdown of many traditional seniority structures. This eventuality too, however, is of small comfort to *today*'s Negro unemployed.

One "preferential" remedy for the present imbalance of opportunity would be the abandonment by unions of past apprenticeship lists, in the manner promised by the Building and Construction Trades Council of Elizabeth, New Jersey, and environs. In October 1963, after Negro picketing and other forms of mass demonstrations, that labor group announced that it was going to replace its apprenticeship lists and give tests on which new lists would be based. Supervising the new examinations would be a joint management-labor apprenticeship committee;

and, significantly, the tests would be administered by "an agency other than unions." Whether the plan is a mirage or not depends on what happens *after* the tests.

In any case, very few other locals can be expected willingly to follow the Elizabeth labor group's lead in compiling wholly new lists. There are civil rights lawyers, however, who maintain that the courts can force a union to revise its waiting lists if prior bias against Negroes can be proved. In a paper delivered at a New York conference of CORE in January 1964, Joseph B. Robison, Assistant National Director of the American Jewish Congress's Commission on Law and Social Action said:

> There is hardly any question that existing seniority rosters and waiting lists—for jobs, union membership or training programs—can be nullified. If they were built up at a time when discrimination was in effect, they are tainted with illegality and cannot be relied on. . . . It follows that seniority rights can never be a legal barrier to remedial action. They are, of course, a potent practical consideration. No union will abandon them willingly. No administrative agency will lightly order their abandonment. But that need not stay us. We may call for abrogation of biased seniority rosters at any time, even during the term of a collective bargaining agreement.

An important and, one hopes, a precedent-making decision in this context was the action of the New York State Commission for Human Rights in March 1964. The commission found Local 28 of the Sheet Metal Workers International Association guilty of deliberately discriminating against Negroes. The local, founded seventy-six years ago, had never had a Negro member. The commission ordered the local to scrap its apprenticeship waiting list and begin a new one. The nine hundred on the current waiting list and all future would-be apprentices would have to apply under a new procedure.

This procedure, as summarized in *The New York Times* March 24, includes these regulations:

> Local 28 and the union-management committee for selecting apprentices must specify in writing the minimum "objective standards, tests and requirements" for apprentices.

These standards must be formally approved by the State Industrial Commissioner before they are put into effect.

The father-son selection system must be ended so that "in no event shall sponsorship by a member or members of Local 28 be adopted as a requirement for apprenticeship training.". . .

Any rejected applicant, if he believes he was the object of discrimination, may have the matter reviewed by the State Commissioner of Education.

In the years immediately ahead there will be more and more calls in the courts for such abrogation or revision of the seniority lists of those unions which have discriminated in the past. Accordingly, unless Congress changes markedly in its ideas and in the pace with which it passes legislation designed to expand the economy greatly, this problem of trying to make up for past bias during present high unemployment is going to lead to increased tension between Negroes and some sections of organized labor.

Ironically, while the public debate continues as to whether "special efforts" to compensate Negroes for past discrimination are "democratic," there is an active trend among *employers* to take color into account when hiring. Before examining this phenomenon, it is useful to dispose of the semantic net in which the issue has been caught. It is often claimed that special privilege will degrade the Negro by continuing his dependence, his second-class citizenship. As one letter writer to the *New York Herald Tribune* asked, "What would we do to his self-esteem if he feels he is being pushed forward regardless of performance?" The basic confusion here is "regardless of performance."

No conscientious Negro leaders, to my knowledge, have advocated placing Negroes in jobs with no concern for their present *capacities* for being trained for a particular function. What is being demanded is that Negroes—in "preferred" numbers—be given the chance to prove they *can* perform in a wide variety of positions so long closed to them.

"This does not mean," says Whitney Young of the Urban

League, "the establishment of a quota system—an idea shunned by responsible Negro organizations and leaders. But, because we are faced with the hypocrisy of 'tokenism,' where the presence of two or three Negro employees is passed off as integration, we are forced, during the transitional stages, to discuss numbers and categories."

Although he calls for "numbers and categories," rather than quota systems, Young is supporting *some* form of transitional selection and recruitment *by color*.

Consider the traditional evasion of employers who are prejudiced against Negroes or are apathetic about equal opportunity. These employers, when pressed, generally contend that their work force is not integrated, or is only minimally mixed, because no qualified Negroes have ever applied for jobs above a low level of competence. Usually Negroes have stayed away from such a firm because they anticipated rejection. Now, as all businesses are becoming subject to pressure, this genre of employer will only be able to prove he is concerned about integrating his staff by going out and recruiting "numbers and categories" of Negroes.

For various reasons an assumption of responsibility for *finding* Negro employees is rapidly gaining adherents among employers. Some act as a result of or in apprehension of boycotts and demonstrations. Others also realize the gains to be made in the economy as a whole if Negroes acquire more purchasing power. And there are some who are making a "special effort" out of a sense of moral urgency. Whatever the motivations, there has been more action toward providing equality by "compensatory" means among employers than among labor unions, despite the "liberal" protestations of the latter's national leaders.

"While the so-called 'moral' sources of social change," says Dr. Kenneth Clark, "are lagging behind—I mean political and labor leaders, educators, and, until quite recently, the churches —more and more hard-headed, realistic businessmen have been moving ahead. It's another source of my belief that major alteration of the Negro's condition is going to come through the imperatives of political and economic power rather than through moral imperatives."

Among employers involved in various "compensatory" approaches, the terms "special" or "compensatory" are seldom used; but that is exactly the concept which is operating both in such federal contract-enforcing stratagems as the Plans for Progress Program of the President's Committee on Equal Opportunity and in the policies of more and more individual businesses not covered by that plan nor by similar programs.

An increasingly characteristic business position is that of Carl Haugen, personnel director of Chase Manhattan Bank in New York. "We've found," Haugen told *Business Week*, "that we can no longer wait for Negroes to apply for jobs. We have to go and seek them out at the high schools and colleges, and let placement people know that we want to see all qualified candidates." Personnel directors are also discovering that it is necessary to advertise on Negro radio stations and in Negro newspapers as well as to utilize such supplemental recruitment help as that provided by the Urban League and its "skills banks" of qualified Negroes in a growing number of cities.

In addition, there is a rise in the number of firms which go beyond intensified recruitment of employees by color. Pitney-Bowes, a Stamford, Connecticut, manufacturer of postage and mailing equipment, has relaxed testing and experience requirements for Negro applicants. According to John O. Nicklis, president of Pitney-Bowes, the firm—which, incidentally, has no unions—has come to the "tentative conclusion" that below-standard educational opportunities for Negroes in the past have to be taken into account. Therefore Pitney-Bowes is now meeting some of its employment needs "by hiring inexperienced Negroes and giving them special on-the-job training." Nicklis has emphasized that his company's policy, however, does not extend to making "a direct comparison of two applicants, one white and one Negro, and choosing one because of his color."

Direct comparison of this sort is, however, beginning to take place in some firms. No business has announced so bold and controversial a means of "preferential" hiring as official company policy, but there are auguries in press reports on business. In the summer of 1963 a General Motors official in Detroit, fearful of a Negro boycott of GM throughout the Northeast, admitted to a *Business Week* reporter: "Today, if two applicants for a job at GM have equal qualifications and one is a Negro, the Negro will get the job." Around the same time a Chicago personnel director told *Newsweek* that when a white and a Negro apply for the same job, "all other things being equal, we'll take the Negro."

Whether or not they hire Negroes over equally qualified whites, more of the firms now zealously seeking Negroes are adopting the Pitney-Bowes position that they will have to alter previous prerequisites of experience and current knowledge for certain job categories if they are to hire significant enough numbers of Negroes. In the process of providing on-the-job training for Negroes with capacity but with undeveloped skills, there may be a temporary decrease in efficiency in some businesses. However, as one unnamed industrialist told *Fortune:* "Make no mistake about it, we're going to have to subsidize Negro employment for some time. But it will be a lot cheaper to do that than to pay it out in welfare"—or, as Charles E. Silberman of *Fortune* added, "in the cost to the community of racial violence."

As for the fear that a company's efficiency may be lessened because some of its white workers are hostile to Negroes, most experience at integrated firms so far has shown that when management makes its hiring policies clear, prejudiced white workers will stay rather than face unemployment or the search for another job which may not be as desirable.

An increasingly typical illustration of employer-directed integration in practice occurred during 1963 when the United States Steel Company, under pressure from the federal government, began opening more job opportunities for Negroes in its Alabama plants and also eliminated separate racial lines of promotion. As a result, some Negroes moved into positions which had traditionally been white, and some, for the first time, became supervisors of white workers.

Resistance from whites was considerably less than the company had expected. "They're going along with the change," a company official explained, "because jobs aren't so easy to get any more." As for white union locals which bristled at the new policy, the company has made it clear to them that "if they don't accept it, we could get less government contracts."

Eventually, in those steel plants, with greater or lesser speed, propinquity will dissolve many of the myths and stereotypes both races nurture about each other. At first white behavior patterns will probably change more readily than white attitudes toward Negroes; but as time goes on, altered ways of acting in relation to a Negro can in some cases begin to change even deeply ingrained attitudes. In any event, what is most important to Negroes is to have access to the jobs.

As United States Steel's efforts in Alabama show, there are instances when a resolute management can alter restrictive union policies, particularly when it can point to the alternative —because of federal scrutiny of employment patterns—of less work for everyone in the plant.

Furthermore, there are businesses that have no unions with which to contend and others which have retained considerable unilateral power to decide entrance requirements and rates of progression of new workers. While it is true, therefore, that unions, especially in traditional crafts, still maintain sizable pockets of resistance, much can be and is being done by employers to initiate fundamental change on their own. (A survey of these directions in business can be found in management consultant John Perry's "Business—Next Target for Integration?" in the *Harvard Business Review*, March–April 1963.)

A variety of "compensatory" devices is also in rising evidence elsewhere in the society. A comprehensive catalogue of developments is not within the scope of this chapter, but the trend is unmistakable. For one example, the New York State Association of Trial Lawyers, recognizing that only five of its thirty-five hundred members were Negroes, decided in December 1963 to set up a scholarship program in the law for minority-group youngsters. A similar plan has been undertaken by the New York chapter of the American Institute of Architects. The State Department, in conjunction with the Ford Foundation and Howard University, has started a project to enlist more Negroes in the United States Foreign Service. In another form of "special treatment," municipalities, Philadelphia and New York among them, are creating referral offices specifically to help Negroes get jobs in a wide range of fields. Early in 1964 the school board of Pittsburgh revealed that it intended to follow a policy of "conscious preferment" in the hiring of Negro employees, including teachers, to remedy the results of past discrimination.

In sum, while arguments continue about "compensatory treatment," more and more employment policy-makers in business and government are proceeding along a preferential line.

Having attempted in this chapter to indicate what *is* happening in this area, I must also re-emphasize that compensatory special efforts for the Negro should be regarded only as a transitional tactic which can at best benefit only a small percentage of Negroes. So far as the black masses are concerned, it would be cruelly misleading to maintain that these special efforts can—now or in the future—be of substantial advantage to *them*, with their presently insufficient skills. To solve the basic employment problems of the Negro underclass, there is no substitute for radically revised educational systems of greatly increased quality for all the dispossessed, and there is no substitute for much more governmental planning as automation accelerates.

I agree, therefore, with Tom Kahn, who has written a major analysis of the "Problems of the Negro Movement" in the Winter 1964 issue of *Dissent*:

> There is the danger that the emphasis on preferential treatment sows the illusion that Negroes can make progress in a declining economy, and diverts attention from the real nature of the unemployment problem. . . . Used functionally in negotiations with certain employers [and unions], preferential treatment can be advantageous; broadcast as a central slogan, it drives a wedge between Negroes and those whites who stand most to gain from a political alliance for economic reform.

My point here, however, has been that some degree of preferential treatment now is both necessary and possible—so long as the larger goal is not thereby obscured or abandoned. Until, therefore, "special efforts" for everyone in the underclass are actually put into operation on a sizable enough basis, the particular problems which afflict the Negro dispossessed point to the fact that it is both too late and too soon to be color-blind.

The continued resistance of many union locals, particularly in the building trades and other crafts, to integration has been clear since this book was first written. Even when new laws have been passed and new court decisions made, whatever integration has occurred so far is, in most cases, token. Accordingly, there will be much more of a direct confrontation between Negroes and labor unions in the decade ahead—a circumstance which further brings into question the "broad-based coalition" for "a new Left" which Bayard Rustin and Michael Harrington, among others, somehow see signs of in the present. Such an eventual coalition is, of course, essential for pervasive social change, but it is self-deluding to expect much real support from most of organized labor in the immediate future.

The way of the immediate future was underlined in the spring of 1965 by Dr. Frank Arricale, Deputy Director of JOIN in New York City: "We are telling the union leaders, 'It's either us or the deluge. Make our Negro and Puerto Rican kids part of the labor movement or your heads will roll in ten years. . . . If you do not open up your unions, you will find that organized labor has a new enemy. Not Wall Street, but the Negroes and Puerto Ricans . . . and those who fight alongside them.' "

For further reading connected with this chapter, I would suggest Herbert Hill's "Twenty Years of State Fair Employment Practice Commissions: A Critical Analysis with Recommendations," *Buffalo Law Review*, Fall 1964.

8

The Creeping Ghetto

You can't get melted if you don't get into the pot.
—Edwin Berry, Executive Director,
Chicago Urban League

Quotas are a deceptively simple attempt to solve a complex problem and just will not work. The only real solution is an open housing market.
—Frances Levenson, Director, National Committee against Discrimination in Housing

"I have been writing the Mayor and the Housing Authority since 1957 trying to get an apartment." The letter to the *New York Amsterdam News*, a Negro weekly, in the winter of 1963 continued: "There are nine in my family and we live in a one-and-a-half room apartment. We have been trying desperately to get an apartment but can't because of the children. We are working people who wish only to have a decent home for our children, but we just don't know what to do any more.

"I have so many letters," the writer continued, "from different people, including the Health Department, the Building Department, the President, and many others that I have written to or have been to see. We get no results. I am wondering if there is anyone who has had this problem, and what they did about it? We just can't take any more."

The millions of Negro poor who have this problem continue

to live in overcrowded ghettos which grow in size as well as in density because of continued Negro migration from the South and because the Negro birth rate is higher than that of whites. (Between 1950 and 1960 the gain in Negro population as a whole was at the rate of 25.4 per cent, while the gain among whites was 17.5 per cent.)

In the past decade Northern city neighborhoods have also become more segregated as a result of the ways in which the majority of public housing and urban renewal projects have been planned and administered. The United States Commission on Civil Rights concluded in its 1963 report that "housing discrimination is perhaps the most ubiquitous and deeply rooted civil rights problem in America."

We have finally realized that urban renewal so far has intensified rather than alleviated the housing problems of the poor, black and white, who have been uprooted. Promised efforts at relocating them in "decent" housing which they can afford have been largely inadequate. For example, only 17 per cent of the total number of families displaced by urban renewal have gone into public housing. The reasons vary. Almost half of these families are ineligible for public housing because their incomes are too high, or, more often, too low, or because of what city planner Chester Hartman has described as "irregular household composition, failure to meet residence requirements, or objectionable social behavior." There are also those who, though eligible, reject public housing because the projects are often so grim and authoritarian.

For whatever reasons, less than one-third of *eligible* families dispossessed by urban renewal have moved into public housing. Among eligible *white* families, only 7 per cent have elected public housing. Since a much larger proportion of nonwhites than whites has been affected by urban renewal and since their incomes are generally lower and their color gives them far less choice in finding new homes, about 25 per cent of the eligible nonwhite families, mostly Negroes, *have* found places in public projects. The rest squeeze into whatever they can find in the expanding "private" Negro slums. Furthermore, whatever integrated communities existed before the invasion of an urban renewal project have rarely been reconstituted afterward. Instead, greater Negro-white polarization has taken place.

To place these figures in further perspective, by the end of 1963, 106 urban renewal projects had been completed since provisions for them were written into the Housing Act of 1949. Already displaced had been 157,000 families and 32,000 individuals—70 to 80 per cent of them nonwhite. Currently being planned or under construction were 1300 more renewal projects. Unless the previous pattern is radically changed, a high proportion of those forced to move by future urban renewal will be added to the segregated slums.

As for public housing, virtually all of it was segregated at the end of the Second World War. By March 1963, according to the Public Housing Administration (*Trends Toward Open Occupancy*, Report #12), almost 78 per cent of the 3028 public housing projects in the 45 states which are involved in the federal program remained segregated. There were 1179 all-white projects, 1174 all-Negro projects, and 675 "completely integrated" projects. (Significantly, the Public Housing Administration defines a project as "completely integrated" if it includes at least one Negro family in what is otherwise an all-white project or one white family in an all-Negro situation.) This segregation continues either by conscious municipal design or as a result of unconcern with integration by local federal housing officials and by those who determine local site location and tenant composition.

A characteristic enclave is in Chicago, where 60,000 low-income Negroes live in a totally homogeneous public housing ghetto which extends for four uninterrupted miles of projects along State Street. At the end of 1963 in Boston, 98 per cent of the Negroes in public housing were concentrated in 7 of the program's 15 projects. In city after city racial stockades have been built with public funds.

Nor is there nearly *enough* public housing. In *Slums and Social Security*, a research report published by the U.S. Department of Health, Education, and Welfare in July 1963, Alvin

Schorr, who wrote the closely documented study, estimated: "If public housing were limited to the lowest incomes, with current resources it could house 2 million of the 32 million we have defined as poor [members of four-person families with total annual income of $2700]. As it reaches above the very lowest incomes, it houses even a smaller percentage of the poor than these figures indicate."

In New York City, for instance, although 230,000 public housing units have been built in the past decade, more than a million people continue to live in what *The New York Times* describes as "a bleak wasteland of broken plaster and fetid hallways, where every day children are bitten by rats." For all these New York slums to be replaced by new public housing would require an expenditure of at least 17 billion dollars.

This is where we are when we talk of arriving at an "open housing market" for Negroes. The urban slums, including those public housing projects which have turned into slums, are growing. The black sections of the slums are increasing even faster. In Phoenix 97 per cent of nearly all that city's Negroes are in a radius of a mile of the railroad tracks or the river bend. In Omaha all but a minute number of the 30,000 Negroes there are crowded into the near North Side. In Newark some 83 per cent live in six of the city's dozen neighborhoods, including three of Newark's most deteriorated areas. Except for 1500 of them, Boston's 63,000 Negroes are jammed into a boomerang-shaped, decaying area of adjoining neighborhoods in Roxbury, North Dorchester, and the South End. In Indianapolis 89 per cent of the Negroes are in Center Township, the "inner city," in homes that are 75 to 100 years old. Nationally, as Tom Kahn has reported, "one out of every 6 Negro dwelling units is dilapidated, obsolete or otherwise substandard, as compared with one in 32 white dwellings."

Therefore, when Robert C. Weaver, head of the Housing and Home Finance Agency, reported at the end of 1963 that the following year should see the beginning of significant dispersion of Negroes "from the segregated ghetto into the general community," I wished he had been much more specific as to how many poor families were to be part of the exodus. What forces, for example, are going to desegregate those four miles on Chicago's State Street?

Clearly, so far as private housing is concerned, nearly all the more sanguine prognoses for an increasingly open market are limited to middle-income Negroes. The rise of fair housing laws, for one example, has little relevance for those Negroes who can't afford to move out of the ghetto. For those who can, for that matter, these laws are underutilized because in most states and cities the administrators of the laws have yet to be given the power to determine on their own initiative—without waiting for complaints—where segregation exists. As a result, evasions proliferate.

A further illustration of the slow rate of dispersion of even middle-income Negroes is the limited help they have received from the late President Kennedy's executive order banning discrimination after November 1962 in certain kinds of federally assisted new and repossessed housing. Among the order's loopholes, in terms of private housing, was its restriction to homes and apartments financed with mortgage loans whose repayment is guaranteed by such federal agencies as the Federal Housing Administration, the Veterans Administration, and the Federal National Mortgage Association. Together, these three affect only about 30 per cent of private home sales.

(In passing, as another index of the discrimination in housing allowed by the government in the past, by 1959 fewer than 2 per cent of the millions of new private housing units whose mortgages had been insured by the FHA since 1934 and by the Veterans Administration since 1944 had been available to nonwhites.)

The Kennedy executive order will not greatly extend private housing integration until it is broadened to include "conventional mortgages," which cover the great majority of home financing. Although there are legal difficulties, this can be done by banning discrimination in financing by *all* institutions in the home mortgage field which are under federal supervision. Included, because their deposits are federally insured, would be most of the nation's banks and savings and loan associations. If this were accomplished, 90 per cent of mortgage transactions in private housing would be covered.

Despite the fact that the majority of mortgage lenders are still able to refuse mortgages to Negroes who want to buy homes in non-Negro areas, an increasing number of previously all-white neighborhoods *are* slowly being integrated. An important element in what success has been achieved are the "fair housing committees" which have been formed to open up their communities. From 1960 to 1963 the number of these committees throughout the country increased from eighteen to more than three hundred.

It is true, therefore, as various city commissions on human rights now emphasize, that more communities are beginning to accept middle-class nonwhite neighbors than many middle-class Negroes realize. And since there are now nearly two hundred thousand Negro families with incomes of $10,000 or more a year, the incidence of middle-class neighborhood integration should grow in the next decade.

Nonetheless, any optimism about this development ought to be severely curbed by a realization of the vast numbers of Negro families left behind. In October 1963 the National Committee Against Discrimination in Housing said it knew of two hundred Negro families which, during the previous year, had moved to formerly all-white suburban neighborhoods in Greater New York. It was also estimated that another hundred or more families had made similar moves without their names having come to the attention of the committee. In addition, about two thousand Negro families within the city of New York had occupied private apartments which had never before been open to Negroes. But in relation to the growing Negro ghettos in New York, the departures were not in the least noticeable.

No *basic* change has taken place in the design reported in 1961 by the United States Commission on Human Rights: "There is an ever-increasing concentration of nonwhites in racial ghettos, largely in the decaying centers of our cities—while a

'white noose' of new suburban housing grows up around them."
It has become fashionable to say that the noose will be broken
because whites will eventually have nowhere else to run. Negroes
must inevitably follow them in greater numbers to the suburbs.
Yet, if present patterns continue, they will follow in segregated
battalions.

Furthermore, as for the cities, the strong likelihood is that in
less than thirty years Negroes will constitute from one-quarter
to one-half of the total population in at least ten of the fourteen biggest central cities. Negroes are already in the majority
in Washington, D.C. Within fifteen years, they are apt to be
in the majority in Chicago, Detroit, Cleveland, Baltimore, and
Saint Louis—with Philadelphia to be added in the next decade.

Clearly an unprecedented degree of governmental planning,
financing, and enforcing of anti-discrimination regulations is the
only way to avoid the continued and deeper entrenchment of
segregated housing patterns, let alone to provide enough low-
income housing to meet the needs of the white and Negro poor.
Without startling new incentives, private builders will remain
chronically uninterested in low-income housing. In the course
of a study on urban renewal for *The New Republic*, Wolf von
Eckart disclosed in September 1963 that as of that date one-half
of 1 per cent of all the housing which has been financed by the
FHA has been aimed at those with an annual income of under
$5000. The figures for private low-income housing built without
any federal assistance are minuscule.

At base, as sociologist Herbert Gans has noted, a far better
solution than massive public housing and other government-
supported schemes to improve and expand low-income housing
"would be to attack poverty directly, to give poor people sufficient incomes that will enable them to buy or rent homes
like everyone else." This solution, of course, also "eliminates
many of the other evils from which the poor suffer" besides bad
housing.

In the meantime, however—and the attack on poverty can
last for decades—there are going to be dense concentrations of
the poor with insufficient, inadequate housing unless compre-

hensive plans are devised and financed to change their living conditions. Such plans will also have to include a wider variety and depth of social services to cope with the problems caused by previous years of slum living—problems which accompany many families to "better" housing.

The alternative is a permanently segregated "underclass" with personalities either squashed or ready for the kind of revolution which will make all previous social upheavals in this country tepid by comparison.

If past errors are not to be compounded, an essential change in direction is toward community-wide planning and away from the project-by-project approach. The federal government is encouraging this concept, but for it to take hold will require the active participation of civic groups with the power to persuade myopic municipal officials.

Among ways of humanizing future housing for the poor in what Chester Hartman describes as "satisfying, heterogeneous living environments" are rehabilitating rather than destroying neighborhoods which can be saved and then providing the residents with direct rental and home-improvement subsidies. It is also possible to allocate apartments in private middle-income buildings for use by low-income families under forms of rent subsidy. In addition, Hartman has pointed out that "families can be given rent certificates which will permit them to go out and rent (or even buy) homes on their own, in any part of the city, in any neighborhood or building they wish to live in." Federal housing officials have, in fact, already begun experimenting on a very small scale with a number of ways in which low-income families can be helped to buy their own homes.

The hardest of all housing problems involve those families at the very bottom who cannot meet the present eligibility criteria of *any* publicly assisted plan to provide low-cost housing. In public housing projects, for example, those criteria (depending on variations from city to city) now exclude large numbers of families with illegitimate children, families with members who are drug addicts or have otherwise broken the law, and families which have owed landlords in the past. "Who," Wolf von

Eckhart has asked, "would rent an apartment to a colored family on relief with a blind father and fourteen children, two of whom are in prison and one of whom is on probation for shoplifting?"

I asked a similar question of the chief housing expert for one of the major civil rights groups. "I don't have the answer," he said. "We have no program for those with the very lowest incomes and the most severe problems. We just don't have the resources. For their desperation to be ended will require an awakening of the society as a whole to how many of them there are and where they are. Sure, what I'm saying is a cop-out. We've all copped out. The amount of money needed to help *them* hasn't even begun to be suggested to Congress."

Within the range of present possibility, however, greater progress can be made toward ending racial segregation in private and public housing. Official "benign quotas" (systems of homeowner and tenant selection aimed at insuring integration) are increasingly suggested. I suspect, however, that discussion of their use is academic. Nearly all civil rights organizations, to begin with, are opposed to quotas for various reasons. Even though "benign," quotas can be used as a guise for tokenism. Fixed numbers, moreover, even when regarded as a transitional stratagem, have a tendency to become rigid.

A more fundamental obstacle is that in most, if not all states, it would be extremely difficult to legitimatize a "benign quota" by law. Even if this *were* possible, anyone excluded by a quota could probably challenge it successfully in court on the ground that a quota does not meet the requirement of equal protection of the laws guaranteed by the Fourteenth Amendment. (A fascinating examination of the constitutional issues on both sides of the question of benign quotas in housing is "The Case of the Checker-Board Ordinance: An Experiment in Race Relations" by Professor Boris I. Bittker of the Yale Law School, *Yale Law Journal*, July 1962.)

In the absence of official benign quotas, what can be done? In private housing, in the suburbs particularly, there will surely be additional variations on the practices already developed in those neighborhoods which contain white residents who do not object to integration but who do not want it to reach whatever "tipping" point will make the community predominantly Negro. Essentially the solution involves informal, voluntary agreements among whites and Negroes to work for a racial balance in the neighborhood by getting buyers in the desired racial proportions for houses as they become vacant. If the system does become inflexible and if anyone feels injured thereby, he can claim discrimination in court, either on the basis of local anti-bias laws or by citing the Fourteenth Amendment.

With regard to public housing, President Kennedy's executive order of November 1962 did bar discrimination in all federally assisted public housing projects built after that date. In addition, the order directed all federal housing agencies to "use their good offices, and to take other appropriate action permitted by law, including . . . litigation if required" to move against discrimination in all existing housing, private and public, which is federally insured or financed. Those "good offices" have been largely unused so far, even though there is strong reason to believe that a federal ban on segregation in all *public* housing built *before* November 1962 would stand up in court.

With regard to future public housing, the quantity is sure to expand beyond the current rate of 35,000 new units a year in view of the long waiting lists at many projects and the huge numbers of the poor who have not yet been included in any public housing plans. As an index, however, of how slow the present pace is toward meeting this demand, the housing bill proposed by President Lyndon Johnson soon after he took office provided for only 240,000 public housing units throughout the country within the next four years. As of now, New York City alone needs at least 200,000 units of additional public housing; but under the administration's bill the entire state of New York would be eligible for no more than 9000 such units during the next four years.

No matter how many new units are built, it is illusory to believe that all future public housing will automatically be integrated under the terms of the Kennedy executive order.

Even though discriminatory policies are not permitted now *after* a project has been built, site selection is a crucial determinant as to whether new public housing will actually be integrated. The Public Housing Authority does not yet have a firm policy of making certain that locations are chosen to encourage integration, but the PHA does say it will usually regard a public housing plan negatively if it can be demonstrated that a site has been chosen with a clear intent to segregate. A resistant municipality, however, can obliquely continue present housing patterns through site-selection in a ghetto neighborhood or a fringe area, without appearing to do so deliberately. The need persists for local groups to bring and maintain pressure on both the municipality and the PHA to insure optimum locations for public housing.

Similarly, as of June 1963 the Urban Renewal Administration now requires that all Community Renewal Programs (long-range, city-wide renewal plans, two-thirds of which are paid for under federal grants) must include affirmative proposals to end housing discrimination as well as to improve the quality and quantity of housing for minority families. Here too, interested local organizations will have to check continually on whether these proposals are sufficient and are enforced. Simultaneously, intensive local vigilance is needed to insure that segregated housing patterns are not continued as an aftermath of projected urban renewal activities which are not part of Community Renewal Programs under the federal definition of that term.

When a community *is* sensitized to the need for integrating present and future publicly assisted housing, practical methods of achieving that aim include not only building new developments outside ghettos but also using "selective" channels of soliciting tenants (such as advertising in the Negro press if the site is in an area previously closed to Negroes) and making the projects architecturally and otherwise attractive enough so that more families, white and Negro, will *want* to live in public developments.

In order to cut across the class segregation which is allied to color division, ways are being developed of combining lower-

and middle-income families in the same project. One approach is to raise the permissible incomes of families in a low-income project so that a family about to rise into the middle class doesn't have to leave. Another is to set up a schedule of skewed rentals in publicly supported middle-income developments, thereby allowing a proportion of low-income tenants to move in. Or the rents need not be skewed and the difference between low- and middle-income rents can be publicly subsidized. An additional method of decreasing class segregation is to allow cooperative ownership of apartments in a project. Not only would new middle-income families be retained, but conceivably this would be another inducement for white families to enter the projects, since the co-op price would be lower than prices in the private housing market.

Even aside from these incentives to bring more whites into projects, additional local action can be taken to desegregate present public housing. Civil rights groups—notably the NAACP—have shown the lead in this area in an increasing number of cities. Though not demanding fixed quotas, the NAACP claims that it is possible to determine by sight if a project is "reasonably" integrated. Accordingly, housing authorities in, among other cities, Baltimore, Jersey City, Boston, and New York have been persuaded to make advancement of integration as important a criterion in a tenant's assignment as any other factor.

In Boston, for example, the Housing Authority has committed itself to denying applicants free choice of projects if a choice is determined by the authority to have been based "on like or dislike of the racial composition of a project, building or community."

Depending on other priorities of need, white applicants in Boston, therefore, are to receive apartments on a first-come, first-served basis; but if, when their turn comes, a vacancy occurs in an integrated or a predominantly Negro development, they cannot decline the apartment on racial grounds—if they want to take advantage of their position on the waiting list.

In New York City the Housing Authority began in 1960 to

keep vacancies open in projects which were racially unbalanced, or becoming unbalanced, until applicants "whose occupancy would further integration" were interested in renting in those developments. This policy has since been abandoned because it runs counter to state laws against discrimination.

Furthermore, denying places to Negro families who need housing is of exceedingly doubtful morality, even if the reason for denial is the achievement of greater integration. The first and overriding desire of a Negro family on familiar terms with rats is to get into a habitable apartment, whether the building is integrated or not. This kind of dilemma involving two vital goals is yet another example of the inadequacies of *any* approach toward more integrated housing for low-income groups at a time when there is not enough housing for *all* low-income families. So long as we continue to deal with basic problems—education, employment, housing—in fragmentary forms, we will continue to get fragmentary solutions which are not, in the long run, solutions at all.

Another illustration, however, of what can be done now—on a limited basis—is the policy of the New York City Housing Authority which "encourages" new applicants for public housing to apply for a project in which their presence will improve that development's racial balance. Those who nonetheless prefer another project state their preference and are placed on a waiting list for that development in the order of their application. (Currently there are 85,000 applicants a year for 6000 vacancies.)

To some extent, the "encouragement" technique is working because, the authority claims, it does have "a list of applicants who have stated their preference for any development without regard to race, creed, color or national origin" of its inhabitants. As a result, when such a white applicant reaches the top of the waiting list and there is a vacancy in a project which needs more whites for balance, he is assigned there.

Clearly, for any attempt at integrating already existing public housing to be even partially successful, the commitment of each particular housing authority or board to this goal has to be made strongly evident to all its subordinates. To be color-blind in the administration of public housing at this point is to perpetuate segregation.

The new "plateau" of race relations, as one NAACP official describes it, requires persuading housing administrators, educators, employers, and government officials to go beyond the neutrality of non-discrimination and instead to adopt positive plans to advance integration. Pending a basic change in the economy, at least some progress toward this end can be made without quotas, benign or otherwise, but no significant advances can be accomplished without thinking in terms of color—and of class.

———————

The contention in this chapter of the need greatly to extend the late President Kennedy's 1962 executive order on housing discrimination is borne out by the fact that, as of the end of 1964, only seventeen per cent of new home construction was subject to those 1962 federal antidiscrimination regulations because only seventeen per cent was financed under Federal Housing Authority or Veterans Administration terms. (See also in this connection: "Bias in Housing—1962 Presidential Order Fails to Aid Integration in Most Neighborhoods," *Wall Street Journal*, July 16, 1964.)

As for the broader subject of housing, race, and class, an especially valuable analysis—and set of prescriptions for the future—is Herbert Gans' "The Failure of Urban Renewal," *Commentary*, April 1965.

9

Integrating Education

In this twentieth century, the uneducated man is not a man. He does not quite exist. In its deep-seated, visceral motivations, the Negro revolt is, in part, a desperate reaction against nonexistence.

—Eric Sevareid, *New York Post*, June 17, 1963

It has been said, correctly, that the schools alone cannot eliminate prejudice, discrimination and segregation. It is equally true that this task will not be accomplished with less than an all-out effort of the schools. Our schools must not be neutral in the struggle of society to better itself. We must not overlook the harmful effects of discrimination on the education of all children. Moreover, within the limits of our control, we must not acquiesce in the undemocratic school patterns which are a concomitant of segregated housing.

—New York City Board of Education "Policy Statement on Integration," June 26, 1963

NORTHERN whites increasingly recognize that education in many predominantly Negro schools in their cities is primarily incarceration. Except, however, for active members of public education associations and other socially oriented groups, their concern is abstract.

The middle-class white does not *see* the inadequacies of curriculum and of teacher attitude in the slum schools. Nor does he feel the fear of Negro parents that their children too will be incarcerated all their lives.

Percentages vary by city, but an over-all guide to the extent of school segregation is an analysis by Robert J. Havighurst, professor of education at the University of Chicago. Defining a racially segregated school as one in which 90 per cent or more of the pupils are of one race, Havighurst told a December 1962 meeting of the American Association for the Advancement of Science that "about 50 per cent of American Negro children are in segregated schools in the South, about 30 to 35 per cent are in segregated schools in the North and West, and no more than 15 per cent are in non-segregated schools."

In the biggest cities the percentage of segregated public schools rises sharply. As of 1963 in Chicago 170 schools were more than 90 per cent Negro, including 56 with nothing but Negro pupils. Moreover, 281 of the elementary and high schools had enrollments more than 90 per cent white, and 91 of those were entirely white. Altogether, 77 per cent of Chicago's schools were segregated. Half of the 214 elementary schools in Philadelphia were at least 97 per cent Negro. In Pittsburgh half that city's Negroes attended schools in which the enrollment was 80 per cent or more nonwhite. Throughout the country comparative achievement records bear out the contention of Meyer Weinberg, editor of the bimonthly magazine *Integrated Education,* that "by and large, the education provided those segregated Negro children was inferior."

At present the most common reaction of whites who are troubled by the imbalance of educational opportunity is to support the idea that schools in the ghetto be greatly improved. There is intense resistance to such plans for desegregating those schools as will affect the traditional "neighborhood school" policy of assigning pupils. This belief in the sanctity of the "neighborhood school" cuts across nearly all shades of white attitudes toward Negroes.

When a radical pacifist I know heard of a proposal to take his children by bus to a school twenty blocks away, his reaction was violent. "They're going to bus my kids out of Greenwich

Village," he came close to screaming, "over my dead body!" This man had participated in, and had sometimes led, nonviolent demonstations against the bomb and against segregation. He considered himself an anarchist and had no race prejudice. Yet I had never heard him as angry and as disturbed on any issue—including the Kennedy-Khrushchev confrontation over Cuba—as he was about the possible removal of his children from their neighborhood school.

As for the average non-radical white of good will, it can be fairly assumed that his spokesman on this issue is *The New York Times* or someone who thinks as the *Times* does. In an editorial on July 18, 1963, the *Times* pointed to the fact that in the borough of Manhattan "Negro and Puerto Rican children . . . total 76.5 per cent of elementary school enrollment and 71.6 per cent junior high school enrollment. Citywide there are 117 elementary schools whose pupils are Negro or Puerto Rican by 90 per cent or more." (The number now is actually 134.)

The *Times* emphasized that these predominantly nonwhite schools cannot be made white: "A satisfactory percentage of integration can be achieved neither by bussing, nor by zoning, nor by governmental fiat, nor by a magician's wand." In an earlier editorial (May 22, 1963) the *Times* had declared: "A basic solution will not come until a fundamental assault has been made on the walls of discrimination in the sale and rental of housing and until more and better jobs enable Negro breadwinners to move out of the slums."

In the preceding chapter I have indicated the length and complexity of the convoluted routes to "open housing." If one accepts the *Times*'s prescription, however, the only course at present, as that newspaper went on to suggest in its July editorial, is for the New York City Board of Education (and, presumably, educational administrators in other large cities) to do its best "with the fullest use of the tried previous methods, which include the open enrollment policy of moving some Negro children to underutilized schools in 'white' or mixed districts. New schools can and must be built in fringe areas. But the best thing it can do for the Negro now is to bring him the best school that can be bought, with money and talent."

A similar conclusion was reached by James B. Conant in his 1961 book, *Slums and Suburbs*: "I think it would be far better for those who are agitating for the deliberate mixing of children to accept *de facto* segregated schools as a consequence of a present housing situation and to work for the improvement of slum schools whether Negro or white."

The *Times*, and those who agree with the *Times*, have found an ally in Joseph P. Lyford, a staff member of the Center for the Study of Democratic Institutions. After researching a Fund for the Republic study of a forty-block area of the upper west side of Manhattan, Lyford disclosed in the summer of 1963: "In my interviews over the past ten months with low-income Negro and Puerto Rican parents in the area, never once has the question of racial percentages been raised as a concern. The parents' interests have been in the type of teachers the children have."

It would seem to me that there is serious doubt as to how truly representative Lyford's sampling is of Negro parents throughout Northern and Western cities. According to the nationwide poll of Negro attitudes directed by Louis Harris (*Newsweek*, July 29, 1963), 71 per cent of those questioned "would like to have their children go to school with white children." Interviews I've had with Negro parents in Harlem and in New York's lower East Side over the past five years substantiate Harris's results. In any case, it is ingenuous to conclude that, whatever they told him, not *one* Negro or Puerto Rican parent in the area Lyford studied was concerned with racial percentages in the schools.

Granted that no one *volunteered* to tell Lyford he cared deeply about whether the schools were segregated. Nonetheless, Lyford's acceptance of his "findings" indicates how unadept whites can be at role-reversal. It apparently did not occur to Lyford or to the *Times* that low-income Negroes who have lost hope of changing their own economic and housing conditions may also not even allow themselves to speculate—certainly not to a white questioner—about the possibility of white society's becoming so concerned with Negro children that actual physical desegregation of the schools will occur in their lifetime.

As a matter of fact, however, since the summer of 1963 an increasing number of Negro parents in New York and elsewhere in the North *have* been acting—by demonstrations and boycotts—to desegregate the public schools. (In the February 3, 1964, boycott of the New York City schools, 44.8 per cent— 464,362—of all elementary and high school students in the city were absent from class that day. In predominantly Negro and Puerto Rican schools the percentage of absentees was much higher, ranging to 92 per cent in central Harlem. On Manhattan's West Side about 70 per cent of the children, including most of the Negroes and Puerto Ricans, stayed out of school. Surely the parents of *these* Negro children were not concerned only "with the type of teachers the children have.")

Nonetheless it does remain true that there are Negro parents who, however much they may passively desire school desegregation, have not yet been recruited into these campaigns. It can be difficult to motivate a Negro past thirty-five or forty, who has been in the ghetto all his life, to expect much immediate change. And in so far as *these* parents do not agitate for school integration, is it conscionable to base an educational policy partly on the diminished expectations of those who have been stripped of confidence that they can change "the system"?

Those Negroes I've interviewed who are voluble about not wanting to wait until open housing and full employment produce desegregated schools would agree with Isaiah Robinson, chairman of the Harlem Parents Committee: "Having a white child sitting next to my Negro child is no guarantee that mine will learn, but it is a guarantee that he will be taught." Or, as an educator in Harlem has predicted: "If white children were put into some of the schools we have here, white parents would not tolerate the conditions there for a moment, and changes would be made very fast."

Isaiah Robinson's approach to school integration recognizes that while the percentage of militant Negro parents is increas-

ing, proportionately there are more white parents who are convinced that if they complain loudly and long enough, they *can*
cause changes in what *they* dislike in the schools. In a racially
mixed school, therefore, the likelihood is that the PTA will be
more effective than in a 90-per-cent Negro school. And in an
integrated school, Negro parents are apt to be stimulated more
quickly by white example to join in the agitation for raised
levels of achievement.

None of these arguments can be expected to persuade white
parents that their children should be "sacrificed" by "reverse
bussing" to integrate the schools at the core of the ghetto. Dr.
Kenneth Clark, a supporter of school integration, agrees with
them. He points out that when the schools to which the white
children are to be transferred are "clearly and woefully inferior,"
nobody gains by the mere physical integration of the classrooms.
In fact, the resultant prolonged protest could lead to a "dis-
ruption of the educational process."

On the other hand, when it comes to transferring Negro students to a middle-class white school, there often arises a rather
sudden solicitude among white parents and educators about the
emigrant's spiritual welfare. The thesis is that a "culturally deprived" Negro placed alongside middle-class white children will
be further damaged psychologically by the realization of how
much farther behind he is than they and also by their hostility
because he is both "different" and "dumb." A corollary worry
is that the level of the class as a whole will fall.

Much of the evidence, however, is in the other direction. As
for hostility, child psychiatrist Robert Coles, in a report, *The
Desegregation of Southern Schools: A Psychiatric Study* (July
1963) concluded that young children of different races get along
with one another naturally and usually ignore adult tensions.
The adjustment takes longer among teen-agers and, in some
cases, may not occur at all. But by the end of a year in Coles's
two-year study, he found, as he later told a New York conference
of the Child Study Association of America, that "even youths
from deeply convinced segregationist homes manage an adjustment to their Negro classmates, and in many cases begin, with

increasing compassion and respect, to see them as individuals."

Yet some observers have reported situations in which white children became even less accepting of Negro transfer pupils than they had been of Negroes before. So far as the Negro child is concerned, however, a key point is made by Warren C. Haggstrom, a sociologist at Syracuse University, in the October–November 1963 issue of *Integrated Education*:

> It is important . . . to remember that the research literature suggests that Negro children benefit in a number of ways from direct comparisons and competition with white children *regardless of the attitudes of white children toward them*. Thus, the extent of interracial friendships cannot be taken as an appropriate index of the consequences of segregation for the Negro personality. On the other hand . . . the fact remains that placing a Negro child in a desegregated school is only the first step of many which will be necessary before he can escape personality damage stemming from his racial membership.

It is only the first step, but it can be an important one. Frederick H. Williams, Director of the Human Relations Unit of New York City's Board of Education, says, "There has not been completed any formal evaluation comparing performances of Negro pupils who moved into desegregated public schools in New York City with those who did not. However, many local reports of the progress of both groups of pupils in *desegregated* schools are encouraging. Where assignment to an all-Negro school has been a disturbing influence for a Negro pupil, the assignment to a desegregated school should remove this obstacle though a period of adjustment may be required.

"Sometimes," Williams adds, "the Negro pupil or parent is not looking at this as a choice between a segregated or desegregated school so much as one between an unsuccessful school and a successful one. In this case, success or failure is judged by the achievement of pupils with reference to the relative merits of program or personnel. It is not unusual then that a child going to a school he *regards* as a better school begins to perform better. The same is true if the parent is convinced of this and transmits it to the child." Simultaneously, according to studies reported by Gertrude Noar, national director of education for the Anti-Defamation League of B'nai B'rith, white children in newly integrated schools frequently improve their grades as a result of teachers' efforts to reach their Negro classmates. Essential to all learning is the teacher's confidence in his pupils' capacity.

In the Robert Coles study of desegregation in Southern schools (released by the Southern Regional Council and the Anti-Defamation League of B'nai B'rith), Coles, a cautious researcher, stated flatly: "We have yet to hear a Southern teacher complain of any drop in intellectual or moral climate in a desegregated room or school."

I am not maintaining that a Negro child can be motivated to greater learning capacity *only* in a desegregated school. It has been proved in some predominantly Negro schools—those, for example, under the jurisdiction of Samuel Shepard in Saint Louis—that unusually committed and resourceful educators can raise educational levels to a marked degree. And a combination of intensified individual guidance, reduced class sizes, enrichment of curriculum, remedial services, extensive cultural experiences through trips, and specialized teacher training can lead to impressive results in "disadvantaged" schools. Particularly important are radically reduced pupil-to-teacher ratios. Many ghetto children need a relationship with adults they can trust.

The raising of statistical indexes, however, evades the basic flaw in the concept of bringing the segregated child "the best school that can be bought with money and talent." June Shagaloff, an education specialist for the NAACP in New York City, accurately charges: "You cannot substitute better conditions for desegregation. There just is no substitute. That's simply separate but equal—it discounts the educational effects of desegregation itself."

James B. Conant has now changed his mind in this regard. "You may be able to educate a Negro in all-Negro schools," he said two years after *Slums and Suburbs* was published, "but you can't make him as good a citizen as you would in a comprehensive school—whether elementary or high school—with people of all races and ability and economic levels."

In 1962 Dr. John H. Fischer, president of Teachers College, Columbia University, said: "I do not like to see administrators playing God to manipulate children in what they think is the best pattern" for integration. A year later Dr. Fischer had come to a different conclusion. "Racial integration," he said, "is one purpose we've got to seek—actively seek—in our society. If we let nature take its course, we will have more segregation and more stratification. I am very apprehensive if we make decisions which separate our society."

Better separate schools are inadequate because *de facto* segregation has the same results on the personality as *de jure* segregation. As the Supreme Court said in its decision of May 17, 1954, declaring the latter unconstitutional, separating Negro children "from others of similar age and qualifications solely because of their race generates a feeling of inferiority as to their status in the community that may affect their hearts and minds in a way unlikely ever to be undone."

"Segregated education," says LeRoy McLoud, Negro principal of the predominantly Negro Lincoln Elementary School in Englewood, New Jersey, "gives the kids the feeling they're not wanted. Which is true—they're *not* wanted. When they get to junior high, they're more concerned with the attitude of the whites and fighting back than concentrating on their studies. The teachers in junior high are mostly white, too, and the kids direct their venom at the teacher: 'You teach me, make me learn.'"

Meanwhile the white children in separate schools, like their parents, do not get to *know* Negroes, except as maids and similar "service" figures. They acquire a distorted image of their own "superiority" and are open to the fears which come from ignorance. One more racially divided generation is thereby assured.

Yet, even among whites who believe these arguments for integrating education are valid, there is recurring doubt that widespread school integration is possible until large-scale housing desegregation has been achieved.

To cope with this doubt, first of all, physical desegregation can take place faster and more widely in the schools than it can in housing because the schools can be made more flexible in this respect than can housing patterns. Changing racial balance in schools need not be as difficult or as lengthy a process as insuring that low-income housing projects are desegregated, making open occupancy laws in private housing really effective, and persuading mortgage-lenders and builders to encourage integrated housing.

Furthermore, if *all* schools in a city were as desegregated as possible and if all were thoroughly improved, an end to housing segregation could be somewhat quickened through what had already been accomplished in the schools. Dr. Dan Dodson, director of the Center for Human Relations at New York University, observes that when a family with children is looking for a new home or apartment, its first question is: "What kind of school will the children be attending?" "If," says Dodson, "the schools in a neighborhood were already both mixed and good," there would be less fear on the part of white parents of what would happen to the school in that particular district if more Negroes were to become their neighbors at any time in the future.

The parents may themselves remain prejudiced, but they will probably be less hasty about moving elsewhere as the neighborhood becomes integrated if they are convinced their children are already going to a first-rate integrated school and if they are convinced that the city's school administrators are committed to a continuing policy of racial balance in the classroom. In this regard, as Dr. Dodson says, "the desegregated school can be the first step toward a desegregated neighborhood."

The essential challenge is to investigate the extent to which it is possible to desegregate public schools in such an area as New York City, where 134 of 581 elementary schools are more than 90 per cent Negro or Puerto Rican, and where, in the borough of Manhattan, Negroes and Puerto Ricans constitute more than three-quarters of the elementary-school enrollment.

I choose New York City because its problem is so difficult that some answers possible there can be made applicable elsewhere. I also focus on that city because its Board of Education was the first in the North to respond to the 1954 Supreme Court Decision. In December 1954 the board formally declared that it intended to prevent the development of any more segregated schools and that it would integrate those already segregated as quickly as possible.

On November 7, 1955, the Commission on Integration of the Board of Education unanimously approved this statement: "This Commission affirms that it is desirable policy to promote ethnic integration in our schools as a positive educational experience of which no child in the city should be deprived." Yet in that year 42 (rather than 134) elementary schools were more than 90 per cent nonwhite. Clearly, despite the avowed intentions of the board and in spite of some effort though the years, school segregation in the city has risen sharply.

In addition, despite the board's repeated pledges to include integration as a major factor in deciding the sites of new schools, of the 81 new elementary and junior high schools opened since 1955, 26 are now 85 to 90 per cent nonwhite and 16 are 85 to 90 per cent white.

In 1955, moreover, a Public Education Association study revealed that sixth- and eighth-grade pupils in predominantly Negro and Puerto Rican schools were more than two grades behind their equivalents in largely white schools. By 1962, according to a follow-up study by the Urban League of Greater New York, that gap had widened. In some cases the Negro children were at least three grades behind.

(Another illustration of the long-term effect of the "education" in many predominantly Negro schools in large cities is a 1959 study of 680 relief recipients in Chicago. Nearly all were Negro and they ranged in age from 16 to 64. The study disclosed that 50.7 per cent were functionally illiterate—below sixth-grade level. Yet only 6 per cent of those functional illiterates had not continued school after the fifth grade. Furthermore, of the 504 in the study who had been exposed to eight years or more of schooling, 191 were functionally illiterate. Nor could this failure of the Chicago public school system be ascribed to the quality of Southern education received by some in the group before they reached Chicago. In its analysis of this survey, the magazine *Integrated Education* emphasized: "*In studies that compared achievement with school attendance, no difference was noted between those who had received all their education in Cook County and those who had not.*")

The dropping farther back of the Negro children in New York was an even greater indictment of *de facto* segregation because it had occurred in a city where, aside from Higher Horizons and Development Guidance projects, 274 of the elementary and junior high schools had been designated by 1962 as "special service" schools. These latter schools are allocated additional texts, supplies, and personnel to reduce class size.

Obviously Negro children were not only still being damaged by the increased existence of segregation, but among only a small percentage of them had the "special efforts" been intensive enough to make their separate education equal.

Admittedly one answer is to pour much more money and much more qualified personnel into the "disadvantaged" schools. But in a city with so many nonwhite pupils, is there any feasible way to desegregate those schools at the same time?

To begin with, as the New York Metropolitan Council of the American Jewish Congress states in its *Program for Integrating New York City's Schools* (1963):

> Integration must not be viewed as an all-or-nothing proposition. It is not something that can be achieved in the same manner in each district and in each school. It may be that integration in an X area in Brooklyn may mean 70% white children and 30% Negro and Puerto Rican, while in Manhattan it may mean 70% Negro and Puerto Rican children and 30% white.

Second, the deficiencies of previous plans for integrating the schools have to be recognized. In New York City the Board of

Education has experimented since 1958 with plans which permitted children in certain nonwhite schools to transfer—with parental approval—to certain underutilized predominantly white schools. (Variations of this voluntary transfer system are being used in other cities as well.) As of 1964 New York City had liberalized the approach to the extent that, if his parents requested, a child in any predominantly nonwhite school could enroll in *any* other school in the city with room for him.

The voluntary transfer concept can be of only limited use in rearranging racial balance. If large numbers of nonwhites in any city were to apply for transfer, there wouldn't be enough room for all of them. Even underutilized schools do not have enough empty chairs to absorb significant numbers of children attending *de facto* segregated schools.

Furthermore, the plan places the burden of initiative on the child and on the parent. A parent already intimidated by an alien power structure and its school system may not have enough resilience to agree to so unfamiliar a way of change. Besides, many Negro parents are no different from those white parents who object to the long bus rides such a voluntary transfer might necessitate. The child not only spends wearying time in transit but has less opportunity to join in after-school activities. And if the school is distant, his parents will be less likely to make close contact with his teachers.

Another negative aspect of voluntary transfers is that, on the basis of experience with this kind of plan so far, the children who accept the challenge are usually superior students and their parents are among the best leadership potential in their community. The "sending" school, therefore, loses some of its brighter pupils and the local PTA loses important strength. It is also difficult for the teachers and student body in a predominantly Negro "sending" school to escape a lowering of morale when outstanding pupils ask to leave it.

Instead of relying on such fragmentary integration devices, programs to desegregate schools will be most effective when they are city-wide and when the full responsibility for their implementation is placed on the school system rather than on individual Negro children and parents.

If a city-wide program of integration, however, is not to cause more white parents to withdraw their children from the public schools, it must simultaneously involve the improvement of *all* schools in the city. If a school has so deteriorated that it cannot be fully rehabilitated, that school should be closed.

With regard to long-range plans, site-selection of new schools is crucial. If a school is built in a ghetto neighborhood or in a fringe area which is soon likely to be swallowed by the ghetto, it will obviously be much more difficult to integrate than a new building away from a segregated neighborhood.

Invariably site-selection aimed at integration will limit the degree to which the "neighborhood school" concept can be applied. Yet there is nothing sacrosanct about the neighborhood-school policy. As the New York Metropolitan Council of the American Jewish Congress points out: "In suburban areas (long before integration became a topic of concern) buses have been provided to bring children to a central school. In fact, the trend has been . . . to the larger, more centralized school where a richer curriculum with more specialized courses, more extensive facilities and faculty, better-equipped science and language laboratories, bigger libraries and better athletic and other recreational facilities . . . can be provided."

Bus time to a centralized school, moreover, can be considerably shortened, by contrast with the time-consuming number of stops it takes to move voluntary transfer students around. Sizable groups of children can be picked up at places which are on a direct route to the centralized school. Under this more functional system, children can still join in after-school activities and be returned home within a reasonably short period of time.

(If cities are to be encouraged to transcend the neighborhood-school concept in their planning for the future, a change in present urban renewal regulations is essential. The United States Commission on Civil Rights has pointed out that "the federal urban renewal law requires a city to pay part of the cost of each renewal project. The city may earn credit toward its obligation by constructing new public facilities, such as schools. But if these facilities derive more than 20 per cent of their use from people living outside of the renewal area, the city loses part of the credit toward its obligation. This discourages any local policy to locate and district a school to promote a racially heterogeneous school population, if, to achieve this objective, more than 20 per cent of the pupils would have to live outside of the renewal area and be included in the school's attendance area.")

Ultimately, as cities continue to grow, the most logical solution is a series of educational parks. In an address at an Adelphi College Seminar on Integration Problems in June 1963, Dr. Max Wolff, a specialist on desegregating schools, likened the grouping concept of an educational park to that of shopping centers and industrial parks. Wolff explained:

> Within its own limits, the educational park, like the shopping center, could be quite decentralized. It could contain buildings of various sizes. Facilities for younger and older children could be kept separate. Transportation to and from the park and supervision within it would permit planning for maximum safety for all the children in an entire community. . . . Educational parks would also be more economical than neighborhood schools. Fewer schools would be needed because gymnasiums and auditoriums could be used continuously instead of briefly each day. In general, more efficient use of facilities and equipment would mean a reduction in the school-plant building program. The concentration of facilities would at one stroke eliminate both the overcrowded school so costly to maintain and the underutilized one so wasteful to keep open.

In July of the same year, Dr. Wolff pointed out other advantages of educational parks in a proposal to Dr. Calvin Gross, New York City superintendent of schools:

> Instead of a redundancy of second-rate facilities in many neighborhood schools, the very finest and most modern equipment can be provided in special purpose areas of the educational center. Science laboratories, unattainable in local schools; libraries, so often lacking or inadequate in neighborhood schools; language laboratories with extensive equipment

can all be made available even to the youngest children. . . .

The educational center will serve all the children of the community, who will have the opportunity, some for the first time, of meeting and working with children of varying backgrounds. The children will stimulate, motivate and challenge each other. In the same way, good teachers will be attracted to the center, because the high-or-low-status schools will have been superseded. The best education and best facilities the city can afford will be available equally to all children of the city.

In a letter printed in the *New York Herald Tribune* on January 18, 1964, Dr. Martin Deutsch, director, Institute for Developmental Studies, Department of Psychiatry, New York Medical College, suggested that these educational parks begin with the fourth grade:

Neighborhood schools, located as far as possible on community borders, should be retained for very young children. There is sufficient evidence as to the association of poverty with learning handicaps to dictate exceptionally high-quality early childhood experience, starting at 3 or 4 years of age. The years after kindergarten would be spent in ungraded, team-teaching classes. Thus, children would be saturated with the basic skills necessary for learning the 3 R's before the beginning of the "school community" at the fourth grade.

Dr. Deutsch also pointed out that a system of educational parks "would effectively reduce the high rate of school turnover caused by high family mobility in lower-income areas. It would stabilize the educational staff and offer a practical basis for administrative decentralization, with each educational park under an official with the rank of deputy superintendent."

It may well take a long time for the idea of educational parks to be widely adopted. In New York City, Stanley H. Lowell, chairman of the City Commission on Human Rights, is able to foresee an educational park at the Polo Grounds, where "you could put half-a-dozen elementary schools, three junior highs and a high school." In most communities, however, considerable persuasion will be necessary before municipal authorities are brought to think—and act—in terms of this kind of long-range planning. However, in New York, as a result of swelling pressure from Negro organizations, which culminated in February 1964 in a one-day boycott of the schools, the Board of Education, in an attempt to prevent the boycott, finally did institute a study of the educational park concept.

In the meantime, even in cities with extensively segregated housing patterns, there are ways to accomplish greater school integration. The "Princeton plan," for one, is applicable when a predominantly white elementary school is reasonably close to a largely nonwhite elementary school. The children in both schools are merged by grades. All the first- to third-grade pupils, for example, may attend one of the two schools, and all the fourth- to sixth-grade students are assigned to the other.

Significantly, the Princeton plan, though first adopted in that city in 1948, has yet to be tried on a sizable basis in any large Northern city. An exception is New York City. There the Board of Education first announced in 1963 that it contemplated applying the plan to a pair of schools in Queens the following year and was considering other possibilities. After the mass organization of Negro parents just mentioned, however, the board suddenly acknowledged, in a report released on January 29, 1964, that at least twenty pairs of elementary schools and ten pairs of junior high schools could be merged under a Princeton plan. (Included in the forty elementary schools were twenty which were 90 per cent or more Negro and Puerto Rican.) The board promised that half of those schools would be rezoned by September 1965 and the other half by September 1966. So far as the boycott leaders were concerned, the number was not nearly enough, but the board's belated decision did prove that mass pressure could indeed accelerate change. (Because of white counter-pressure, the board later began to vacillate as to the exact number of schools to be paired immediately, but the significance of the discovery that more than a couple of schools *could* be fused will not be forgotten by the Negro community.)

Clearly, in many communities a preparatory period of parent education is wise before a Princeton plan goes into effect. Mrs. Ellen Lurie, a member of a local New York school board and a researcher for the Parents' Action Committee for Equality, has suggested a "school linkage" approach during the orientation period. For a year or more before the plan begins, the staffs of both schools can hold regular joint meetings to plan curricula, while parents' associations also meet to work on mutual improvement of the two schools. Other possibilities are: "joint concerts, joint art exhibits, joint grade projects (if the fourth grade is studying New York City, both schools can do it together)."

Pupils in each school could visit "the neighborhood surrounding the other. They could go on common trips. They might even bus in to the partner school (if bussing is required) for a two-week period . . . and at the same time, a grade on a different level could be visiting the other school." In her unpublished paper "School Integration in New York City," from which I have drawn this suggestion, Mrs. Lurie underlines that "an attempt must be made during the entire school year to bring home to parents and staff at both sets of schools the individual contributions of each . . . with the goal of preparing both schools to actually pair up as soon as practical."

In a Princeton plan, moreover, there is not the same kind of "acceptance" problem which confronts isolated voluntary transfer students in predominantly white schools. The youngsters affected in both schools not only do not lose their friends in the fusion but also, as Mrs. Lurie observes, gain a double neighborhood to share with youngsters they would not otherwise have gotten to know.

It is also possible to extend the Princeton plan to a whole district or to several districts. This "area-pairing" technique, the American Jewish Congress advises, "can be used in fringe areas with neighboring white and minority group residential concentrations. Adjacent school districts, one serving predominantly white children, the other serving predominantly Negro and/or Puerto Rican children, could be rezoned as one district and the several elementary grades divided between them."

In order to change the racial balance of elementary schools deeply impacted within segregated neighborhoods, extensive "area-pairing" or other forms of rezoning will inevitably involve bussing and a degree of reverse bussing. Again, reverse bussing of whites into the worst schools of the ghetto is impractical until those of the presently inferior segregated schools which should not be closed entirely are brought up to the city's highest standard, and, for that matter, beyond it. It may well be that some of the children in these areas will not be desegregated until new centralized schools are built outside the ghetto—another reason for greatly increased emphasis on "educational parks" in planning new school construction.

Even in the most segregated neighborhoods, however, changes can be made toward integrating junior high schools. After elementary school, bussing is already widely practiced in most communities, and there is no reason why segregated primary schools should continue feeding into segregated upper schools. Under a city-wide plan a board of education can insure more racial balance in junior high schools, first by changing the feeding patterns from elementary schools and then, if necessary, by closing junior high schools in the ghetto and building new centralized replacements. Obviously, once the junior high school is integrated, the senior grades will also be.

In any case, depending on particular neighborhoods and particular cities, there are many variations of the plans I've outlined which can be practically instituted. It need not be true, *The New York Times* notwithstanding, that "a basic solution will not come until a fundamental assault has been made on the walls of discrimination in the sale and rental of housing and until more and better jobs enable Negro breadwinners to move out of the slums." If the *Times*'s editorial writers were Negro, I wonder if they could remain that patient while another generation of their children, even in the best of all possible separate schools, grew up segregated.

Although there are major moves which can be taken now to integrate education, there must first be persistent pressure on school boards and parents throughout the community to make them realize what those steps are. Proponents of these plans will also have to remember—and continually to make clear—

that no program is worth supporting unless it increases the educational opportunities for all the children in a given system. There will then come the struggle to get the additional financing required by any move to upgrade and desegregate schools, and that kind of campaign involves political organization.

One other serious problem remains. To what extent can the courts be expected to call for positive efforts at desegregation and to what extent are the courts likely to block such efforts? In October 1960 a group of parents in New Rochelle, New York, brought a federal court suit against the New Rochelle Board of Education. They charged that their children were being deprived of their constitutional right to equal education because they were forced to attend a segregated neighborhood school.

Among the arguments of their attorney, Paul Zuber, was a distillation of the claim that *de facto* segregation, however it has been caused, is as unconstitutional as the *de jure* segregation outlawed by the United States Supreme Court in 1954. Reporting on the case for the United States Commission on Civil Rights, John Kaplan of the Northwestern University Law School wrote that Zuber's complaint "was based upon this simple syllogism: A neighborhood school in an all-Negro area will be all-Negro and, therefore, segregated. The state cannot constitutionally compel any student to go to a segregated school. Therefore, the application of the neighborhood-school policy to an all-Negro residential area is unconstitutional."

Federal Judge Irving R. Kaufman did not decide the case on this basis. He ruled for the parents on the grounds that the New Rochelle Board of Education had deliberately maintained segregated schools through gerrymandering and discriminatory transfers. He did not rule that the existence of a predominantly Negro school is in itself evidence that a school board intends to maintain segregation. Additional evidence was required of *deliberate* attempts to segregate, and in the New Rochelle case it was supplied to the satisfaction of the court.

Accordingly Zuber has concluded, and some other civil rights lawyers agree with him, that extensive research will have to be done in each case of *de facto* school segregation to accumulate proof of deliberate maintenance and creation of that segregation. Zuber would prefer, and in this he is joined by nearly all Negro leaders, that the "right" case be brought to the United States Supreme Court in order to establish that intent to segregate need *not* be proved—that forcing a Negro child to attend any *de facto* segregated school is within the context of the 1954 Supreme Court decision that separate Negro schools are harmful to Negro children and therefore unconstitutional.

So far state courts and the lower federal courts are divided on the issue of whether the mere existence of a segregated school is cause for remedial action. In October 1963, for example, in the first Federal Appeals Court decision which positively upheld a neighborhood-school policy to be constitutional, three justices in the Federal District Court in Chicago unanimously upheld and praised a ruling ten months before by Federal District Court Judge George M. Beamer in a Gary, Indiana, case of alleged school discrimination. Parents of 111 Gary school children had asked that city officials be enjoined from maintaining racially segregated public schools. Judge Beamer had decided that the Gary school board was not deliberately trying to foster segregation and "furthermore, requiring certain students to leave their neighborhood and friends and be transferred to another school miles away, while other students, similarly situated, remained in the neighborhood school, simply for the purpose of balancing the races in the various schools would in my opinion be indeed a violation of the equal protection clause of the Fourteenth Amendment."

The Appeals Court agreed with Judge Beamer that Gary, Indiana, school district boundaries had not been drawn "for the purpose of including or excluding children of certain races," and that, therefore, the neighborhood-school policy in Gary could not be overturned.

Alexander Bickel may be correct in his January 4, 1964, prediction in *The New Republic* that the judicial process in this area can be expected to restrict itself "to fashioning narrow remedies only, in cases where *de facto* segregation turns out to be the product of conscious school-board action. . . . No significant judicial intervention is to be looked for in the more numerous cases where segregation in the schools reflects not the actions of a segregationist school board, now or in the past, but conditions in the community, plus normal educational policies, such as residential zoning, ability grouping, and the like."

On the other hand, in April 1962 a United States District Court in the Eastern District of New York denied a petition by the school board of Hempstead, New York, to dismiss a segregation complaint by Negro plaintiffs in that city. The court declared:

> The central constitutional fact is the inadequacy of segregated education. That it is not coerced by direct action of an arm of the state cannot, alone, be decisive of the issue of the deprivation of constitutional right. Education is compulsory in New York State. . . . The educational system that is thus compulsory and publicly afforded must deal with the inadequacy arising from adventitious segregation; it cannot accept and indurate segregation on the ground that it is not coerced or planned but accepted.

As of this writing, the extent to which the courts will insist on positive efforts to bring about integrated schools is unclear. Similarly murky is the extent to which they will allow such efforts as are begun by the initiative of state educational authorities and local school boards. Nonetheless, by the end of 1963 four states—New York, New Jersey, California, and Illinois— had declared that each school board within their borders did have a duty to prevent segregation in the public schools, no matter how it had become entrenched.

These policy statements were issued in New York by the New York Board of Regents and the New York Commissioner of Education; in California by the California State Board of Education; and in New Jersey by that state's Commissioner of Education. Illinois, however, became in June 1963 the first state in which *legislation* was passed requiring all school boards to revise or change existing school zones to eliminate public school segregation.

Yet, as white parents go to court to claim that specific ways of changing these zones deprive *their* children of equal protection of the laws under the Fourteenth Amendment, there will continue to be conflicting decisions in both state and federal courts—unless and until the Supreme Court makes a decision as to whether *de facto* segregation, deliberate or not, is unconstitutional.

(In June 1963 the California Supreme Court ruled that "even in the absence of gerrymandering or other affirmative discriminatory conduct by a school board, a student under some circumstances would be entitled to relief where, by reason of residential segregation, substantial racial imbalance exists in his school." But in January 1964 a New York State Supreme Court Justice barred the transfer of pupils in Malverne, Long Island, to achieve integration, declaring: "While the United States Constitution forbids segregation by law in the public schools, it neither forbids racial imbalance nor compels racial balance.")

In the absence of a clear determination in the courts as to the steps communities may lawfully take to *promote* school integration, many school boards in many states will remain "neutral," neither adding any new segregation patterns nor working purposefully to change those which already exist.

If non-deliberate *de facto* school segregation remains constitutional, we have an exceedingly long way to go before our children cease to be divided by race, at least while they are in school.

———

Since this chapter was written, Judge J. Skelly Wright of the United States Court of Appeals for the District of Columbia, has predicted that the Supreme Court will eventually rule directly on the constitutionality of *de facto* school segregation "if the problem persists, and if the states fail to correct the evil." The problem is getting worse, and most states and communities are not likely to correct the evil voluntarily. Judge Wright expects that the Supreme Court, if it rules, will decide that such segregation is indeed unconstitutional and may then require city and suburban school districts to merge to attain racial balance.

10

Come Out, Come Out,
Wherever You Are

If the white world could understand how the non-white has had hostility trampled into him for a hundred years, then the white world would begin to understand the problem they have given us to unravel in the lives of these children. Maybe they'd understand how hard it is to convince a kid, in the face of all his home and community influences, that he really belongs in the same world a white man belongs in. —Samuel Shepard, a director of elementary education in Saint Louis, quoted in "Not Like Other Children" by Bernard Asbell, *Redbook*, October 1963

Of every 100 youngsters, we still drop from school 30 or 35 who lack even rudimentary learning mainly because we don't know how to teach them. In thousands of cases we don't even know how to talk to them well enough to get them to listen.

—Dr. John H. Fischer, president of Teachers College, Columbia University, in a March 1964 address to the National Association of Independent Schools

THE school is in central Harlem. The sixth-grade class is all Negro. A young white teacher, who volunteered to work in Harlem, is having trouble maintaining discipline. She

school systems, Benjamin Solomon, a research associate at the Industrial Relations Center, University of Chicago, has written in *Integrated Education* (August 1963):

> Though segregation would clearly seem to be inconsistent with any meaningful professional credo, there are few instances of serious and persistent organized protests [against] segregated education among teachers in northern and western cities. The widespread accommodation by teachers to *de facto* segregation suggests a limited belief in the educability of Negro children; lack of encouragement of high aspirations; acceptance of low standards, inferior physical conditions, lack of supplies, and the like; ignorance or even collaboration with anti-Negro bias in curriculum and materials; lack of understanding of or concern for the impact of segregation on the education of Negro or white children.

There are also teachers who are explicitly hostile to children of a class and culture alien to them. In one lower East Side school in New York an eight-year-old Puerto Rican girl with a slight heart condition was absent for two days in the winter of 1963. Her mother knows only a few words of English, and the note she sent to explain her child's absence was illegible. The teacher, enraged when he read the note, ripped it up in front of the class. The girl was told to bring another note, but she was too ashamed to tell her mother what had happened. For two weeks the girl had to write, "I must bring a note from home," thousands of times during class time. The teacher, incidentally, had no knowledge of the child's heart condition. Three months after school had opened he had not yet "had time" to examine her file. The same teacher was accustomed to refer to the girl as a "bean-eater" and a "pig," and he once refused to handle the youngster's notebook "because it must have germs."

When the girl's mother protested to the principal and asked that the girl be transferred to another class, the principal refused because "we can't set a precedent of a child winning a victory over a teacher." Finally, because of pressure on the principal by a social agency to whom the mother appealed, the girl was transferred. The teacher, however, is still in the school.

Another principal on the lower East Side, in addressing a meeting of Puerto Rican and Negro mothers who had complaints about their children's low level of achievement, said he would speak briefly "because you won't understand me anyhow." He did tell them they should be grateful the school took the trouble it did with such "slow-learning children." An administrative official of the Board of Education assigned to the same area later characterized the complaining mothers as "not ready for freedom."

Teachers' hostility to their charges occasionally breaks into violence. In the course of any school year there are at least a dozen stories in the *Amsterdam News,* a New York Negro weekly, about white teachers who hit Negro pupils, and no one knows how many other instances are not reported.

In the *New York Post* of September 6, 1963, Mrs. Joan Charles, telling of her teaching experiences in a Negro high school in the Bedford-Stuyvesant area of Brooklyn, recalled that a day after she started in the school a veteran teacher advised her, "Don't hit Leon because his mother comes to school and objects." Another time, after a boy had swung at a classmate, Mrs. Charles saw a teacher take the offender and bang his head against the wall several times. "I won't say," Mrs. Charles added, "that these children weren't problems. But this was declared, open war, and the teachers usually won, because they were bigger. And the horror of it is that you accept these things— it becomes the norm. . . . I honestly felt these teachers hated the children."

An illustration of the rage this military-police approach to discipline can generate is a letter from a Negro teacher to the *Amsterdam News*: "If our children did not carry weapons to protect themselves from white sadists in disguise as teachers, the race would become extinct within twenty-five years. I feel that every child should be equipped with some kind of weapon every morning he leaves home for the battlefield."

The violent teachers are not in the majority in slum schools, and the culturally deprived do not fight a physical battle a day; but too many classrooms in depressed areas *are* run as if they were custodial barracks. In this context, as well as in every other area in the life of the Negro poor, I use a term such as "culturally deprived" uneasily. Because it does keep recurring in the literature on education, I can't avoid the term, but I agree with Dr. Kenneth Clark that these children should instead be called "socially denied children or rejected children." For Clark "the term cultural deprivation masks the fact these are human beings who are not in just some God-given state, but are deliberately and chronically victimized by the larger society in general, and by educational institutions specifically."

Consider, as another example, the remarkable recommendation two years ago of Dr. Carl Hansen, Washington, D.C., superintendent of schools, that corporal punishment be administered to unruly children in certain circumstances.

Mrs. Vernon Ayer, principal of a Harlem school for more than twenty-five years before her retirement, said of the Hansen proposal: "These children have already been beaten enough. That's the trouble with them. Instead of instilling a sense of obligation, a beating often releases a boy from any feeling that he has to act differently. He feels that by taking the beating, he has paid the price. I used to say to them, 'I won't let you grow up like that,' and even the ones that were the hardest to reach would listen to me and know that I cared what happened to them."

Nor are all behavior problems as difficult to deal with as many teachers in slum schools believe. Mrs. Ayer remembers a boy who was exceedingly hard to handle in the morning; but after lunch he invariably calmed down. She discovered that the child rarely had anything to eat for breakfast or the night before. He was "difficult" because he was hungry.

John Niemeyer, president of the Bank Street College of Education in New York City, writes in *Programs for the Educationally Disadvantaged* (1963):

Certain schools will need to take on some of the responsibilities which are usually thought of as belonging to social agencies and not the school. One elementary school in Philadelphia, for example, has won the cooperation of police and milkmen to the extent that the school learns early in the morning of any child who has been locked out of his home for the night. Such a child is greeted by the principal, given a hot shower and breakfast, and put to bed for several hours. This may seem a far cry from the usual role of the school, but children of this type in this particular school had proved to be drastic disrupting forces and obviously learned nothing during the schoolday.

There are other principals such as the one in Philadelphia and Mrs. Ayer in Harlem, and there are excellent, sensitive teachers in slum schools; but they are in the minority. Furthermore, even if a Negro child does have a capable teacher, he sees comparatively few Negroes in positions of authority in most Northern school systems. In New York City, for instance, only 8.3 per cent of all the teachers are Negro and less than 1 per cent of the 3000 supervisory school personnel are Negro. In the 1962–1963 school year there were no Negroes among the city's 835 principals.

The result, Mrs. Josephine Jones, who has taught in Harlem for twenty-three years, has pointed out, is that "the pupils do not feel a sense of relation and identity, much less a feeling of security. Neither does the pupil feel that a Negro teacher can protect him in the event of serious trouble. He feels that he is on his own, alone, frightened, frustrated and tottering precariously in an adult, white-controlled world."

Even, however, in a segregated school within a system in which supervisory Negroes are rare, it has been repeatedly demonstrated that when teachers do care and do believe their students can learn, not only do achievement levels rise but behavior problems also decline. After three years of Higher Horizons in New York, the principal of a high school involved in the project reported: "In the past, students from 43 [the Higher Horizons junior high which feeds into his high school] were our worst behaved. More teacher and administrative time was spent on them than on any other group. Since we had the project group, this has changed. Not a single student in the project group has been reported to the Dean's office for discipline. Today they are our best behaved."

The question remains, however, whether the teachers in Higher Horizons and similar types of "enriched" programs throughout the country have enough understanding of their pupils beneath and beyond their care for them. While it is important to prove that slum children can learn and can be motivated to *want* to behave well, are there alternative ways of teaching which more fully recognize the positive elements as well as the liabilities in the "culture" of the deprived?

In his chapter on Higher Horizons in *The Culturally Deprived Child* (1962), Frank Riessman of the Department of Psychology and Psychiatry at Columbia University, noted:

> The concept of the *slow gifted child* is not considered by the Program, and one has the feeling that the able children who are selected resemble more the traditional, fast symbolic learners. The possibility of discovering a new kind of talent characterized by different ways of learning and thinking is by-passed by the Program, which appears to have a middle-class model in mind; the aim is to give the deprived children the experiences the more favored children have had, in the hope they might then develop along the lines of these children. Rarely considered is a genuine pluralism where children of diverse backgrounds would be encouraged to develop very differently in light of their specific strengths and particular learning styles.

Riessman clarifies his concern about underestimating the "slow" child by underlining that slowness can indicate a way of learning that is based on caution, thoroughness, or "an emphasis on the concrete and physical." A child may be slow "because he can't understand a concept unless he does something physically, e.g., with his hands, in connection with the idea he is trying to grasp." Slowness, of course, can also represent intellectual inadequacy, but "even here we have to be very careful to check all possible blocks, not only the obvious emotional disturbances. There may be other types of blockage as well, such as auditory blocks, reading difficulties (not of emotional origin), antagonism to the teacher, etc."

Many teachers, however, regard all slowness negatively, forgetting that "while our culture emphasizes speed, there is really no reason to assume that gifted, creative people have to learn rapidly or perform rapidly."

Riessman is also critical of the Higher Horizons attitude toward intelligence tests. The program does recognize the limitations of the standard IQ determinants as applied to culturally deprived children, and accordingly a nonverbal intelligence test has been used for Higher Horizons pupils, along with other ways of measuring achievement. However, Riessman charges: "The Program does not appear to realize that the deprived child's difficulty with tests is not simply verbal inadequacy or lack of familiarity with standard words. This is one factor, but equally important are his lack of basic test-taking skills, insufficient practice, little motivation, and absence of rapport with the middle-class examiner."

While the inadequacies of standard IQ tests, particularly with regard to slum children, is increasingly recognized among educators, these and similarly middle-class-oriented tests remain entrenched in many school systems. How many middle-class white parents have even thought about, let alone have come to the point of agreeing with, the contention of Professor Allison Davis of the University of Chicago: "Half the ability in this country goes down the drain because of the failure of intelligence tests to measure the real mental ability of children from the lower socio-economic groups, and because of the failure of the schools to recognize and train this ability"?

One of the most flagrant injustices caused by the tests involves those students for whom English is a second language when they enter the schools. In November 1963, 5000 of these children in the New York City schools were given IQ tests in their own language. A fourth of them scored in the 80th and 90th percentiles, but many of these high-scoring children were being taught at the time in the lowest sections of their grades.

The most widespread harm done by these tests encompasses those native American children who are victims of class bias in education. As Dr. Patricia Sexton in *Education and Income* (1961), and other researchers have consistently proved, children from poor families score less well on IQ and the usual achievement tests than children of higher economic classes. It is largely on the basis of these tests that children begin to be placed on different "tracks" early in their school careers. By the time they are in secondary school, they have been routed toward "academic," "general," or "vocational" programs.

The track system with its "ability" groupings is a major reason why, as Dr. Kenneth Clark says, "public education in America within the last three or four decades is no longer an instrument facilitating social mobility, but has become probably one of the most effective techniques in maintaining class differences and cleavages."

The "ability" groupings reinforce the self-fulfilling prophecy of underachievement for the slum child in several ways. In addition to what this form of segregation portends for the future of the lesser-rated children, those with already negative images of themselves are further confirmed in the low estimate they have of their worth. No matter what euphemisms a teacher uses to disguise the fact that, for a school year and longer, children have been split off into "brighter" and "less bright" groups, the members of each group know and are affected by the difference in status.

Those who are second-rated, moreover, are deprived of the particular kinds of intellectual stimulation they might have received from the "brighter" children. With regard to whether the latter, as their parents fear, will be held back by being in a heterogeneous class, much of the research on this question, as noted by Maurice J. Eash in *Educational Leadership* for April 1961, indicates that "the brighter children did not appear to suffer when left with average and low ability students, at least through elementary school." And it is in elementary school that the fundamental damage is done to the disadvantaged child.

The effect of the track system on teachers is emphasized by Dr. Martin Deutsch in his chapter in *Integrating the Urban School* (1963):

It is objectively very difficult to get away from differing sets of expectations for the children in different tracks or groups.

These expectations seep into the teacher-child interaction and into the learning process. A tendency develops to reduce the stimuli presented to conform with the expectations of the child's performance. When a particular child answers a question correctly, instead of consciously raising the demand level for him, the tendency is to keep this level constant for a period of time and thus adjust to the performance expectations of the group. So what is developed is a kind of compression system.

A frequent contention, however, is that a homogeneous group is more easy for the average teacher to instruct. This thesis, as Aaron Lipton, principal of the R. J. Bailey School in Hartsdale, New York, points out, "matches the weaknesses of teachers rather than the facts of educability, and brings in its trail the danger of stereotyping the average child at a level of performance far below his true capacities."

Another objection to tracking is that for all the children involved it reinforces the already far too strong tendency throughout the society for people to see others and themselves in terms of group characteristics. Alongside the clannishness of the slum children and their parents is the snobbishness of the "bright" youngsters and *their* parents. If a basic goal of education is to stimulate the growth of individual creativity, homogeneous grouping begun in elementary school is an especially effective way to subvert that goal.

Those Negroes and whites who are now agitating for desegregated and improved schooling for the disadvantaged have—with some exceptions—been underestimating the corollary need to attack "tracking." As a result, track systems remain in effect in most urban school systems. In New York City, as part of its reaction to rising complaints by Negroes about the inadequate education their children are receiving, the Board of Education finally did announce in March 1964 that as of the next fall, the school system would abandon group IQ testing. Instead, new achievement tests in particular subjects are to be administered and the Educational Testing Service in Princeton, New Jersey, has been commissioned to devise a color-blind method of appraising general learning capacities. The track system, however, remains in force.

I do not intend, within the compass of this book, to attempt a comprehensive series of suggestions as to how schools without rigid track systems can best function; but I do want to indicate that there *are* alternatives to the prevailing class divisions in the schools. One way of bypassing the traditional track system has been suggested by Inge Lederer Gibel in the November 1963 *Harper's*. It involves grouping the children in different ways throughout the day: "The child who excels in math will very likely be poorest in art. Let every child have a chance to be at some time in the 'best group' and in the 'worst group,' and it will still be possible to let each advance at his own pace."

A variation on this idea for schools where the initial cleavage is very pronounced is outlined by Frank Riessman. He advocates a grouping for part of the day: "For a few hours you take out the ten children in the class who are not doing as well as the other youngsters. Immediately, you find that among these ten there are one or two who do better than the others. They stand out and they respond much more confidently in the new group. After a few weeks you can take the two who have emerged and put them back in the main class for the entire day. Then, after a period, we may see two more children emerging to the top in the smaller group. This is a simple matter of group dynamics. The teacher who works with these ten children should stress role playing, visual aids, and other methods of learning that are attuned to these children's style of learning."

In addition to breaking down the track system in graded schools, more school systems are eventually likely to adopt the ungraded elementary school plan in which all children are advanced on the basis of individual rates of growth and achievement, without the competitiveness endemic to present ways of grouping.

These changes in orientation will require more teachers, smaller class size, and, most importantly, teachers who recognize different learning styles and do not patronize the seemingly "slower" children. Nor does the end of the customary pigeonholing mean that educational standards should be in the least diluted. In elementary grades, for example, the criteria for the mastering of all the basic learning skills must be no lower in teaching the deprived child than in teaching middle-class children. A teacher who is not convinced that low-income children have as much capacity to learn as any other children is a menace in the slum school.

Even with regard to IQ tests, for instance, the research of psychologist Ernest Haggard and others has shown that if disadvantaged children are properly motivated and if their attitude toward the test situation and the examiner is responsive, they can quickly be trained to achieve markedly higher scores even on the usual middle-class-biased tests. The teacher should also realize, however, that these tests do not discover the particular strengths of the low-income child. The role of the school, as Patricia Sexton emphasizes, should be to "reach out to the child 'where he is' and bring him into the center of our culture [while] respecting what is good in *his* culture and offering him what he needs to know to survive and thrive in ours."

Training teachers to know and respect what is "good" in the low-income child's culture does not mean a romanticizing of slum life. There is, first of all, no clearly homogeneous lower-class culture. In any one street, in any one building, there is a wide range of values, behavior patterns, and goals among the poor. However, it is possible—with this cautionary observation in mind—to speak of qualities which can frequently be observed among children of the low-income class.

The negative qualities have become familiar through all the books and articles on "breeding grounds for delinquency." Slum children tend to be parochial and suspicious about most things and people outside their highly circumscribed area of movement. Self-discipline is not one of their more marked characteristics, and they are more likely to express hostility in immediate physical terms than is the middle-class child.

On the other hand, it is also possible to generalize that slum children are apt to be more emotionally spontaneous and direct than their middle-class counterparts. When they do enter into a relationship on their terms, there can be a depth of loyalty and commitment which is not as common as among the more competitive children of the "upper" classes.

Edgar Z. Friedenberg, associate professor of education at Brooklyn College, expands on Patricia Sexton's concept of "reaching out" to these children by emphasizing that in order to make real contact with them, the school "would have to accept their language, and their dress and their values as a point of departure for disciplined exploration, to be understood, not as a trick for luring them into the middle class, but as a way of helping them to explore the meaning of their own lives. This is the way to encourage and nurture potentialities from *whatever* class."

The key phrase is "a point of departure for disciplined exploration." A teacher who indiscriminately accepts all the values of lower-class life styles is as harmful as a teacher who is stiffly committed to middle-class values and criteria. To begin with, children of any class have to be taught to accept the consequences of their behavior. A permissive attitude which allows slum children to disrupt a classroom is stupid. But discipline need not be humiliating or brutal.

Similarly, it is both patronizing and damaging for a middle-class teacher to pander to the anti-intellectualism he may find among some low-income children. One of his responsibilities is to explain and demonstrate to his students that not all *their* values are commendable and that not all middle-class values are to be automatically suspect or scorned.

It is of small value for the lower-class child to be "understood" if he is not also given the chance to find out for himself, and as late in his school career as possible, whether he wants to specialize in academic work or in varyingly less abstract studies. To make a choice, he will have to have as solid a background in reading, verbalizing, and all the other "middle-class" skills as any child. He will have to know how to take tests, how to apply for a job or for a college admission interview. He can, however, be effectively guided in this direction, while retaining those of his lower-class values which are positive, if, from the start, his teachers know what those values are and how to channel them.

It is Frank Riessman's conviction that a teacher who is sensitive to differences in life as well as learning styles "will begin to see why the deprived child is hostile, what he expects of her, why he wants her to prove herself. The teacher will come to learn . . . how she can utilize his in-group loyalty, informality, equalitarianism, humor, and the like. She will come to understand why he does not need 'love' but respect. And finally, she will be able to interpret in a new light much of the behavior which appears negative. What previously appeared to be emotional imbalance and supersensitivity to minor frustrations can now be seen anew."

The teacher, however, also must be attuned to recognize the real deprivations in a slum child's background. It makes excellent sense, for example, to include nursery schools in compulsory free public education so that disadvantaged children can begin to get compensatory education as soon as they can absorb it.

Riessman claims that there is a danger in overemphasizing preschool preparation for the slum child because such a plan "carries with it the implication that not much more than remedial work can be done with these youngsters in the school proper. It is another way in which the school can shirk responsibility."

There is no reason, however, why this implication *has* to be part of preschool preparation. Attendance at a well-staffed public nursery school can save a child much needless confusion and hurt when he does start school. It is true that there are more stimuli for a child in a slum home than are generally acknowledged. The spontaneity which many lower-income children show is, as Riessman points out, "a trait not ordinarily associated with a history of deficient stimulation." It is also true, however, that while lower-class children exhibit vivid, informal verbal expressiveness among themselves, they are often deficient in certain basic areas of verbal knowledge which a middle-class child acquires from his parents before he begins school.

A parent who returns from a day of demeaning work to an

overcrowded home is not likely to have the energy or the inclination to read picture books or play verbal games with his children. What conversation many slum children have with adults is frequently limited to receiving directions.

To take an illustration from an unusually deprived home, a five-year-old Negro boy who entered an integrated kindergarten in Westchester, New York, two years ago was tested and "found" to be mentally retarded. Asked to name an animal, he said, "Shoe." Asked to show where his nose was, he had no answer, This "dullness," however, was not inherent in the child. Apparently hardly anyone ever spoke at all in his home. After receiving special help, the boy went into the first grade, where he functioned at the average level of the class as a whole. If that youngster had been reached in nursery school, he might not have needed special aid in kindergarten. And if he had gone to a school where no compensatory education was given at all, he might well have been left in a "mentally retarded" class throughout his school years.

As it happens, that kindergarten was in Greenburgh District 8 in Westchester, where *each* kindergarten pupil is closely studied during his first weeks in school. If his academic prognosis appears to be poor, he is then given both academic and emotional help for the rest of the year. This practice of intensive research into the new pupil and his family is becoming more common throughout the country, but it is not nearly common enough.

A teacher who is aware of the strengths and weaknesses in the lower-class child's background can go on to work much more successfully with him than is now customary in slum schools. In his *Redbook* article in October 1963, "Not Like Other Children," Bernard Asbell has written of Mrs. Bailey Bishop, who teaches first grade in a predominantly Negro school in Chicago. Her children's IQ scores are low and their homes are culturally deprived by any standards. Mrs. Bishop ignores IQs and has no patience with such concepts as a standard first-grade vocabulary.

Mrs. Bishop knows that her children will be alert and receptive when they are interested in a subject. Her first task is to awaken that interest. When Asbell walked into the classroom, the children were reading about space capsules and oxygen. They knew what "weightlessness," among other words not in first-grade lists, meant. Mrs. Bishop had made the children curious about the concepts of gravity, weight, and weightlessness. Once curious, they were eager to find words for what they wanted to know, and they remembered those words.

There have been similar results in a fifth-grade class in central Harlem. Children came into a science class with poor reading skills and a distinctly limited vocabulary. Their teacher first interested them in the new subject matter by visual means. He showed them several experiments in electromagnetism, let them work the experiments themselves, and built up in his class a science vocabulary which considerably exceeded in length and complexity the standard Board of Education fifth-grade list.

The same children's reading teacher then used the words they had learned in science class to spur them in their lessons in language. She had them organize the new words in groups of sentences and in other ways and thereby she too turned a concrete set of experiences into an aid to teach more abstract knowledge.

Another example, related by Frank Riessman, is that of the substitute teacher who overheard two Negro children arguing about who was darker and why. "Do you want to talk about that?" the teacher asked the class. They did, and she went into a long discussion of physical anthropology, genetics, and race. The children were absorbed and, she recalled, "they wouldn't let me erase the words from the board until they had carefully copied them down."

Riessman has been a persistent advocate of the creative use of role-playing as another means to activate the interest of low-income children. In a May 1962 speech at a Washington conference on the education of disadvantaged children, Riessman told of the apparent inarticulateness of a group of slum children when he asked them why they were angry at their teachers. When, however, he set up a role-playing situation in which

books were given to 7000 Detroit elementary school students in the 1963–1964 academic year.

In New York the curriculum center at Mobilization for Youth, a multiple-purpose social agency on the lower East Side, has been creating readers aimed directly at Puerto Rican children. In one, A Place of My Own, Rosita lives in a crowded apartment, yearns for a place where she can be by herself, and finally constructs a home of her own out of a box which she places on the roof of her tenement. Her happiness is contagious, and each of her brothers and sisters builds a place of his own.

The draft of another, Benny and the Bomberos or the Stickball Game, begins with a group of children playing ball in the street and being yelled at by a truck driver. The ball gets lost, and in trying to retrieve it Benny starts up a fire escape which suddenly swings away, leaving him hanging high in the air. A fire truck comes to the rescue. "A huge man in a blue shirt picked up Benny gently. The man carried Benny down the ladder. On the ground Benny felt good. 'We have fires to go to,' the big man said to Benny. 'You must not climb on the building again.' Benny said, 'NUNCA, NEVER.' Benny felt good."

The history texts used in most public schools are as distorting for white and minority children as are the elementary readers. Here too reform has been slow. The magazine Integrated Education quotes from the Illinois School Code: "History of the Negro race may be taught in all public schools." "Is this really a privilege?" the editors ask.

In the summer of 1963 one hundred Negro students and teachers picketed the Chicago Board of Education. Among the signs they carried were: "Include the Negro in History!" and "Is History White?" They rejected any plan to teach Negro history as a separate unit. "We want to see," said one demonstrator, "Frederick Douglass, Henry Highland Garnet, Benjamin Banneker, and Nat Turner mentioned along with Washington, Jefferson, Franklin, and Paine."

Not only should Negro history be included in history courses given throughout the school system, but all teachers should be required to read a series of basic books concerning the cultural and historical backgrounds of the minority children in the school system. As a move in this direction the New York City Board of Education, in the fall of 1963, inaugurated a series of lectures on the Negro's role in American life for teachers enrolled in an in-service training course. At one of the lectures James Baldwin pointed to the absence of any indication in the usual lower-school text of how the Negro felt about slavery. "If you pretend," Baldwin told the prospective teachers, "that I hauled all that cotton for you just because I loved you, you're mad."

While new history books are being developed and published, supplementary texts for present books can at least be prepared by individual school systems with the aid of experts in Negro history. In Detroit in the spring of 1963, the Board of Education issued a new fifty-two-page booklet, *The Struggle for Freedom and Rights*, as a supplement to the history book in use in that city's eighth grades. The latter, *Our United States*, had been criticized by the NAACP for showing the Negro as a "dependent, servile creature." Actually, *Our United States* should have been scrapped and additional booklets substituted until a completely new text was ready, but the introduction of the supplement did at least provide eighth-graders with a more accurate knowledge of the achievements and trials of the American Negro.

As in everything else related to the "Negro problem," it will take pressure to bring changes in elementary readers and history texts. Acquiring superior teachers for the culturally disadvantaged child is a more complex problem. "It is clear," says Dr. Harry Rivlin, dean of teacher education at the City University of New York, "that even the most imaginative superintendent and the most cooperative board of education cannot solve the problems of urban education until the schools get an adequate supply of skilled and understanding teachers, and then makes optimum use of these teachers' abilities."

The suggestion of paying additional salary to induce a teacher to work in a "difficult" school makes little educational or moral sense. (Admittedly, the ultimate goal is to make extensive enough city-wide changes in a school system to eliminate "difficult schools," but until then the problem of teacher recruitment for slum schools will remain vital.) If a teacher can be interested in working at such a school only by an extra yearly increment, he is unlikely to be the kind of teacher the low-income child needs. There should be extra compensation for those schools—but in the form of more teachers and specialists, smaller classes, and additional teaching materials.

There is also the proposal that since the schools in disadvantaged neighborhoods usually have a disproportionate percentage of substitute and new teachers, a school board should no longer allow teachers with regular tenure to select the schools in which they want to work or to request transfers from slum schools.

A teacher *forced* to work in a slum school is bound to communicate his hostility to his pupils. The transitional answer is to use as many qualified teachers as volunteer, train new ones specifically for teaching low-income children, and, when necessary, retain able though unenthusiastic teachers until they can be replaced. By and large, a restive regular teacher is preferable to a complaining substitute in that the former can presumably communicate more information and skills to his class if he has any pride of profession.

As for recruiting new teachers for the disadvantaged, I agree with Edgar Z. Friedenberg that licensing requirements should be changed "to include a certain flexibility of mind, spontaneity of character, conceptual independence and joy in the presence of the young—broad categories all, and crude, but as such within the scope of projective testing today." And no matter where he is to be placed in the school system, the attitudes of a teacher on race should also be determined, so far as is possible.

Not that being free of bias is enough. As has been noted, a teacher of the deprived should also know minority history and culture and should be aware of the positive and negative elements in lower-class ways of life. For those already teaching, some of this knowledge can be absorbed by reading, by mandatory courses, and by regular required visits to the homes of the children in their classes.

Much more can be done to *prepare* prospective teachers. A particularly useful model in training teachers for work with low-income children is a project under way at Hunter College. A full description of the Hunter plan is provided by Vernon F. Haubrich, an assistant professor of education at the college, in his chapter in the Columbia Teachers College Publication *Education in Depressed Areas* (1963).

Part of the Hunter plan is that "prospective teachers should be specifically prepared in schools where they will eventually teach." In many sections of the country it will not be possible to have a student do field teaching in the system, let alone the school, in which he will begin his career. But it should be possible to train a future teacher in an actual classroom with disadvantaged children rather than in the characteristic university "laboratory schools," populated largely by children of the faculty and carefully selected pupils from the surrounding community.

The Hunter project is composed of volunteers. All the schools in which they are trained, Professor Haubrich notes, "have the classic problems of truancy, behavior difficulties, high teacher turnover, problems in language proficiency, low measured scores on verbal IQ tests, and a high percentage of families on welfare."

The students not only work a large number of hours under supervision in the schools, but they also get to know the community as a whole through regular visits to community leaders, social agencies, public housing developments, tenements, and the like. In the school itself the student teachers meet systematically with the school's regular personnel—guidance counselors, remedial reading teachers, truant officers, supervisory personnel—to learn from the pragmatic experience these professionals have acquired in years of working in depressed areas.

(I should note in passing that long-term experience in these schools is no guarantee that all the professionals on the staff have the quality of knowledge and understanding which slum children need. Therefore, more thought should be given to changing the automatic requirements in many school systems for promotion in schools with a high percentage of low-income children. Tenure and the mere passing of formal examinations will not insure that a school in a depressed area gets the best kind of supervision. A new set of criteria based on assessing a principal or assistant principal's specific skills in reaching the children in these schools should be substituted for present methods of promotion.)

There is an increasing number of teacher-training programs aimed at giving future teachers direct experience in the slums. Hopefully, as they learn how to reach low-income children, the student teachers will lose whatever stereotypes they started with concerning the "educability" of the disadvantaged and concerning the learning process itself. The degree of the need for these teachers is shown by an estimate made for the Ford Foundation by the Great Cities School Improvement Studies. In 1960 one child out of three in this country's fourteen largest cities was culturally deprived. By 1970 one out of every two children being educated in a big city will qualify for that classification. Unresolved is whether there will be enough teacher-training programs —and enough teacher volunteers—to meet the needs of those children in time.

More effort is also needed to recruit increasing numbers of minority youngsters into the teaching profession. This can be begun through concentrated encouragement by teachers in low-income schools of those pupils who appear to have the capacity for a teaching career. One way of intensifying the motivation of youngsters with this kind of potential is the Homework Helper program instituted by Mobilization for Youth in New York City. High school students within Mobilization's project area on the lower East Side are trained and paid to tutor neighborhood elementary school youngsters with academic problems. In the process, the tutor's own sense of achievement is heightened and he has the unprecedented experience of being rewarded materially for intellectual achievement. The federal government can also help greatly through scholarships and tuition subsidies to encourage youngsters of all colors and classes to prepare themselves for teaching as well as for other community service professions.

Focusing on the need for more and better-qualified teachers in depressed areas ought not to obscure another way in which the school can function more usefully—an expansion of its hours of operation. In New York City's all-day neighborhood schools, for instance, children with working mothers or with academic or personality problems benefit appreciably from an after-hours program in the school. There isn't, however, enough money in the school budget to establish nearly as many all-day neighborhood school programs as the city needs.

In Flint, Michigan, Charles Stewart Mott, a philanthropist, has provided funds so that schools in that city can remain open after regular class hours. In the additional time the schools provide a broad range of recreation programs and classes—advanced and remedial. At night parents return to the schools with their children for more courses and recreational activities. During summer vacations classes and play programs are continued at the schools.

Unfortunately there are not enough Charles Stewart Motts to go around, nor do most cities yet have ways to obtain the extra funds required for creating "community schools." With foundation help and with a growing municipal awareness of their worth, there *have* been major advances in this direction in some cities—Detroit and New Haven among them. But there are not enough such schools, just as there are not enough trained teachers for depressed areas, and not enough actual desegregation of schools. Far too many slum children still fit Joseph Lyford's description: "They act like leaves blowing in the street. They don't know they're important and no one is telling them."

11

The Circle of Failure

In the decades from 1870 to 1914 the American slum was merely the stopping place on the way to a job and a future. Today the slums fester with a frightening sort of permanence. We stockpile metals, rare minerals, ores and various other materials. What about the human resources? —Ralph McGill

The white man, he's not taking advantage of you in public like they doing in Birmingham, but he's killing you with that pencil and paper, brother.
> —A Negro boy in San Francisco, in *Take This Hammer,* a documentary distributed by the National Educational Television and Radio Center

Nearly a million young people are leaving our educational system each year before completing even elementary or secondary school. . . Two-thirds of the unemployed have less than a high school education. One of every twelve workers with only elementary schooling is unemployed compared with only one of seventy college graduates.
> —President Lyndon Johnson, report to Congress, March 9, 1964

ONE out of every three youngsters now in the fifth grade drops out of school before he is graduated from high school. While 75 per cent of white Americans now finish high school, only 40 per cent of the nonwhites do. Since the machines which are taking over more and more jobs now have, on the average, ability equivalent to a high school education, the future of the dropout is clear and grim.

"If present trends continue," says Thomas J. Watson, chairman of the board of International Business Machines, "by 1970 the United States will have in its cities more than a million and a half young people untrained, unemployed, and frustrated to the point of danger."

In this context there is reason for distinctly limited comfort in the fact that more salaried positions are opening for Negroes in professional, technical, administrative, sales, clerical, supervisory, and other white-collar positions. Despite this rarefied progress in recent years, the vast majority of employed Negroes are in low-income jobs. (As of 1963, 47 per cent of white workers were in white-collar positions, in contrast to 17 per cent of the Negroes in the work force.) And in most cases, whatever his job, the Negro earns less than a white who does equivalent work. Nor are Negro college graduates immune from this racial imbalance of income. A Negro male who completes four years of college can still expect to earn less than a white male with no more than eight years of elementary school. All in all, the median pay of the Negro worker in 1962 was only 55 per cent that of the white worker, a closing of the gap by just 1 per cent since 1947.

It is easy enough to continue marshaling statistics to outline the extent of the quicksand which is just ahead of many Negro youngsters and which has already entrapped their parents. The most frightening single statistic is that while 15 per cent of our youth population (sixteen to twenty-one) is Negro, more than half of those unemployed in that age range are black.

Grotesquely, the myth persists among many middle-class whites that even if advancing technology is making it more difficult for the poor to "improve" themselves, most of them, particularly the nonwhites, are lazy, prefer to exist on welfare, and drop out of school because they are inherently incapable of learning the more complex skills one must have to compete successfully in today's job market.

The problem of the poor, however, is not lack of will to work, but is rather lack of opportunity to get the training and the kind of work which will bring them a sense of achievement and a decent income. Similarly, as I noted earlier, youngsters drop out of school not because they can't or don't want to learn, but because they believe, usually correctly, that the instruction they're being given is not relevant to their needs.

There was considerable publicity in July 1963 when the National Education Association inaugurated a "crash" program to induce dropouts to return to school. Federal funds were provided to allow 600 guidance counselors in 62 communities in 23 states and the District of Columbia to go on a door-to-door campaign to recapture dropouts. The counselors netted 75,000 youngsters—12½ per cent of those who had left school from January 1, 1963, to the end of the school year. Quickly more and more of those 75,000 left school again, and at the end of 1963 it appeared certain that nine out of ten would be back on the streets. Why?

"Too many of them," Secretary of Labor Willard Wirtz has answered, "see their older brothers out of jobs, even though they completed high school, because there are not enough jobs to be had. Others found their schools still overcrowded and not geared to train them for jobs that are available."

In the previous chapter I focused on how the circle of failure is first drawn tight in the elementary schools. It is also necessary to consider a later solidification of failure—vocational education in the public schools. Throughout the country, while one-third of academic high school students drop out before graduation, two-thirds of those enrolled in vocational classes never finish high school.

The Taconic Foundation in March 1962 released a report by Mary Conway Kohler, *Youth and Work in New York City*. Her primary conclusion applies to the majority of vocational high schools throughout the country.

Only a fraction of students who enter vocational high schools receive any realistic and practical preparation for work. . . . It is extremely questionable, and certainly never has been demonstrated, whether the training absorbed by vocational high school graduates is useful to them in getting employment and advancing on the job. It is doubtful whether the enormous investment in the vocational schools and the high cost of instruction is bringing the expected return.

After much pressure, a Referral Committee of the Building Industry was set up in New York in 1963 to accelerate the placing of more Negroes and Puerto Ricans as apprentices and journeymen in building-trades unions. After five months of operation the committee reported that most of its members were shocked "that boys who were graduates of our Vocational High Schools or who had at least two years in these schools could not spell such words as 'brick,' 'carpenter,' 'building trades,' etc., or could not add inches and feet."

The Referral Committee was emphasizing defects in the applicants' education which had *preceded* their training in vocational schools. As for instruction in specific job skills, in one vocational high school in New York students in automotive shops are learning about engines from ten-year-old cars. In another, boys learn to repair radios with tubes instead of transistors. In a third, prospective airplane mechanics are taught on piston rather than jet engines.

A fundamental fault in conventional methods of vocational education within the public school system is that they continue the "tracks" begun in the elementary schools, which further widen and entrench class differences, particularly for minority children. There has been a trend away from separate vocational schools, especially in the Western states; but in too many of the big cities with rising Negro populations there is a far too early separation between academic and vocational pupils (often with a gray no man's land of "general education" programs in between).

An important study of vocational education was released in

October 1963 by the Public Education Association in New York City, with the help of a grant from the Taconic Foundation. The study, *Reorganizing Secondary Education in New York*, is applicable as well to many other school systems.

The disadvantages, the report states, of dividing students between separate academic and vocational high schools are: 1) children are forced to make a vocational choice before they're ready to, often as early as the eighth grade; 2) once set on either the vocational or the academic "track," the child finds it difficult to change, even when a shift in his own interests or a reassessment of his abilities indicates the need for a change; 3) starting specific vocational education at too young an age leads to inadequate concentration on the basic skills of writing, reading, arithmetic, and oral communication; 4) less time is given to social studies, "which are indispensable tools for understanding the responsibilities of citizenship in our complex society"; and 5) vocational students are not well enough prepared for "the broad skills and adaptability which are now required by rapid changes in technology," so rapid that in the decades ahead a man may have to learn a new occupation three or four times in his working life.

Finally, this extension of the "track" system encourages "*de facto* segregation by the placing of a great predominance of lower socioeconomic group members in a separate vocational school," thereby making it impossible for young people "to meet and work together in an educationally desirable and democratic atmosphere."

Among the recommendations of the study were: develop a single system of high schools with a basic but flexible curriculum to replace the present separate schools; encourage students to defer training in specific vocational skills until after high school, or at least until the last two years of high school; and offer vocational exploratory programs for all students (including those college-bound youngsters who may find nonacademic pursuits more satisfying eventually but who avoid looking into those fields because "of the status factors inherent in the present vocational-academic system").

The suggested curriculum flexibility would include provisions "for the needs of the rapid learner, the slow learner, the 'late bloomer,' and other students with special problems." The study also recommended programs by which employers and government would enable students who are not going on to college to work at jobs on a part-time basis while they continue their vocational education after high school.

In addition, the study contains a plan which could be utilized throughout the country:

> The school system, through its guidance, training and placement personnel, should assume responsibility for all young people until they are 21 years of age, employed full time or enrolled in an institution of higher learning. It is proposed that this be an informal rather than a legal obligation. The high school system should encourage the return of both graduates and dropouts for guidance and vocational training or retraining as the need arises. Procedures should be established so that employers notify school authorities when a youth loses his job or for some other reason becomes unemployed.

Another proposal concerns the establishment of "community skill centers" to "provide the specific vocational skill training for students which would supplement the proposed . . . vocational exploration courses in the high schools." These centers would be available "for high school or post high school students, for [adult] unemployed persons needing retraining or for local employees interested in upgrading their skills or preparing for new jobs. The training, insofar as possible, should be on an individual basis, adapted to the pace of the student, and should be open for his use either day or night. In addition, business and industry would be encouraged to use the skill centers as part of their own on-the-job training programs." In less densely populated sections than large cities, these could become "area skill centers."

What of the low-income youngsters who have no interest in vocational education and who want to go to college? I am not focusing here on ways to motivate the slum child to consider a college education, having indicated in the previous chapter some of the solutions in elementary schools to the problem of changing a child's negative self-image and low expectations. When an eighth-grade Negro pupil in Middletown, Connecticut, announced in class a couple of years ago that he intended to be a lawyer, his predominantly black classmates howled with laughter. In present educational systems it may sometimes be too late to counteract the self-imprisoning irony in that laughter by the time a Negro is already in high school.

Among those of the poor who now do want to attend college, the route is frequently blocked because of insufficient finances or because of inadequate high school training or below-standard grades. A vastly increased program of federal scholarship aid would help solve the first obstacle, but not the other two. Responsibility, therefore, also rests on the colleges themselves, according to the principle underlined by Dr. Homer D. Babbidge, president of the University of Connecticut: "In a society that has shifted its concern from *de jure* to *de facto* conditions, the burden that befalls a socially responsible institution is to pierce the veil of surface equity and make some positive effort to provide not only 'equality of opportunity' but 'opportunity for equality' as well."

Dr. Babbidge has suggested that the colleges can abandon "some stiff-necked notions of equality for the kid for whom so little has been done." He advocates "setting aside certain formal admissions requirements; providing special and extra tutorial, counseling and personal encouragement; providing extra financial aid to obviate the need for part-time work; permitting a lighter class load over a long period of time." The latter idea would involve a five-year undergraduate course as a means of making up for educational deficiencies caused by inferior elementary and secondary schools.

What may be an important pilot project in encouraging more children of the poor to *prepare* for college has been instituted by the City University in New York City. The project involves two tuition-free plans for disadvantaged students who would be selected for the project on the basis of "evidences of strong motivation and qualities of leadership and creativity" although their secondary-school grades were not up to the university's admission standards.

As described by Robert H. Terte in *The New York Times* of February 19, 1964:

> One plan calls for assigning 500 "special matriculants" a year for the next five years to two or more of the university's community colleges. While attending the two-year institutions the matriculants . . . would receive special counseling, remedial work in summer sessions and limited programs, where necessary, to enable them to continue in the colleges' programs.
>
> The second plan, developed in cooperation with the Board of Education, would establish "development centers" in five high schools primarily for selected students "who had not thought of going to college." The two-year program of these "schools within a school" would stress reading, writing, study skills and speech.
>
> All students who successfully completed the center's program would be admitted to the City University. [The City University includes Brooklyn, City, Hunter, and Queens Colleges as well as the Bronx, Queensborough and Staten Island Community Colleges, together with the new Kingsborough and Community College in Manhattan.]

In all planning about altering the educational system—from elementary school up—so that there will be real opportunity for equality, the major emphasis must be on reaching the mass of low-income youngsters. A danger in Higher Horizons, in college scholarships for high-ranking Negroes, and in similar approaches is that, as they succeed, the white community, its conscience soothed, does not recognize that surface amelioration is not enough.

In an exceptionally perceptive article, "Dropouts: A Political Problem," in the August 1963 issue of *Integrated Education,* S. M. Miller, a professor of education at Syracuse University, writes: "Helping the talented few is not solving problems of discrimination and avoids direct confrontation with a basic issue of contemporary American education. It may well be that our efforts at guided individual mobility may result in providing enough mobility to enough people so that pressure for real, basic, pervasive social change will not take place."

Throughout the entire spectrum of what must be done—from getting the funds for better schools to providing many more jobs in the economy as a whole—the basic lever for change is organization for political pressure. Any discussion of the problem of the Negro and of the poor which ignores politics is academic. And if there is to be mass support for "real, basic, pervasive social change," it is not going to begin with large numbers of the white middle class. As an entity, the dispossessed alone know how badly they live. The "underclass" does have the potential power to move the majority, but only the Negroes among them have begun to utilize that power, as yet in a limited and fragmented way.

Noel Day, executive director of the St. Mark Social Center in Roxbury, Massachusetts, and one of the most militant spokesmen for Negroes in Greater Boston, points out: "It is one of the ironies of the process of ghettoization in the North that it has created an immense concentration of power within a limited area and structured a situation where discontent can be shared easily and quickly."

The sharing of discontent, however, has to be increasingly channeled into specific programs, political action, and, where necessary, civil disobedience if the discontent is not simply to fester and if we are not to have a permanently and increasingly divided country.

THREE

12

Organizing for Action

> All this hollering over integration don't mean noth-
> ing to me. All them Negroes who are doing it hope to
> git something for themselves. All this stuff don't help
> people like me. I'm going to be working in a laundry
> all my life and there's no way to git out of it.
>
> —A Negro in Harlem, quoted in *The
> New York Times*, August 12, 1963

Where Negroes have no problem in registering
to vote, many nonetheless don't bother. In the ten largest Northern cities, from 25 to 50 per cent of eligible Negro voters are not
registered. When they do bother, the vast majority—Roy Wilkins puts the figure at 79 per cent—vote as Democrats.

How are more Negroes to be motivated to vote? Obviously
the most powerful stimulus to increased registration will be the
ability of a political candidate to convince the apathetic that he
is primarily concerned with *their* interests and that he has a
program which, if implemented, can bring basic changes in the
way they live, the kinds of jobs they can get, and the quality of
education their children receive.

To begin with one of the possibilities of accelerating the recruitment of Negroes for political action, there must inevitably, for the reasons cited at the end of Chapter 4, be more Negro candidates. To tell those Negroes who are distrustful of whites that it is "undemocratic" to vote by color would appear to them to be wildly ironic in view of what has happened to them because of their color.

In any case, Negroes are not represented in any equitable proportion in local, state, and national political power structures. So long, therefore, as Negroes are forced to remain residentially segregated, they can at least use their concentrated power potential to insure the presence of more black faces in legislatures and in executive offices.

One fear among many whites is that the growth of politics by color will result in more Adam Clayton Powells. It may, but here again the question is one of alternatives. So far as the Negro in Harlem is concerned, it is much easier to support Powell than to support any of the other possibilities offered up to now.

Powell continues to be re-elected because he is a Negro and because one of his roles is to make all whites uncomfortably aware that he is a Negro. "Most Negroes," as Roy Wilkins observes, "are in no position to talk back to white folks, but Congressman Powell is, and he does. That is the reason he's a hero up there in Harlem."

There is little illusion among his constituency that Powell is morally superior to the general run of politician. In fact, the kind of "race pride" which elects Powell partly reflects the cynicism among many in the ghetto who see how almost anyone goes about "making it" in the white world. Expert at detecting white hypocrisy, Powell's supporters admire his ability to use power as white men do.

They would applaud his having told Professor Eric Goldman on NBC-TV's *The Open Mind:* "I have a special responsibility of being the *equal* of every white man in the House and in the Senate." "Equal in evil as well as in good?" Goldman asked. Powell's answer proved how thoroughly he has absorbed the ethics of the majority. "It's not evil," said Powell, "if it is legal."

In addition, Adam Clayton Powell is more than the equal of the majority of whites in his accumulation of material comforts, and this "success" too is a factor in his mass support. "When Powell travels first class," Ernest Dunbar has noted in *Look*, "many a humble Negro travels with him vicariously." Another dividend—a daydream—comes from voting for Powell.

Not all Powell's strength is drawn from compensatory identification with him. Despite the large amounts of time he spends in Puerto Rico, Powell's presence has long been felt in Harlem in concretely visible terms. Since he was twenty-two, when he led a mass movement to end a ban against Negro doctors in Harlem Hospital, Powell has been active, locally and nationally, in many specific anti-discrimination campaigns.

He forced Consolidated Edison in New York to upgrade Negro workers; he was instrumental in getting the city's bus lines to hire Negro drivers and mechanics; and he was among the first to pressure white merchants along 125th Street in Harlem to employ more Negroes.

On his occasional visits to Washington, Powell has exposed discrimination in a number of government agencies and has leveled a minatory finger at railroad unions on the same count. Moreover, although the Harlem community at large may not be aware of the importance of the project, the $250,000,000 federal grant he obtained for Associated Community Teams—a pilot program for a domestic peace corps in Harlem, staffed by Negroes—has had valuable initial results. In short, Powell, for all his deficiencies, continues to convince his constituency that a Negro in office will *do* more for Negroes than a white man will.

It is easy enough to fault Powell's leadership on moral grounds and to lament that an A. Philip Randolph in Powell's position would have done much more to enhance the Negro's "image" among whites. Powell's inability to rise above the moral level of his white political colleagues is not, however, seen as a failure by his supporters, not only because of their cynicism about politics but also because they have long since come to the conclusion that being a "good" Negro is not in itself going to change the way most whites feel about and act toward Negroes, good and bad.

Yet Powell *has* been a failure—at understanding what needs to be done beyond treating "the problem" with palliatives. Powell's followers, for instance, point to his record as chairman of the House Education and Labor Committee. In the Eighty-seventh Congress he was able to get fourteen bills passed in fourteen months—an impressive numerical achievement. Powell did help push through the compromise Minimum Wage Bill, the Manpower Development and Training Act, and the Juvenile Delinquency and Youth Offenses Act. But, neither in Congress nor in his contacts with his constituents, has Powell clearly and consistently indicated how inadequate these bills are. Nor, for another example, has he been prominent among those who have advocated and supported practical plans for improving curricula, teacher-training, and the kinds of rezoning which would make possible faster integration of the schools.

Powell has failed in one of the most vital functions of a legislator: he has not educated his constituency on the issues most relevant to them nor has he stimulated them to do their own thinking and planning on these issues. Yet although *The New York Times* and others of Powell's critics have condemned him for his absenteeism, his junkets, and his increasing "black nationalism," Powell's failure to orient his electorate and to spur them to more organized, long-term action for basic change is not commented on in the white or Negro press.

When opponents, moreover, have been selected to run against Powell—and this would also apply to most other Negro machine politicians—they have been no more able educators and organizers for basic change than Powell. Having, therefore, been given no real alternatives to the coruscating Congressman who *does* tell the white folks off and who has engaged in *some* visible activity to diminish discrimination, the majority of Harlem's registered voters have had no real reason not to vote for Powell.

We may indeed have additional Adam Clayton Powells as pressure grows for more Negroes in office, but even an Adam

Clayton Powell cannot draw enough of the black masses into the political process. In his Congressional district, charismatic as Powell is, at least half the population over twenty-one is not registered. Therefore, for political action to become meaningful enough to convince more Negroes to vote, not only more black leaders are required but also black leaders of a different order from Powell.

Before suggesting where some of these qualitatively different leaders can be found, I think it necessary to point out that in the initial stages of stimulating more Negroes to participate in politics, the formation of all-Negro parties or all-Negro slates is not as automatically outrageous as *The New York Times* and other opponents of aggressive color-consciousness maintain. If such parties and slates are simply forums for bombast, they are, of course, of no use except perhaps to reduce the blood pressure of their members. But insofar as race-consciousness is going to help get greater numbers of Negroes involved in political activity during the transition period before a wholly open society (if that millennium occurs), all-black political movements can increase the awareness among some Negro poor of what the issues are, and can also get them used to using their votes.

For example, there is a nascent organization, the Freedom Now Party, formed by a group of Negro radical intellectuals "with an all-black slate and a platform for liberation." Its 1963 call to action included as an essential element of that party's platform a program "to create the basic economic changes needed to guarantee well-paid jobs for all. It's not enough to call for 'equal opportunity' when jobs, decent housing and schools are scarce even for whites."

New York attorney Conrad Lynn, who first announced the party's formation on August 28, 1963, made a point of emphasizing: "Today the Negro is at the bottom of the power structure. As he rises, he cannot help but lift the status of every other fellow American who suffers from existing evils."

In explaining the all-black nature of the Freedom Now Party, LaMarr Barron, acting chairman of the party's Michigan committee, has emphasized the following.

We are not racists; we do not want to oppress or exploit anybody because of their race or color. We are not anti-white; we know there are some whites who favor Freedom Now too, although unfortunately they are still few in numbers and power. We will gladly cooperate, after we have formed our own power, with any non-Negro persons, movements or parties that have the same goal we have.

But we want to control our own destiny, whoever we cooperate with, and that means we want to control our own political movement, work out our own political policies and tactics, have our own leadership. The best way to assure this is by having our own all-black party. This will also safeguard us against betrayal by whites, which has been the sad story of our people the last 100 years. We call this self-reliance, not racism.

We believe in the equality of the races, but until conditions of genuine equal opportunity are achieved, we think the best way to promote equality is through our own independent, self-controlled political action. Meanwhile I am not going to lose any sleep if white liberals don't understand or like it.

Clearly the Freedom Now Party, if it grows at all, will be extremely limited in numbers and power unless it reveals organizing skill and compelling leadership of unprecedented proportions. It could, however, be a small step in the direction of enrolling more Negroes in political action and in underlining the economic goals of that action.

The growing possibility meanwhile that the Muslims may finally engage in political activity can also have some positive results if that sect concentrates less of its energies on preaching hatred of whites and more on uniting with other Negro groups on particular programs for changing the conditions under which Negroes live.

At the end of 1963 there were increasing signs that the Muslims were muting their excoriation of whites to some degree and that they were planning more active cooperation with other Negro organizations. It was also evident that in many cases this cooperation might be accepted on a local basis.

When Akbar Muhammad, youngest son of Elijah Muhammad, leader of the Muslims, returned to the United States in

1963 after studying in Egypt and elsewhere in Africa, he told a Harlem rally in July: "We are not a racist group, but lovers of the black people. I don't hate any man because of the color of his skin. I look at a man's heart. I watch his actions, and I make my conclusions on the basis of what he does rather than how he looks." Akbar Muhammad went on to call for more cohesion among American Negroes: "No one group can obtain the maximum of freedom for the black man in America, but we can if all groups unite."

Admittedly, as long as rage at whites is a basic part of their stance, Muslim involvement in politics, on a narrow or broad basis, will appear to buttress the barriers against integration. But if the Muslims, with whatever strength they are able to muster, can be marshaled politically to help achieve more Negro opportunity to be equal, it may turn out that they will have aided in the creation of an objective situation in which their preachment of hatred will be much less effective. In other words, if in alliance with other Negro-led groups, Muslims could help elect in certain ghetto sections "race" men who were also aware that the pragmatic route to equality is in the achievement of more and better jobs, education, and housing for all the poor (including the white dispossessed as a practical political tactic), any resultant changes which brought those goals nearer could also lead to less black bitterness on which the race-hate doctrines of the Muslims could feed.

There has been no pronouncement as yet from the Muslims as to how they might focus their potential political strength. The Freedom Now Party, however, has a specific goal of electing from 25 to 50 Negro Congressmen within the next few years. It will indeed require more than that party alone to propel that number of Negroes into Congress. But on paper, in view of the large and growing numbers of Negroes in the big cities, it is certainly possible for more Negro Congressmen to be elected, and it is also possible to achieve other expansions of Negro political power, particularly as legislative reapportionment increases the value of urban votes. Malcolm X, who has broken away from the Muslims to form his own black nationalist political movement, is accurate in his emphasis on the fact that "Negroes still don't understand the power of the ballot in the North." As he announced his split with the Muslims in March 1964, Malcolm X said that one of his goals was to make Negroes understand that "Negro voters have it in their power to decide next November whether Johnson stays in the White House or goes back to his Texas cotton patch." For even the mesmeric Malcolm X to translate that "understanding" into a political movement, however, will require his devising a much more specific and realistic political program than he seems capable so far of producing.

White politicians, in any case, are already acutely aware that Negroes possess a balance of power in certain municipalities and that the Negro vote can be crucial in such states as New York, California, Pennsylvania, Illinois, and Michigan. For example, the late President Kennedy, who amassed huge pluralities in Negro precincts in 1960, won Illinois by only 9000 votes out of 4,757,000 cast, Michigan by 67,000 out of 3,318,000; and Missouri by 10,000 out of 1,934,000. In the city of Chicago, to pinpoint the Negro swing balance in Illinois, Kennedy received 64 per cent of the city's total vote but won 81 per cent of the Negro vote.

With regard to white candidates, a counter-argument to the value of the Negro swing vote is that as white resistance to Negro militancy increases, resentful white voters can swing elections the other way to candidates who agree with them that Negroes are moving "too fast." However, neither major party is likely to nominate such a candidate for a national ticket in view of the vital number of electoral votes in those Northern states where a candidate must at least profess agreement with the urgency of action toward "freedom now" to get both the Negro and the white liberal votes which are necessary to carry those areas.

In local contests another ironic corollary of residential segregation is that by virtue of the concentration of their numbers Negroes are more visibly intimidating to white politicians who cannot afford to lose all Negro support than is the anticipation of white resistance elsewhere in the district. Of course there are many large political divisions in which the Negro is in such a minority that he can be ignored with impunity; but where he has the power of numbers he must be reckoned with. Negroes are beginning to learn that they can use their ghettoized power for bargaining purposes much more effectively than has been the case so far.

To return to the possibility of increasing the Negro power of numbers through all-black organizations, there are, in addition to the Freedom Now Party, the Muslims, and the Malcolm X organization, more and more local Negro-led units, many of them still inchoate, which are gearing for political action. Nationally, this small, fragmented trend toward all-black political organizations can have only slight effect. I have mentioned this phenomenon, however, because it is persistent and, as I suggested, because it can be of transitional use in getting some of those Negroes who are presently apolitical into the habit of thinking in political terms.

As these all-Negro formations, moreover, also educate their recruits about the economic measures which have to be applied throughout the society, more potential allies will have been gained for that large *integrated* political fusion for full employment and concomitant goals which is being planned by such strategists as Bayard Rustin and other tacticians in SNCC, CORE, the Southern Christian Leadership Conference, and elsewhere in the civil rights movement.

I shall come back to the difficulties of setting up an ultimate alliance between black and white poor, the labor movement, and other possible sectors of power, but I point out here that I don't think planning in this direction is going to result in a third party. Pragmatically, the necessary legislative measures will come, if they do come, through reshaping of the Democratic Party.

In local situations, enlisting more Negroes in politics will have to include the taking over of Democratic organizations in the ghettos. In most cases now, whether local clubs are "reform" or "regular," it is a waste of effort to try to persuade the alienated to join those organizations. With few exceptions, the most meaningful pressures for change in the daily existence of the "underclass" have been initiated from outside the present political structure.

In New York City, for example, the Democratic organization is "liberal," includes a substantial proportion of "reform" clubs, and is integrated to a comparatively high level. Nonetheless, whatever increase has been made in motivating the Negro masses to act for themselves has been stimulated by direct-action demonstrations called by such groups as CORE and new protest organizations.

The first effective rent strikes in the city began autonomously in Harlem in the winter of 1963–1964. Local political leaders "endorsed" the action only after it had begun. Similarly, the most striking dramatizations of the need for change in the city's public school system has come from NAACP and Urban League exposés; from other forms of pressure by those groups; from CORE (and its demonstrations); and from increasing activity (including a boycott) by ghetto leaders who are not political functionaries.

The same pattern is evident in other Northern cities. Usually, whenever sizable numbers of previously apathetic Negro poor have been moved to organize, they have been led not by local Democratic leaders, but by direct actionists who have appealed to them on the basis of working on immediate changes in specific local problems of education, employment, and housing.

It is, therefore, from the direct-action movement that political take-overs of present political organizations in the ghettos can come. I do not mean that mass direct action should cease, but rather that, simultaneously with more cohesively planned demonstrations, the actionists should devote their energies and power to forming political clubs which can challenge the existing organizations, including most middle-class "reform" clubs, in primaries. In this way, militancy channeled into both direct action and political techniques should be able to draw more of the alienated into "the movement" while also strengthening the foundations of the new alliance being worked toward on a national basis.

Direct-action demonstrations will continue and will be intensified, in any case, not only because they have proved to be the most effective way of awakening the black poor, but also because there are some changes which need not and should not be postponed until they can be accomplished politically.

As Martin Luther King said after his failure in Albany, Georgia, in December 1961, "We attacked the political power structure instead of the economic power structure. You don't win against a political power structure where you don't have the votes. But you can win against an economic power structure when you have the economic power to make the difference between a merchant's profit and loss."

A common rebuttal by white "friends of the Negro" to the increase of Negro militancy through economic boycotts and other forms of harassment is that of James P. Mitchell, former Secretary of Labor and now human relations coordinator for San Francisco. In the January 3, 1964, issue of *Time*, Mitchell is quoted as warning: "Militancy could quite easily antagonize important people who are now prepared or preparing to do something. What Negroes have to remember is something they tend to forget: that they are a minority, and that they can only achieve what they want with the support of the majority."

I have seen no evidence that Negroes ever forget that they are a minority. Nor do they forget how slow "important people" have been to act. It is the contention of the direct-actionists that the majority must be confronted again and again with the nature of Negro demands before they really understand those demands. Secondly, where the Negro has power, it has been demonstrated again and again that changes can be made without waiting for the voluntary "support" of the majority.

A further illustration of white lack of understanding of so fundamental a fact at this stage of the "unfinished revolution" is the assertion by even as astute an historian as Oscar Handlin in the *Atlantic Monthly* for March 1964.

Sit-ins and street demonstrations are the only recourse in those areas of the South where the Negroes are excluded from political decisions and due process of law. But the same devices, used in Boston, New York, Philadelphia, and Chicago, reflect a misreading of the situation with unfortunate consequences. Negroes in those cities do have legitimate means of making their wants felt, and when they move outside those channels, they are likely to arouse antagonism that makes it more difficult to attain their immediate and ultimate goals.

On the contrary, the "misreading" is by Professor Handlin. Most beginnings in recent years toward change for Negroes in Northern cities have been as a result of their first moving "outside those channels." In this respect Dr. John C. Bennett, president of Union Theological Seminary, is a far more accurate historian of the present than is Professor Handlin. Speaking of the situation in New York, Dr. Bennett has pointed out that "the white people of New York are so far removed from the real dynamics of the problem that the Negroes have to apply more and more pressure. Without pressure, the white people always postpone. They never do enough."

Wyatt Tee Walker, executive secretary of the Southern Christian Leadership Conference, agrees: "We've got to have a crisis to bargain with. To take a moderate approach, hoping to get white help, doesn't work. They nail you to the cross, and it saps the enthusiasm of the followers. You've got to have a crisis."

Walker speaks of his experiences in the South, but his point is perhaps even more applicable in the North, where white resistance to Negro equality is more subtle, more rationalized than in the South. In the North, therefore, pressure to break through white evasiveness has to be greater.

Furthermore, in the North it is still harder to recruit the Negro masses than it is in the South because the Negro poor have been made much more cynical by their experiences with *de facto* segregation in cities where the laws are on their side. Accordingly, when they *are* moved to act for themselves, their enthusiasm for remaining in the ranks will be sapped all the more easily by waiting for "important" whites "who are now prepared or preparing to do something."

In addition, as I've tried to illustrate throughout this book, the problems to be resolved are too urgent to allow for more waiting until the majority recognizes that urgency. Nor, psychologically, is it possible for those Negroes committed to direct action to wait. Despite polls and despite the claims of some clergymen, editorial writers, and political figures that a significant change has taken place in the attitude of the majority of whites toward Negroes, that change has been far too small. The proof is the acuteness of the present crisis in race relations.

What the majority has not yet fully realized—and what only continued mass action will bring them to acknowledge—is that Negroes are demanding rights which are theirs. The concept of whites "conceding" or "granting" rights which already belong to Negroes is at the core of white confusion about Negro relentlessness. The point has become a cliché, but consider how obscured it can be in a specific instance.

In the fall of 1963 much criticism by white "friends" of the Negro was directed against Mrs. Gloria Richardson, head of the Nonviolent Action Committee in Cambridge, Maryland. After intense pressure by that committee to desegregate Cambridge, including its public accommodations, the local power structure finally decided to put a city charter amendment to the voters. If passed, the amendment would have opened public accommodations to Negroes. Mrs. Richardson urged her followers not to vote for that amendment, and as a result it was defeated.

Time magazine, reporting the story in its October 11, 1963, issue, termed Mrs. Richardson a "zealot"; added that "officials of other civil rights groups begged her to change her stand"; and concluded: "It all seemed a strange brand of leadership, particularly at a time when, in some parts of the U.S., her fellow Negroes were shedding blood in their struggle for the right to vote."

Yet in the body of the story *Time* had quoted Mrs. Richardson as having insisted it was wrong to submit "the constitutional rights of our people to the whim of a popular majority." *Time* failed to understand the neo-colonialism involved in letting a white majority determine whether Negroes were to exercise rights to which they were already entitled. For Mrs. Richardson to have agreed to this compact would indeed have been a "strange brand of leadership."

Or, as Dick Gregory puts it, "no Negro made the Constitution. It was all engineered by the white minds of America. Had we anything to do with it, you might say we'd tricked you. But we didn't, and you told people all over the world it's a just constitution. All we're saying now is TELL US."

So long as whites fail to understand this basic distinction between what they are "ready" to do and what they are constitutionally obligated to do, direct-action techniques will continue. Waiting for the courts to point this distinction out to the majority is much too slow a process, because the courts are limited in their enforcement powers to the extent that local communities can conduct a variety of delaying actions—including their own deliberately stalling recourse to the courts. Obviously cases must continue to be brought to court to reaffirm Negroes' rights, but for Negroes actually to get these rights will require supplementary direct action for years ahead.

I must re-emphasize that some of these rights will be empty when obtained if there aren't enough jobs to go around and not enough public expenditure for improved education and better housing. But a great deal can be and has been accomplished within the limitations of present possibilities, through direct-action techniques. In more and more cities Negroes are winning a higher share of what jobs are available by demonstrations and selective buying campaigns as well as by the threat of direct action. In case after case white employers who might have been "prepared or preparing to do something" have indeed been resentful of being pushed into immediate action; but when the economic pressure has been sizable and persistent enough to cut profits, most of them have yielded.

To cite one of hundreds of examples, a Philadelphia "selective buying" campaign, begun in 1960 and eventually involving 450 Negro ministers as organizers, resulted in the opening of some 3000 jobs to Negroes by the middle of 1963. By that time twenty-four concerns had been subjected to a boycott or had been threatened with one. Although some resisted, all of them eventually improved employment opportunities for Negroes. In a city in which Negro unemployment is more than twice that of white unemployment, 3000 jobs is not an impressive figure, but at least 3000 more Negroes have been able to live somewhat more comfortably than before.

Similarly, lie-ins, sit-ins, and picketing have ended discrimination at scores of new private housing developments throughout the North and West. In the context of the total housing problem for the poor, these victories for comparatively few, largely middle-class Negroes are slight; but again, there has at least been that much more momentum toward open housing as a result of direct action. And the gains made thereby have served to stimulate additional demonstrations by other groups elsewhere.

A particularly revealing illustration of the value of direct action is the New York City rent strike, which first received widespread local publicity in December 1963. There had been abortive rent strikes before, but this movement, started on November 1 in sixteen Harlem buildings, was better organized than its predecessors. By mid-December, it had grown to include 58 buildings and 850 families. A month later 300 buildings with 5000 families were involved, and the strike had begun to spread to the lower East Side, Brooklyn, and the Bronx. Its leader was a Negro, Jesse Gray, who had been a tailor before training himself as a community organizer.

Since the turn of the century New York City officials had regularly and earnestly promised decisive action to make slum apartments habitable. Laws were passed, building codes were strengthened and even enforced to a greater or lesser degree, but living conditions in sections of the ghettos remained appalling. By June 1963 Joseph Lyford had predicted: "Only when the Negroes have sit-in demonstrations in New York—when they lie down on the stairways in some of the slums in which they live—will they get better housing."

Under Jesse Gray's direction, the Harlem rent strikers did not lie down on stairways. They simply refused to pay rent. *The New York Times* editorialized on December 26, 1963:

> The rent strike building up a head of steam in some Harlem areas used methods that cannot be condoned to eliminate housing abuses that cannot be endured. The answer to better housing conditions is not the anarchy and lawlessness implied in a rent strike but the strict enforcement of the Building Code.
>
> Nonpayment of rent is inexcusable, but the rotten conditions that induce it must not be ignored. . . .

Yet were it not for the "inexcusable" methods the *Times* could not condone, the tenants who joined the rent strike would have had no alternative but to wait for "strict enforcement of the Building Code" at some vague future date. Mr. Gray's strike did not suddenly lead to resplendent renovation of the buildings involved, but, as a result of the way the strike dramatized slum living conditions, not only were newly diligent inspectors in larger numbers assigned to the buildings in question but new plans for legalizing rent strikes under certain conditions were started both in the city courts and in the state legislature.

In one resultant decision by a New York City Civil Court judge, the right was upheld of thirteen striking tenants to refuse rent to a landlord for apartments where serious violations of the building code existed. The strikers were directed to turn the rents over to the court. The offending landlord could then apply for the money only if he agreed to use it to correct those violations. Mayor Robert Wagner meanwhile proposed legislation which would in effect make rent strikes legal if conditions in a building constituted a major threat to public health and if the tenants agreed to pay the rents into a special fund which the city would use to make necessary repairs and provide necessary services—for which the landlord would be charged. Another bill introduced as a result of the rent strike provided that if a tenant does not have the "substantial benefit of the dwelling," he cannot be evicted or forced to pay rent.

The legislation, even if passed, will be no more effective than the present building code unless Jesse Gray and others like him keep large numbers of tenants in readiness for a strike if conditions do not improve or, if once improved, they deteriorate again. It is Gray's intent, reported in *The New York Times* for December 31, 1963:

> . . . to organize every slum tenement in Harlem. Each building would have a tenants' committee and the committee would call a strike whenever it believed that intolerable violations of the housing laws were ignored by the landlord.
>
> Then the committee treasurer would collect the rents and, instead of paying them to the landlord, would put them in a special account in a bank. The rentals would be held in an escrow account until the strike ended. [Or unless the courts or new legislation directed that the special fund be administered by the city or by a judge.]
>
> Mr. Gray hopes to force the city to take over tenement buildings under receivership laws. He knows that the owners often do not have funds to rehabilitate the buildings. The eventual solution, he believes, is a massive drive by the Federal government to eliminate slums.

Mr. Gray, therefore, would appear to be the kind of indigenous leader who knows both the values and limitations of short-term direct-action techniques, while also being aware of where the long-range solution lies. It is this type of leadership which could combine demonstrations and strikes with organizing the strikers and their sympathizers into neighborhood political groups.

Another illustration of the necessity of mass direct action when authorities are slow to move has been the use in New York City of the threat and the actuality of a school boycott to accelerate integration in the public school system. As I pointed out in the chapter on "Integrating Education," segregation has steadily risen in New York's schools, despite repeated proclamations by the Board of Education that its "intent" was to desegregate the schools as completely and swiftly as possible. Only after it was clear to the board that thousands of Negro parents were organized to press for their demands did it finally decide to apply the Princeton plan to more schools, begin to make major changes in the feeder patterns of junior high to senior high schools, start to study the educational park concept, and agree to the "elimination of the group intelligence test and the substitution for it of more valid indicators of ability."

Although direct action in the form of rent strikes and school boycotts has shown tangible results in New York City, what case can be made for those demonstrations which not only fail but further divide whites and Negroes? On June 18, 1963, for instance, as a result of an NAACP-directed boycott of the Boston public schools, over 8000 of the city's 28,000 junior- and senior-high-school students stayed out of class. Instead, they received instruction in Negro history and in the theory and practice of nonviolent resistance in ten "freedom schools" set up for that day in churches and social agencies.

The demonstration was caused in part by the refusal of four of the five members of the Boston School Committee—particularly its chairman, Mrs. Louise Day Hicks—to admit to the existence of *de facto* segregation in the public schools. The one-day boycott and other tactics, including an all-night sit-in at school committee headquarters, did not cause the committee to change its mind.

Moreover, the election for the school committee the following November revealed widespread white hostility to the NAACP's actions. Mrs. Hicks swept the field. The other members of the committee were also re-elected, but the only one sympathetic to the NAACP position, Arthur Gartland, ran far behind the rest of the incumbents.

A surface conclusion from this Boston experience would be that the boycott had been a failure and had actually created a wider split between the black and white communities than existed before. The leaders of the boycott believe, however, that theirs is the only route to ultimate victory. One of them, Noel Day, points out: "The boycott was a success in terms of getting the Negro community organized for action. It was never as united before the boycott as it has been since. Educationally, therefore, the boycott was very valuable, and as we call further boycotts, along with other kinds of direct action, we'll be able to make our strength felt more and more effectively."

And, in fact, when the entire Boston public school system was boycotted on February 26, 1964, 20,000 out of 92,000 pupils stayed out of school. Included in the total was the vast majority of the 14,000 Negro students in the system.

"It may come to the point," a young Negro actionist in Boston told me before the second boycott, "that we will have to tie up the city to prove how serious and how strong we are. I mean masses of people, standing immovable, in the key streets in the business section. Before the boycott, we couldn't have recruited enough people to make that sort of dislocation work. Now we can."

It is true that, as Negro action becomes more provocative, community tensions are more rawly exposed. But attempts to mute these tensions by delay and by compromises which cannot satisfy basic Negro needs will only postpone a much more explosive and bitter confrontation.

Another example of how a short-term failure insures the need for more, not less, direct action, was the Chicago school boycott of October 22, 1963, as a result of which 224,000 elementary and high school students (51 per cent of the total elementary and 38 per cent of the high school enrollment) stayed out of school to dramatize the conviction of Negro leaders that Superintendent of Schools Benjamin Willis was insufficiently sensitive to the amount of *de facto* segregation and to the poor education for Negro pupils in the Chicago schools. As in Boston, the boycott did not convert the Board of Education.

On the surface a second Chicago school boycott on February 25, 1964, appeared to have been a failure by contrast with the huge turnout the previous October. This time 172,000 students remained away from school—a drop of 52,000. However, the second boycott also involved a conflict between militant Negro actionists and entrenched Negro political figures in Chicago, along with the conservative leadership of the city's NAACP. Negro leaders in the local Democratic power bloc, including Negro Congressman William Dawson, opposed the second boycott in order not to have Democratic Mayor Richard Daley further embarrassed. The NAACP, having mildly supported the first boycott, also refused to participate in the second.

Of most significance was that Negro ward politicians—including five of the six Negro aldermen on the City Council—organized a countermovement to persuade Negro parents to send their children to school on February 25. (Schools in the ward of Alderman Kenneth Campbell, an anti-boycott leader, were, however, 90 per cent empty on that day.)

The fact, therefore, that as many as 172,000 pupils—most of them Negro—stayed out in the face of opposition from the traditional Negro power structure presages a determined assault on that power structure by the young members of CORE, the Student Nonviolent Coordinating Committee, and other civil rights groups which coordinated the second boycott.

Attacking what he termed "field hands" among local Negro politicians who, he claimed, "fronted for Daley and do his dirty work," boycott chairman Lawrence Landry, a twenty-eight-year-old Negro sociologist, warned that unless Mayor Daley fired Superintendent of Schools Benjamin Willis, there would be a Negro boycott of the November elections, thus damaging Daley's national status in the Democratic Party if President Lyndon Johnson were to lose a significant number of Chicago votes. Landry also began to plan weekly boycotts of the "worst" schools in Chicago and pointed out that his group would now speak for the city's Negroes on housing and welfare as well as on school problems.

In Chicago, then, the boycotts have not yet caused basic changes in the schools but they have helped organize the Negro community to work for change and they have provided the initial momentum for a political realignment in that community.

Until they have enough positive political power of their own to elect more people of their persuasion to the Board of Education, it may turn out that in order to bring about root changes in the Chicago school system, Negro parents may have to threaten to keep their children out of classes for weeks or months. "Responsible" white liberals deplore this tactic because of the delay it causes in a child's education. But what else are Negroes to do when what Oscar Handlin calls the "legitimate means of making their wants felt" do not lead to sufficient action? Furthermore, is there any doubt that if more than 200,-000 Chicago public school pupils were to remain out of school for a month or two months, basic changes would result quickly? And if their parents were to be convicted of breaking the law by encouraging a long-term boycott, is there enough jail space in Chicago to accommodate them?

In a situation such as Chicago's, it has become unrealistic to expect Negro parents to continue permitting inferior education for their children while waiting for "legitimate means" to work. They are beginning to learn from their two boycotts that, as Jesse Gray has said of the New York rent strikers, "Once you've got thousands of people not paying rents [or not sending their children to school], it's not a legal problem. It's a political problem." It is a political problem even when Negroes do not yet have enough power to change the Board of Education, as is shown by the fact that the local Democratic machine in Chicago has now been made fearful that Negroes already have enough potential negative political force—if they are fully organized—to injure that machine by withdrawing support from it.

Throughout the North, unless greater positive political power is achieved by Negroes more quickly than would seem to be possible and unless more whites become able to imagine themselves Negroes so that they can look at the schools, for example, as Negro parents do, not only will there be more direct action in the years ahead but a larger proportion of it will also take the form of civil disobedience.

One answer to the frequent question, "How can anyone decide *which* laws he will disobey?" has been given by many young demonstrators in the South whose civil disobedience has led to an ultimate decision by the Supreme Court that some of the local ordinances they broke were not lawful to begin with.

But what of those laws which will stand up in court? How can you justify breaking laws which in themselves are not unconstitutional? The answer is that if a man is willing to pay the consequences—jail and/or fine—for breaking a law he considers unjust or unequally enforced, there are situations in which he may feel that this is the most effective witness he can make for justice. Radical pacifists who refuse to pay income tax are in this category, and so are those Negro parents who protest laws which force them to send their children to *de facto* segregated schools.

To those who contend that mass civil disobedience, even when conducted in a disciplined, nonviolent manner, is an invitation to anarchy, Martin Luther King replies that he is more interested in justice than in order. Whites will not be able to persuade him—and those who believe as he does—to change that position so long as order in a community exists simultaneously with mass Negro deprivation.

There is rising concern among both whites and Negroes that direct action, including civil disobedience, may cease being nonviolent if major changes are too slow in coming. In the summer of 1963 Dr. King said: "The Negro is shedding his fear. My main concern is that this fearlessness will not become violence. I dare say that 85 per cent of the Negro population, if not 95 per cent, does not adhere to nonviolence or does not believe in it. They are allowing the nonviolent movement to go ahead because it's working."

The lack of belief in nonviolence as an all-encompassing philosophy is also true of a majority of the workers in the nonviolent movement itself. For all but a comparatively few, nonviolence is a tactic, not a way of life. After a two-and-a-half-year study of Negro college students in the Washington, D.C., area who had participated in demonstrations, Dr. Frederic Solomon, a teaching fellow in psychiatry at Howard University's College of Medicine, told a conference at the university in November 1963; "To these students, nonviolent techniques seem like a good strategy and their reason for not striking back when being physically abused is that it would 'hurt the movement.'" He cited what a twenty-one-year-old demonstrator had told him:

> I keep quiet when I'm getting beat up. Inside, I may be thinking, "God, if you are up there, now is the time to lend a hand. I believed in you for a long, long time." . . . but most often, I think to myself, "I'll get you one day. I'm going to chop you up one day. When I get the chance, I'm going to shoot you." Even though I try not to show how angry I am in my face.

As I mentioned at the beginning of this book, those whites are deluded who believe that a basic motivation of most non-violent demonstrators is to "save" the white man from his own self-corroding prejudices and fears. Some members of SNCC and CORE, and probably most of the ministers in the Southern Christian Leadership Conference, do believe that whites can be changed by "redemptive love." But most of those being recruited into mass direct action, particularly in the North, would agree with what Stokely Carmichael, a Howard University student, said at a 1963 SNCC–CORE conference: "We are not the redeemers of the nation. All we want is our civil rights."

In "Will Commitment to Nonviolence Last?" in the April 1963 issue of *Liberation*, Carleton Mabee, director of the Social Science Division at Delta College in Michigan, and a close student of the nonviolent movement, quoted a staff member of SNCC: "Slitting the throats of ten Mississippi legislators would be worth more than having ten thousand put in jail for nonviolent action."

Another demonstrator told Mabee: "My motivation for being in the movement is hate. I am an existentialist like Sartre. I just believe in *engagement*." And Norman Hill, National Program Director of CORE, admitted, Mabee wrote, that "there is a violent spirit in much nonviolence and it will not be easy to reduce it, he believes, because for some time to come, as the decline of segregation frees Negroes from their inhibitions, they will release more of their hostility."

Mabee concludes his article by observing that the participants in the nonviolent movement so far are mainly youths and the fact that "youths are naturally less disciplined than adults" makes their continuing nonviolence all the more impressive. "Their commitment, however," he adds, "will not necessarily continue. If they accept nonviolence merely as a tactic, as probably over ninety per cent of them do, their commitment is likely to continue (whether the movement turns increasingly to political activity or not) only if they receive a vigorous training in nonviolence and achieve a fair number of victories over segregation."

Mabee, then, joins Martin Luther King, James Baldwin, and other Negroes who warn of violence if those victories are not large enough and do not come soon enough. The warning is partly in itself a tactic to frighten the white folks, but it also reflects genuine worry.

It is difficult, however, to conceive of any disciplined, large-scale attempt to organize Negroes for violence unless frustrations spiral to such a height that large sections of the Negro poor will finally follow such leaders for want of any other way to release their bitterness and hatred.

Until desperation becomes that inflammable, no organized movement for violence is likely to take hold because even the most fiercely anti-white Negroes know violence will not work. This knowledge may not hold a man back when he sees a policeman beating another Negro or when he considers himself insulted by an individual white man. Nor does this knowledge deter some Negroes in the South and North from arming themselves for self-defense. But I have heard of no group which professes to believe that a Negro "army" can go on the offensive and achieve anything but their own destruction, however many white lives are lost in the process.

I do not make this point to bring comfort to whites who fear a Negro uprising. There may well be an increase in urban guerrilla warfare. But I do want to place the persistent warnings about Negro violence in a more realistic context. Mass Negro violence will only come, if it does, when it appears to be clear that none of the rational alternatives—demonstrations or court decisions or politics—are making basic enough changes in the way most Negroes live.

We are still in a stage at which these alternatives provide hope. On September 25, 1963, Bayard Rustin spoke at Community Church in New York concerning the future of the Negro movement following the March on Washington and the deaths by bombing of four Negro children in Birmingham. Among those in the audience were Muslims and a number of young Negro radicals who had been writing and speaking of the "bankruptcy" of nonviolence.

At one point in his address, Rustin shouted: "If there is a man here who advocates violence, let him stand up!" There was silence, and Rustin continued: "Let him stand up and I will show you a man who is prepared to do NOTHING—but talk." No one stood up, and in subsequent conversations I have had with those Negroes who feel nonviolence is becoming a useless tactic, all admitted the violence they did advocate was either defensive or a last, desperate self-assertion by immolation. No one believed the Negro could *win* if violence were sustained to the point of a mass racial clash.

There is still time, therefore, before, as Dr. John Morsell of the NAACP puts it, there will either be "violent reaction . . . or a profound and total disillusionment with all the processes of democratic government and the Negro will simply withdraw into an isolated, white-hating minority indigestible in the body politic."

This time can be best utilized in increased political action and more direct action—the former aimed at achieving programs for full employment and increased public expenditures for schools and housing, among other goals; and the latter used to accomplish short-term changes which will also serve to sustain the hopes of the Negro community.

In both politics and direct action a major problem is finding leaders with the capacity to bring more alienated Negroes into the movement. Additional organizers will come from civil rights groups, college students, and, increasingly, lower-class Negroes with leadership potential. Finding more of this last group, how-ever, can be considerably accelerated by using the skills of a relatively new order of social worker. Furthermore, some of these social workers themselves can become effective organizers of political and direct action.

Dr. Kenneth Clark, in an address to a New York conference of the old order of social workers on November 18, 1963, greatly disturbed his audience by asserting that the civil rights struggle had become "primarily a political one and has gone beyond the point where it can be influenced significantly by social workers." He added that social workers had been bypassed in the Negro's struggle for equal rights because they had permitted "a stagnant, stinking, corrupt structure to exist for years."

It is true that the traditional social-work approach, when it was not palpably "middle-class colonialism," focused too often on individual problems without taking sufficiently into account and trying to change the social and economic conditions from which the individual problems had emerged. As one of the new breed of social workers observes, many of those in his profession still, "quite unconsciously, see their jobs as a sedative for social ills rather than a good hard push for change."

Another count in Kenneth Clark's indictment of customary social work is his statement in the January 1963 issue of *American Child*:

> Voluntary agencies tend to retreat behind restricted defini-tions of programs or resort to such transparent jargon as "the hard to reach" in futile attempts to obscure the fact that those who are most desperately in need of their services are the least likely to be offered or given them. Indeed it is ironic to note the number of social agencies that restrict their in-take to those "who can accept help" or "who are ready for help."

An important shift of emphasis, however, has been taking place in the conception of social work in depressed areas. Basic to the newer concept is the obligation of the agency or team of workers to search out the most alienated and also to guide the neighborhood into organization for social change.

While individual case work may continue, an essential goal of this approach is to create the conviction within a low-income community that it *can* act collectively for itself in relation to the schools, the city government, urban renewal planners, and all those other outside forces which up to now have seemed no more responsive to the desires and concerns of the dispossessed than the weather.

Among examples of this way of stimulating the poor to take power is TWO (The Woodlawn Organization), organized in the fall of 1959 in a 90-per-cent Negro neighborhood on Chicago's South Side by sociologist Saul Alinsky as one of the projects of his Industrial Areas Foundation. TWO has since forced many changes in a projected urban renewal plan for Woodlawn. One result of its pressure is that demolition has been restricted to housing that cannot be rehabilitated instead of the whole neighborhood's being razed to construct middle-class housing which present residents cannot afford.

Through church and informal block clubs, more than half the 82,000 population of Woodlawn has been drawn into TWO. Among its other accomplishments, Elinor Richey has pointed out in "The Slum That Saved Itself" (*Progressive*, October 1963), TWO has "forced slum landlords to repair buildings, exposed and boycotted dishonest merchants, conducted voter-registration drives, and fed thousands during a welfare crisis."

Alinsky began by finding natural leaders in the community. Elinor Richey describes the process:

> . . . leaders in the sense of people with a following. Every-where angry little groups clustered around some respected spokesman: a hairdresser, cigar stand operator, mechanic or fry cook, each one castigating some facet of injustice. Sporadic instead of planned, isolated instead of joined, these were but guerrilla war cries. The task was to channel the power of this wafting, wasted fury into an offensive strong enough to force the city to listen to Woodlawn's demands.

> Soon these natural leaders were heading block groups affiliated with Alinsky's "Temporary Woodlawn Organization." Enlisted also were the established groups; union and trade

associations, social clubs, business organizations, churches, youth groups, and fraternal orders.

At one point a few years ago, TWO rounded up forty-six busloads of Woodlawn residents and brought them to City Hall to register. "Many of them," Alinsky recalls, "were weeping; others were saying, 'They're paying attention to us.' 'They're recognizing that we're people.'"

In Harlem finding ways to organize the community to act for itself has been a primary goal of both Associated Community Teams, the domestic peace corps operation there, and Harlem Youth Opportunities Unlimited. With the aid of a $230,000 federal grant and another $100,000 from the city of New York, the latter group has engaged in an intensive eighteen-month period of research and planning to devise a demonstration project for the youth of central Harlem which will require extensive federal financing (as much as $100,000,000). During the course of its research HARYOU also set up several pilot programs, among them a number of social-action projects.

The final plan, submitted in January 1964 by HARYOU in collaboration with Associated Community Teams, emphasized that any workable demonstration project to alter Negro youngsters' image of themselves must include—along with radically improved educational opportunities—"intelligently planned action for social changes with the youths themselves playing a pivotal role."

A similar approach is at the base of the Community Organization division of Mobilization for Youth, the three-year demonstration project on New York's lower East Side which started in 1962 with a $13,500,000 budget provided by federal and city sources along with help from the Ford Foundation.

Mobilization has a multitude of programs, from training youngsters in work habits and skills to suggesting curriculum changes in the neighborhood's schools. The most vital of its achievements so far, however, has been the ability of its Community Organization personnel to reach many Negroes and Puerto Ricans (adults and youngsters) who had had no previous contacts with other agencies on the lower East Side.

By various means many of these disaffiliated low-income people have been encouraged to form action units of their own, guided at first by Mobilization for Youth but intended eventually to function autonomously. Picketing and other forms of demonstrations are among the methods utilized by these groups —and encouraged by Mobilization—to fight discrimination, exploitation by slum landlords, and the inefficiency of city agencies.

One of the units, Mobilization for Mothers, has brought a number of previously alienated parents into active participation in school affairs. They maintain pressure on principals to raise the educational standards of the schools, and when a teacher or a principal is found to be prejudiced against Negro or Puerto Rican children, Mobilization for Mothers gathers its own members and other elements in the community to protest to the local assistant superintendent of schools and, when that doesn't work, to the Board of Education.

In terms of organizing the "underclass," there is an additional consequence of what Mobilization for Youth and similarly oriented agencies have begun. In what Frank Riessman calls a "revolution" in social work, increasing numbers of indigenous personnel are being hired to staff these programs. These recruits are nonprofessionals who live in the neighborhood and have the capacity to relate to the disaffiliated on a different and, in certain areas, more effective level than is possible for a professional social worker. The indigenous worker knows the problems of the neighborhood by experience. He has easier access to the "unreachable" than the professional is likely to have, and he faces none of the barriers of communication which often exist between the middle-class social worker and the poor.

Indigenous personnel are being used in a wide variety of roles —among them, guiding parents into active participation in school affairs; advising women on relief on how to deal with welfare and other agencies; and helping organize autonomous neighborhood groups for protests against bad housing, police brutality, and discrimination in employment in local stores.

Frank Riessman, a member of the training department of

Mobilization for Youth, estimates that "in light of the tre-
mendously expanded need envisioned in the next decade in the
helping professions—social work, teaching, nursing, etc.—there
is no reason why we cannot anticipate the employment of a
minimum of four to six million nonprofessionals in these fields."

Furthermore, a greater percentage of youngsters in slum neighborhoods can and should be motivated to go into social-service
work as professionals in view of the fact that more and more
former job categories are being swiftly decimated by automation.

It is from this expanding nucleus of indigenous service workers, nonprofessional and professional, that yet another sizable
source of leadership in political and mass direct action can come.
Not all, to be sure, will have the temperament or the driving
interest to extend their energies into political organization and
demonstrations. But experience in Mobilization for Youth and
other action-oriented agencies has already indicated that many
indigenous workers do become enthusiastic participants in and
organizers for social action.

They are also particularly qualified to find and develop leaders among the dispossessed. Frank Riessman points out in an
unpublished report, "The Revolution in Social Work: The New
Nonprofessional," that indigenous personnel "have a somewhat
unique opportunity to develop leadership in community people
who hitherto may have been overburdened with responsibilities
or problems and whose leadership potential has gone unrecog-
nized . . . through their informal personal contact they can
begin to encourage the expression of leadership and can provide
a kind of leadership 'training'—they can invite the parent or
tenant to a PTA or a House Committee, informally discuss
the meeting for days and weeks afterwards and reinforce any
latent desire the individual evidences to participate more
actively."

In sum, there is a large and growing reservoir of potential
leaders for political and other forms of social action among those
who know the problems and needs of the Negro first-hand: civil
rights actionists; the "new" social workers (particularly those
who are members of minority groups); the nonprofessional, in-

digenous personnel in social agencies and in other community action programs; and members of the "underclass" itself.

Whether leadership sources are fully utilized depends on the extent to which they are organized for maximum effectiveness, first in their own neighborhoods, and then as part of a national alliance which could be formed from existing civil rights organizations, the less somnolent sections of organized labor, and other groups of the underprivileged in addition to Negroes. With regard to the all-black units, as I noted before, even if they do not join in such an alliance, they will have at least stimulated their followers to think in terms of positive action. A Negro voting for Malcolm X for Congress is more valuable to himself and to everyone else than a Negro in the ghetto who is convinced there is *nothing* he can do to change himself and the ghetto.

Since this chapter was written, Mobilization for Youth in New York has been stifled by a combination of politicians and real-estate interests partly because Mobilization had encouraged rent strikes, picketing, and other forms of nascent community action *by* the poor themselves. The experience underlines Charles Silberman's point that those who want basic social change cannot expect the present government and the rest of the present establishment to help make their revolution for them.

Similarly, the clear indications that "community action" in the War on Poverty is, in most cases, not going to be led by the poor themselves further reveals both the need for the poor to insist on being their own policy-makers, inside or outside of government programs, and also the need for the poor to organize politically so that the government which does assist them financially will become responsible to *them* because more and more of them will be *in* the government.

The need for new leadership of the poor from the poor remains acute. The late Malcolm X could have become such a leader. Others must be found.

13

Beyond Civil Rights

> It will prove to be impossible to approach the equality of opportunity for Negroes without reviving and renewing the progressive movement in American politics, which has been quiescent for some ten years.
>
> —Walter Lippmann, *Newsweek*, July 8, 1963

> The poor in America are unorganized and largely mute. They exert no pressure corresponding to their numbers and to the severity of their plight. They are the least revolutionary proletariat in the world.
>
> —Gunnar Myrdal, *Challenge to Affluence* (1963)

> There are a half-million Negroes in our state working for less than fifty cents an hour. There are nearly a million unorganized Latin Americans in our state working for less than fifty cents an hour. . . . Civil rights means more than just doing something for the Negro . . . we can't win in Texas against the money changers that run the temple, called the state government, with just organized labor.
>
> —Hank Brown, President of the Texas AFL–CIO, in an address at the AFL–CIO convention in November 1963

WITH Negroes demonstrating in the streets, threatening and executing boycotts of businesses and schools, and otherwise thrusting themselves into the consciousness of whites, the "Negro problem" is loomingly visible. The problem of poverty, beneath and beyond the civil rights issue, is still, however, relatively easy for the affluent to evade.

The subject of poverty, to be sure, is being increasingly discussed in magazine articles and books; but the statistics cease to be astonishing after a while, and even case histories and pictures of individuals in the "underclass" are not immediate enough to be acutely disturbing to those who are not poor.

Soon after taking office, President Lyndon Johnson proposed an "unconditional war on poverty" and urged Congress to allocate a billion dollars for that war in the fiscal year beginning in July 1964. But even if Congress were to vote an annual two or three billion for this purpose, the sum would result in only token skirmishes. Within the possibilities of present American *Realpolitik,* no Congress within the coming decade is going to vote enough money for a radical attack on poverty unless enough of the poor organize to change the composition of Congress. As a Senate aide asked early in 1964, "How are you going to get most of these legislators that interested in the problem? No one around here really knows any poor people personally."

The estimated number of our "unorganized and largely mute" poor, as Gunnar Myrdal describes them, differs according to one's definition of poverty. In January 1964 the President's Council of Economic Advisers reported that there were 35,000,-000 Americans in poverty. (The council regards as poor those families with annual incomes of less than $3000 and unattached individuals who earn less than $1500 a year.)

In its April 1962 report, *Poverty and Deprivation in the U.S.,* the Conference on Economic Progress estimated the number of American poor at 38,000,000. The conference used an annual income of $4000 as the cutoff figure between families which are poor and those which are not. It also considered "unattached individuals" to be poor if they earned less than $2000 a year.

In addition to the 38,000,000 poor, the Conference on Economic Progress considers 39,000,000 more Americans to be living in a state of deprivation ("above poverty but short of minimum requirements for a modestly comfortable level of living.")

This group includes 37,000,000 with family income between $4000 and $5999 and 2,000,000 "unattached" with annual incomes of from $2000 to $2999.

So far as the Negro is concerned, the key paragraphs in *Poverty and Deprivation in the U.S.* are:

> More than 60 per cent of nonwhite families were living in poverty in 1960, contrasted with 28½ per cent of white families. . . . Almost 80 per cent of the nonwhite families were living in poverty or deprivation, contrasted with about 52 per cent of the whites.
>
> Looking at unattached individuals in 1960, about 66 per cent of the nonwhites were in poverty, contrasted with 52 per cent of the whites. . . . More than 80 per cent of the nonwhites were living in poverty and deprivation compared with less than 65 per cent of the whites.

Although nonwhites, of course, are not exclusively Negro, the bulk of that category is composed of Negroes. What has to be remembered, however, is that while there are proportionately more Negro than white poor, at least 75 per cent of *all* the poor are white.

The root of the problem is education and employment. It will not be enough to bring political pressure for as full employment as is possible under automation without also demanding huge amounts of public expenditure for improved education and for adult retraining. From now on, an increasing percentage of the jobs available will require high levels of skills.

What makes the prognosis for those currently out of work so bleak is that in 1963 two-thirds of the 4,322,000 recorded as being unemployed and seeking work had not finished high school and one-fifth had less than a sixth-grade education. There are other millions of Americans who have more education but who, without retraining, will not be equipped for the changing job market in the years ahead.

As for the children of the poor, the inferior education they are now receiving and the high dropout rates from the schools insure—unless there is major change—that most of those who are now born into poverty or deprivation will end their lives in the same condition. In New York State, for example, Dr. James Allen, Jr., the State Commissioner of Education, estimates that by 1970 there will be one low-paying, unskilled job available for every five youths who have less than a high school education.

If the poor, the underemployed, and the unemployed are to be organized to work for change in their own situation and to make their children's future more viable, the initial stimulus will come from the Negro movement because it already has a dynamism and a nucleus of organization. A major educative task among the leaders of that movement now is not only to recruit greater numbers of the Negro masses but also to emphasize the identification of the black poor with all the poor.

In her 1946 novel, *The Street*, Ann Petry sketched the beginning of this identification in a young Negro mother who goes to visit her son in the children's shelter. He had been apprehended for an act of delinquency which was directly related to the poverty in which he and his mother were living. The woman looks about the waiting room, noticing first that "it was filled with colored women, sitting in huddled-over positions." Gradually she realizes there are some white mothers there too: "They were sitting in the same shrinking, huddled positions. Perhaps, she thought, we're all here because we're all poor. Maybe it doesn't have anything to do with color."

It would be greatly misleading to tell the Negro poor that color has *nothing* to do with the way they live, but their perspective could be broadened by a recognition of how many non-whites are in economic traps similar to theirs. As of now, however, the Negro poor are far too preoccupied with survival and with the particular afflictions of being black to think in terms of a potential alliance between them and the white poor.

More and more of their leaders, however, *have* reached this point of recognition. Mrs. Gloria Richardson, as head of the Negro civil rights forces in Cambridge, Maryland, speaks of what has happened to the low-income whites who caused most of the disturbances during her group's demonstrations for equal rights: "When there was trouble, and the cops picked up on one of *them*, they'd be much rougher on him than us. That's because they're poor."

If it is going to be a difficult process for Negro leaders to convince those in the black ghetto that they have grounds for union with the white dispossessed, it will take an even longer time, as conditions are now, before low-income whites realize their community of interest with the Negro underclass.

In a column in *The New York Times* for November 10, 1963, James Reston, surveying the complexities and some of the successes of integrating neighborhoods in the prosperous Cleveland suburb of Shaker Heights, ended by writing: "Other Cleveland suburbs, however, are not the same and in many ways not so generous as Shaker Heights. Paradoxically the poorer areas are less generous with the Negro than the rich and, particularly where the Polish and Slovak populations come in contact with the Negro, there is much greater tension."

There is nothing enigmatic about the harshness of attitude toward Negroes in most poor white neighborhoods. Aside from the parochialism endemic to enclaves of the poor of any color, there is the very real fear among unskilled and semi-skilled whites that they will be the first victims of the accelerated Negro drive for job equality. There is the further truism that a white who is already low in status is often driven emotionally to "need" someone lower than he to look down on.

Largely ignored by organized labor and having as yet no indigenous leadership of their own, low-income whites gravitate, when they move at all, to politicians who capitalize on their prejudices. In the South, and increasingly in the North, those of the white dispossessed who do vote are supporting candidates who appear to promise continued racial segregation.

Ironically, Senator Richard B. Russell of Georgia, leader of the Senate segregationists, complained in a CBS-TV interview on July 17, 1963, that the condition of "the 20 million white people who are at the bottom of our economic heap is worse than that of our 20 million Negro citizens." He lamented that these white poor are being overlooked because they lack the "articulate" leadership of the Negroes and because comparatively few of them vote. Although his figure of 20 million white poor is too low, the Senator's analysis was correct so far as it went. The white poor do lack leaders, particularly leaders who can show them the need to unite on a class basis with all the alienated.

One of the beginning indications of awareness by the poor white of what *he* has to do to change his situation was a declaration in November 1963 by Berman Gibson, a leader of the unemployed miners in Hazard, Kentucky. In view of the severe poverty in eastern Kentucky, Gibson was enraged when the House Appropriations Committee that month rejected a $45,-000,000 public works plan for the region. It was a small enough expenditure of funds and would have provided only a thousand jobs over a four-month period.

"There's going to be nothing put through Congress to help the people," Gibson said after the Appropriations Committee rejection, "unless we get organized to do it. The 45 million wasn't enough; the people down there need more than a thousand jobs for four months. They need something permanent that they can depend on—and if we don't get it we are just going to have to get on the streets like the colored people."

In January 1964 Gibson led a delegation of miners to Washington. They talked with Congressmen and Federal officials and picketed the White House until one of President Johnson's aides finally met with them. Significantly, the miners' delegation received organizational help during their Washington visit from the Student Nonviolent Coordinating Committee. Members of SNCC and CORE also supported the picket line and were among the sponsors of a public rally. When the Kentucky miners decided to establish a permanent Washington base for lobbying and fund-raising, a SNCC member volunteered to be executive secretary and set up the miners' office in SNCC's Washington quarters.

Other examples of how the tactics of Negro civil rights actionists are beginning to influence some white workers in the South —admittedly a very small percentage of the unorganized so far— are included in the January 12, 1964, issue of the Retail, Wholesale and Department Store Union's *Record*. Describing the sudden increase in successful organizing drives by unions during the past year in the traditionally resistant South, the *Record* cites these possible auguries for the future:

> At a dairy in Winston-Salem, when the management refused to negotiate, a white worker took the floor to say, with an embarrassed grin: "Why don't we stand up and fight like them . . . like them Freedom Riders. . . ."
>
> At a feed mill in Charlotte, civil rights activity by the Negro workers brought grudging respect from white mechanics who had refused to join the union for 20 years, and this new respect plus old grievances brought them into the union.

Union organizers in the South are under no illusion that the majority of the unorganized white workers support the Negro drive for equality, but there is growing evidence that at least some of those in the white labor force have reached the point at which they recognize the need to adapt the Negroes' methods to their own problems.

James Pierce, who is in charge of Southern organizing for the AFL–CIO Industrial Union Department, tells of a plant in Statesville, North Carolina—Southern Screw Company—which had been impossible to organize for twenty-five years. After intense civil rights campaigns were begun in the town by Negroes, Pierce recalls, "We put out a leaflet at the plant. . . . I admit to some surprise at the result—one-third of the cards were signed and returned in three days, and by the end of the month we had petitioned for an election . . . we won it by 2 to 1." Pierce adds that the remark, "If the Negroes can do it, we can," is increasingly being heard in Southern organizing drives.

Illustrations of white labor commitment to *solidarity* with Negroes are much harder to find, but there are signs. The RWDSU *Record* reports:

> At a dairy in North Carolina, a committee of white workers leading the organizing drive listed workers they could trust [and] wrote down the names of every Negro worker in the place. "They got guts, and we need them," one committeeman said.

And at the annual AFL–CIO meeting in New York in November 1963 a delegate from a plumbers' union in Texas stated: "We will take our stand with the Negro, with the Latin American, or in ten years we'll not stand at all in our state."

As a matter of fact, an indication of what could be accomplished in an alliance which transcended racial divisions is the Democratic Coalition in Texas. Formed in June 1963, it includes some elements of organized labor, "independent" white liberals, Negroes, and PASO (The Political Association of Spanish-Speaking Organizations). The previous April, PASO and Local 36 of the International Brotherhood of Teamsters had organized a political revolt in Crystal City, Texas, which swept out of office the Anglo-Saxon minority which had always controlled the town. Elected in their place were five Mexican-Americans as Crystal City's Mayor and Council.

The vote potential at present of the Democratic Coalition is nearly half the total number of ballots cast in Texas in the 1960 Presidential election—500,000 Mexican-Americans, 400,000 union members, and 350,000 Negroes. In order for that potential to be fully realized, the coalition will have to undertake a huge job of conversion and persuasion among each element in the putative alliance and will also have to face the formidable opposition of the "regular" political and economic power structures in Texas. In any case, it is one initial design for the kind of fusion of forces which could take place in other sections of the country.

An illustration of some Negro thinking in the direction of forming new and broader alliances was the speech Bayard Rustin gave to the fourth annual conference of the Student Nonviolent Coordinating Committee, held in Washington, D.C., in December 1963. One of Rustin's contentions was that whites in SNCC and in other civil rights organizations should consider a new role for themselves as the civil rights movement broadened its goals to "join with other dispossessed groups in demanding basic social and economic reforms."

Among the projects Rustin suggested for Northern white actionists was that they work within their own communities to amass support for economic boycotts of Northern firms with economic power in Southern cities. In this manner they could begin to get more of the trade unionists and the white middle class in the North to come into an alliance with Negro workers in the South. The alliance would first involve a boycott, for example, of the nationally distributed products of Dan River Mills, the economic foundation of Danville, Virginia, a city which had been particularly resistant to integration.

From support of the boycott, this fusion of some among the Northern white middle class and trade unionists could go on to back specific regional and national political programs based on what Rustin calls "bolder concepts of social welfare, urban reconstruction, and economic planning."

Rustin's speech included another example of a new role for the white actionist:

> I would like to see some white people not put on jeans and go to Mississippi, [an act] which is for them a very simple job with all the glamour of being deeply associated with the Negro struggle. I challenge them to do something less glamorous and more real—to go into the white ghettos of the North, into West Virginia, into Kentucky, and identify yourselves, live on $20 a week like SNCC workers do, get to know those people, and get the white unemployed to join us in this struggle. Because, my friends, when the day comes that the white unemployed of this nation, using the spirit of the Negro movement, go into the street and adopt its tactic of dislocation and mass action, we are on our way to the first stage of a political alliance.

A few weeks later SNCC revealed that it was planning to send young white staff members into white Southern communities to organize the unemployed to act for themselves.

At the Washington conference of SNCC Rustin made a particular point of urging his listeners to overcome their cynicism about organized labor as a force for social change:

> I do not care how devilish the trade union movement is. One has to look at it the way one looks on the devilment of one's wife or cousin. It is part of our family; we cannot get along

without it. This conference was in part paid for by it, but that's only the beginning. . . . My proposal, therefore, is that a number of you, black and white, need to seek out responsible places in the trade union movement or to challenge the trade union movement wherever you are by organizing workers into tiny little units of ten people, whatever you can get. . . . Get men organized to demand their rights and to support the trade union movement effort to revitalize itself. . . . They are not doing enough. It is up to us to get them to do more.

In his speech, however, Rustin did not consider the question of how basic and widespread the trade union movement's "effort to revitalize itself" actually is. First of all, organized labor is decreasing in numbers. According to a Labor Department report in December 1963, total membership of unions with headquarters in the United States had dropped to 17,630,000 in 1962—a decline of 487,000 in two years. The figures for AFL–CIO unions showed a decline from 15,100,000 to 14,800,000. "The drop in membership," the Labor Department pointed out, "has been due to declining employment caused by structural shifts in the economy and lagging demand for the products of industry, rather than worker disaffection with the labor movement." But, it added, "there is as yet no evidence of a resurgence of organizing spirit comparable to that in the late 1930's and the early 1940's."

Labor's organizational failure is made clear by remembering that there is a work force in this country of at least 70,000,000 people. There have been and continue to be campaigns to organize more of the professional, technical, and clerical workers whose proportion of the work force increases along with automation. So far these campaigns have had indifferent success.

Notwithstanding the previously indicated rise in organizing activity in the South, labor unions throughout the country continue to be particularly weak in their efforts to organize workers with the lowest incomes, many of whom are members of minority groups. Nor has organized labor been concerned with the unemployed, including those of the unemployed who were union members when they lost their jobs. The concept of organizing the unemployed as a political force has entirely eluded labor officialdom—with a very few exceptions.

The Center for the Study of Democratic Institutions has published *Labor Looks at Labor*, a revealing discussion among a group of unidentified trade-union leaders from the United Auto Workers. One of them made the crucial point: "We have raised the trade-union member in many instances practically to a middle-class status, and he is the type we now deal with. Recently, a fellow came into our office from the research department of a large bank and asked us what had happened to the workers at Douglas after the big lay-off a couple of years back. We had to tell him that we didn't have the vaguest idea. When they got off the check-list, they were beyond our ken. And nobody else seemed to know what happened to them either."

As for low-income workers, another participant in the discussion asked whether there wasn't a tendency "on our part as a labor organization not to want to bother with certain people because it is beneath our dignity as staff representatives to sign a contract with a $1.35 wage rate in it. Aren't we a little ashamed to have people know that we associate with that sort of agreement? This is one of the things that has made Hoffa successful. He will go out and organize car-washers and negotiate a contract for $1.35 an hour, whereas we have a tendency to look only at those who are making $3 and $4 an hour so that we can have some pride in the type of agreement we negotiate. We have been forgetting the guy way down below who is really getting kicked in the face. Nobody is doing anything about him except Hoffa."

A. Philip Randolph has warned that, if labor continues to ignore the unemployed and the underpaid, it will "degenerate into a mere protection association, insulating the 'haves' from the 'have-nots' in the working class." In their speeches most labor leaders pay some rhetorical heed to Randolph's concern; but in actuality there are few major signs of "revitalization" of the labor movement in this context.

Following the 1963 AFL–CIO convention in New York, John

D. Pomfret, labor reporter for *The New York Times*, wrote a gloomy analysis of the current dynamism, or rather lack of it, in organized labor. In the *Times* for November 21, 1963, Pomfret noted that "a substantial number of the delegates appeared to be genuinely concerned with labor's problems," but

> . . . many union leaders have difficulty dealing with the broader problems that confront labor. They travel around the country negotiating contracts and settling internal problems. Many of them, immersed for years in the details of contracts, find it difficult to think in the general terms required by some of the large problems they face.
>
> Then, too, the unions have a disadvantage in their structure. The important element is the national union, not the federation. The federation has limited resources and virtually no authority over its constituents.
>
> Many of the problems the unions face, however, will require concerted action. The federation has been able to keep unions from quarreling to a remarkable degree, but it is open to question whether it can make them work together.

Pomfret interviewed one national union president, who apparently preferred not to be named, and the latter's statement focuses on a fundamental difficulty in any plan which counts on immediate help from much of organized labor in mobilizing the poor for political and social action: "Our organizations are essentially defensive. Even when we seem to be initiating, what we are doing is reacting to pressure from the outside—from the employers, for example, or the community or the Negroes." The problem, therefore, is whether the civil rights movement can bring *enough* "pressure from the outside" to activate the present leadership of organized labor to seek out the dispossessed.

Complicating the problem even further is the fact that, in 1964, there is only limited hope of radical change in the quality of labor leadership as older officials retire. In *The New York Times* for November 13, 1963, John Pomfret pointed out accurately that "unions do almost nothing to assure that talented men are brought along, preferring in most cases to leave the selection [of new leaders] to political processes that are primitive and random."

An additional reason why organized labor at present has a re-stricted potential for any new broad coalition is the fact that, as labor expert A. H. Raskin pointed out in *The Reporter*, De-cember 5, 1963, "in its present role . . . it is becoming a politi-cal company union, tied to the Democrats but with little evident ability to influence their policies."

Many of organized labor's programs for full employment, for example, are well conceived, but labor so far has shown little desire to press hard enough for these programs when that pres-sure might mean a serious break with a Democratic administra-tion. The quality of the alliance envisioned by Bayard Rustin and by others of his persuasion in civil rights groups would re-quire a labor movement which would be a great deal more in-sistent in its demands for social and political reforms than cur-rent labor leaders have been. What is necessary is the kind of insistence which would lead organized labor to support—much more often than it does now—candidates with bold programs for change, even when those candidates are in opposition to regular Democratic party choices.

In fact, a "revitalized" labor movement would, in collabora-tion with civil rights groups and other elements of the new alliance, *search out* the most qualified and radical (in the de-notative sense of the word) candidates and help finance their campaigns.

I am not sanguine about so basic a change occurring within most of the labor movement during this decade. It may be that if enough pressure is put on the more restive and social-action-oriented sections of organized labor, the "new populism" can get the support of an important minority of the labor move-ment. There is a likelihood, moreover, that as unemployment grows among previously stable segments of the industrial labor force, there may also be increasing pressure from *within* certain unions to force them into more militant social and political activities. It is illusory, however, to count on the majority of organized labor to be in the vanguard of the alliance for which Rustin calls.

What if no such alliance can be put together in significant

enough numbers within the next decade or so to bring about orderly change? One possibility, as has been suggested, is the presence of a permanent inert underclass, much of it on the dole.

Another possibility is contained in a paper, "Towards a Corporate America," delivered by Professor Andrew Hacker of Cornell University at the fifty-ninth annual conference of the American Political Science Association in New York in September 1963. Professor Hacker speculated that as accelerated automation contracts that part of America which is "protected by the corporate umbrella," the other part, "the society of losers, may grow in number and power with increasing rapidity. . . . If this pool grows to substantial proportions, if it finds political leadership, if it gives vent to its resentments and frustrations, then, and perhaps then only, will a force arise to challenge the great corporate institutions. For then power will meet power, the power of a mass movement confronting the power of machine. The discard heap the machine created may arise to devour its progenitor. . . . The resolution will not be a pleasant one."

14

The New Equality

The means are at hand to fulfill the age-old dream: poverty can now be abolished. How long shall we ignore this underdeveloped nation in our midst? How long shall we look the other way while our fellow human beings suffer? How long?

—Michael Harrington, *The Other America* (1962)

There will be a Negro President of this country, but it will not be the country we are sitting in now.

—James Baldwin

IT IS because the awakening of the white conscience and the achievement of civil rights are not enough to bring the Negro fully into this society that the fundamental goal of "the movement" must become the acquisition of power, particularly political power.

In a September 29, 1963, column, Walter Lippmann distilled the present state of "the unfinished revolution." Lippmann wrote: "It is probable, therefore, that while the Negroes will prevail in regard to the first wave of their grievances, the removal of the badges of slavery, no substantial improvement of their general economic condition is likely to come soon. For this will require the conquest of dire poverty, and the country is not now ready for such an undertaking."

The country is not ready and Congress is not ready. Without some form of powerful neo-Populist alliance to accomplish basic change, the country will be no more ready in 1970, and the likeli-

hood is that there will then be at least 11,000,000 unemployed
—some 13 per cent of the 87,000,000 work force projected by
the Labor Department for the beginning of the next decade.
Joseph Lyford of the Center for the Study of Democratic Institutions is more pessimistic. He estimates there "may very well
be" 14,000,000 unemployed by 1970.

As Michael Harrington says, the means are at hand to end
poverty, and so are the plans. It is not within the scope of this
book to present a detailed blueprint for socioeconomic change,
nor, in any case, am I an economist. However, a variety of resourceful proposals are available. Gunnar Myrdal has broadly
outlined a direction for the future in *Challenge to Affluence*
(1963). Among the sources for more specific plans are John
H. G. Pierson's *Insuring Full Employment* (1964), Michael D.
Reagan's *The Managed Economy* (1964), Robert Theobald's
Free Men and Free Markets (1963), Congressman Henry
Reuss's *The Critical Decade* (1964), and the Conference on
Economic Progress's *Key Policies for Full Employment* (1963).

All I propose to indicate here in part is the scope of what
could be accomplished for those most in need if the country and
the Congress were made ready. In addition, for example, to
much more adequate tax-reduction programs to increase purchasing power among low- and middle-income groups, a vast
program of construction is vitally needed—including housing,
schools, hospitals, public health and rehabilitation centers, and
urban transportation systems. Required would be a long-range,
comprehensive federal program, much more ambitious than any
yet proposed and involving federal loans, financial guarantees,
and direct grants-in-aid to state and local governments.

In education alone, while local school-bond issues and budgets
are being defeated all over the country, at least two million children go to school in outmoded, hazardous buildings. There is
currently a shortage of at least 125,000 public school classrooms.
School buildings with an average of more than 25 pupils per
classroom now contain 22,000,000 of the 40,200,000 children in
school. There are 10,600,000 youngsters in schools where the
average class size is more than 30. Meanwhile the population

increases. Frank E. Karelsen, president of the Public Education Association in New York, has estimated that a minimum annual national expenditure of $4,000,000,000 for the next five years is needed for the most essential improvements in school buildings, classroom materials, and the hiring of more teachers (including more fully qualified teachers). If, as is being increasingly advocated, compulsory free public school education should be extended to include junior college, additional funds will be needed for that purpose. As for colleges, a February 1964 report by the Ford Foundation's Educational Facilities Laboratories warned that by 1970 there will be a shortage—at present rates of construction—of more than a million seats in American colleges and universities. The report urged greatly increased planning and financial commitment by the community, and that means primarily the federal government, if we are not to have a growth of "academic slums" in the 1970s.

The lack of national planning on all levels of education has caused the situation described by Robert Hutchins: "We have been content to regard education as the responsibility of 50 states, which have delegated their duties to 40,000 local school boards. The result is that we are the only country in the West without an educational system. We have a lot of schools, but no national policy, or national plan, or national thought in regard to them." It is partly because of the absence of national standards that, as Hutchins adds, "in 1960 almost four million children between the ages of 13 and 17 were not in school. In 1960 more than eight per cent of the population 25 years of age or older had not gone beyond the fifth grade. Forty per cent had not gone beyond the eighth grade. Only half had finished high school."

As part of national planning, a much more comprehensive program is also required to train and retrain dropouts, the millions of undereducated adult unemployed, and those whose present skills will soon be obsolete. We also have to recognize, as John I. Snyder, president and chairman of U.S. Industries, Inc., emphasizes, that our present retraining techniques are inadequate in terms of making a significant number of the hard-core unemployed re-employable. New methods must be found.

If retraining, moreover, is to cope successfully with growing structural unemployment, this country will have to devise adaptations on a mass scale of the Swedish policy by which the government does more than pay the cost of retraining workers. When jobs die out in a particular locality, the Swedish government finances the transportation to and rehousing of displaced workers in more economically viable areas.

Greatly increased federal planning will also be essential with regard to developing additional methods by which the unemployed can be helped to find jobs. The United States Employment Service, for example, should become much more of a *national* job placement and counseling service. As Edward T. Chase points out in the March 1964 issue of *Progressive*, "Today, the U.S. Employment Service is federally financed but run by the states. Its operations are locally oriented and its offices stigmatized as 'unemployment offices' rather than centers for employment." Chase recommends:

> A reformed U.S.E.S. would provide up-to-the-minute regional and national employment trends information in all its 1,900 offices; expert interviewing, testing, counseling, and placement services for all skill levels; and a real source of information on job openings. The latter could be achieved by making it compulsory for larger firms to list openings with the U.S.E.S. (but with no compulsion that firms have to hire only applicants referred by the U.S.E.S.).

In Sweden, incidentally, all employers are required to inform the National Employment Service in advance—usually two months ahead—of impending shutdowns, thereby easing the readjustment of the work force. As for Chase's suggestion of a source of "up-to-the-minute regional and national employment trends," the present situation, as Dr. Arthur F. Burns of the National Bureau of Economic Research has pointed out, is that there is a "deplorable" lack of statistics on job openings. He recommends that a clearing house of national statistics on job vacancies be established by means of automation. With the aid of electronic computers, Professor Burns explains, "an unemployed worker expressing his need or preference to an officer of an employment exchange might be referred in a matter of hours, if not minutes, to a list of potential employers, outside his community if there are none in his own, who need that type of employee. Employers could be served in a similar way." Although employers should be expected to pay part of the cost of such a computer information service, the plan could not get under way without an initial federal grant and continued federal support.

Also part of any comprehensive campaign to diminish the size of the "other America" is an increase in federal and local minimum wage levels, an extension of minimum wage legislation to many more of the sixteen million workers not now covered, and a rise in unemployment benefits together with an expansion of the number of those entitled to such benefits.

Social services for the underclass are also grossly inadequate. For example, according to the Department of Health, Education, and Welfare, only one out of every six of the country's impoverished children is currently reached by the aid for dependent children program. In only fifteen states, moreover, at the end of 1963, was it possible for families to receive this form of public assistance payment when a parent was unemployed. "In all the other states," Dr. Ellen Winston, Commissioner of Welfare, noted, "no matter how needy the children may be, such aid is limited to families in which the father is dead, incapacitated, or absent from home."

For those past the age of work, an extension of social-security coverage and a rise in social-security payments are essential, along with an increase in other forms of protection. Currently, eight million of the elderly have no hospitalization insurance at all and most of the other ten million are inadequately covered. Far too many of the old in America have to live their last years on a minimum of income and dignity. Yet, Gunnar Myrdal notes in *Challenge to Affluence*: "In Sweden all persons over sixty-seven will now, in stable currency, be guaranteed an income which, up to a fairly high level, shall amount to two thirds of what they earned in their best years. . . . The United States is equally rich as Sweden. Most Americans believe they are much richer. They could certainly afford to be more generous to the old generation."

What of those who are not old but who will be incapable of being relocated or of being retrained—those who are psychologically unable to begin again in a new area and those whose educational deficiencies are so great that they can acquire only limited technical skills? There have been suggestions that the government become a master employer of these underskilled workers rather than allow them to vegetate on relief.

The government as an employer could provide jobs in the construction of public works as well as in soil-conservation, flood-control, reforestation, and other socially useful services that do not require high levels of skills. In addition, some of these men and women could be trained for various forms of social work, as outlined in the chapter "Organizing for Action."

Nonetheless, the great likelihood, as automation increases, is that sizable numbers may be left for whom there will not be enough hours of work, whether governmentally or privately supplied, to guarantee a reasonable income.

What may be the ultimate answer, but the one most difficult to implement politically, is that of Robert Theobald in *Free Men and Free Markets*. He proposes "a basis of distribution of income which is not tied to work as a measure." Much of his book is devoted to proving that "we can have meaningful leisure rather than destructive unemployment; a socially determined rate and process of development rather than forced and destructive maximum rates of economic growth; a flexible decentralized socioeconomic system rather than a destructive movement toward centralized, dictatorial rule."

There is no point in my summarizing here the nature of Professor Theobald's plan because, although it is economically feasible, we are far from the point at which anyone who is now in Congress would vote for this essential element in it:

> We will need to adopt the concept of an absolute constitutional right to an income. This would guarantee to every citizen of the United States and to every person who has

resided within the United States for a period of five consecutive years, the right to an income from the federal government sufficient to enable him to live with dignity. No government agency, judicial body or other organization whatsoever should have the power to suspend or limit any payments assured by these guarantees.

I have mentioned Professor Theobald's approach primarily to indicate how unprecedentedly bold and far-ranging economic planning for the age of automation will have to be if poverty is to be ended. Within the possibilities of the pragmatic present, however, it is going to be difficult enough to amass the political pressure to achieve the more limited, incomplete list of programs for economic and social change which have been outlined in this chapter as well as to convince Congress of the logic of greatly reducing armament expenditure now that we have achieved "overkill" capacity, in order to transfer those funds to programs designed to meet human needs and to create many more jobs than are now possible in the increasingly automated defense industries.

There is, moreover, an additional area of major concern. I touched on it in the discussion of Norman Mailer's theories in the chapter on "The Mystery of Black." Essentially the concern is that even if the transformation of the black and white underclass into moderate affluence can be accomplished, the *quality* of American life, as now reflected in the emotional grayness of the middle class, would not be any different.

Unless the values of the society are changed, such social critics as Paul Goodman and A. J. Muste warn, we will have an integrated society in which poverty may no longer be a problem but which will continue to be based on acquisitiveness, peace-through-terror, and the shallowness of inner imagination which is revealed by the kinds of television programs which have the highest ratings.

There is, however, a prospect that if, through socially oriented planning, the economy of abundance which is possible with automation can be extended to all, the resultant change in the distribution and definition of work could alter our values. It is that kind of society in which the constitutional right to an income advocated by Professor Theobald would not necessarily carry with it the connotation of large numbers of the citizenry vegetating on the dole.

Professor Theobald recognizes that "the guarantee of an income only provides freedom *from* want, freedom *from* complete dependence on an employer, and freedom *from* the necessity of complete conformity to the prevailing views of society. An Economic Security Plan can only give a man the means to be free; it will not ensure that he will use those means. The discovery of the proper uses of freedom is the fundamental task of the remainder of the twentieth century. It is already clear, however, that we have the ability to be the modern Greeks, with mechanical slaves taking the place of human toil, if we can find a way to use abundance to our advantage."

Even without the adoption of the Theobald prescription for an economic security plan, the economy can be so altered as to make feasible the hope of Gerald Piel, publisher of *Scientific American*: "The liberation of people from tasks unworthy of human capacity should now begin to free that capacity for a host of activities now neglected in our civilization: teaching and learning, fundamental scientific investigation, the performing and the graphic arts, letters, the crafts, politics and social service."

If, for example, the very process of education—aside from the provision of more classrooms and teachers—were to be much more deeply explored and changed to awaken the full capacities of our children, they need not grow up as emotionally and intellectually blocked as most of us are. For them, as they become adults, the increased expanse of leisure time made inevitable as automation increases would be a further means of growth not, as would be the case with many of their parents, of further stultification.

In such a society, moreover, with its increasing emphasis on employment in human services, many of those ideas of Paul Goodman which appear impractical now would be entirely workable. In the October 5, 1963, issue of *The New Republic*,

Goodman called for alternative educational opportunities for youngsters who, for various reasons of temperament and interest, prefer not to continue within the formal educational system.

Now, as Goodman knows, "all must go to school—or drop out of the economy." But in a society in which the technical and professional jobs which require extended schooling are easily filled and there is a surplus of labor which can be paid for doing socially meaningful work, it would be possible to provide such alternative educational opportunities suggested by Goodman as:

> . . . improving 50,000 ugly small towns; youth work camps in conservation and urban renewal; countervailing mass communications with hundreds of little theatres, little radio, local papers . . . community service like Friends Service and Peace Corps. In such concrete activities, directly useful in society, millions of youth could find educational opportunity more tailored to their needs.

The point is that planning need not be synonymous with regimentation. A democratically planned economy, based on the application of resources to the meeting of the genuine needs of all Americans, can provide much more diversity of opportunity for meaningful work and leisure than now exists. Poverty can be eradicated without creating overstuffed homogeneity. On the other hand, a fragmentarily planned economy, such as ours now is, cannot solve the human problems of automation and will not allow most of the poor to escape from their ghettos.

Accordingly, Bayard Rustin could not be more cogent in his recurring advice to today's civil rights actionists to "think in terms not only of mass action but of a political and economic program which will alter the outdated assumptions now held by the majority in this society" and to "think of how to find and encourage the greatest possible number of allies in what must be done."

Their numbers are few. The projected broad new alliance is inchoate. But if the thrust of Negro demands for the new equality continues to increase—and there is every expectation that it will—the momentum for extending "the movement" into political action will also be greatly accelerated.

Although the odds at present are heavily against a major re-education of the electorate within this decade, the civil rights actionists may startle us again. The ultimate irony in American race relations may yet be that the bitter insistence of the Negro revolt will have provided the initial impetus for basic social and economic change for all Americans. Having gone beyond morality to power in order to achieve its aims, "the movement" may have begun to create a society in which morality will be the normative principle in action.

Epilogue

Since this book was written, I have become even more convinced that basic social and economic change is essential if there is to be a "new equality" and that this change is not going to occur at first as the result of the kind of broad-based coalition being called for by Bayard Rustin. I have dedicated this book to him in gratitude for what he has taught me, but at this point in time the situation does not allow me to agree with his analysis of what must be done now. (See Rustin's "From Protest to Politics" in the February 1964 *Commentary*.)

The stubborn fact is that not nearly enough of today's labor leaders, churchmen, and white liberals yet realize that, as Joseph Lyford emphasizes, "The demand of the civil rights movement cannot be fulfilled within the present context of society. The Negro is trying to enter a social community and the tradition of work-and-income which are in the process of vanishing for even the hitherto privileged white worker."

For labor to be part of any meaningful coalition, there will have to be a new kind of organized labor. "Ways must be found," Ben Seligman notes in the Winter 1965 *Dissent*, "to organize and represent workers thrown out of jobs by automation; ways must be found to organize and consider the millions of ill-paid 'marginal' workers who scrape along on the minimum wage and suffer the consequences of racial discrimination. Perhaps new structures will be needed, amalgamated unions of workers cutting across industrial lines, just as in the thirties the CIO cut across craft lines. But the time to think, to worry, to discuss is now, when there are still a few years of grace."

There is no more time of grace for millions now in the underclass, and time is swiftly running out for their children. A labor movement which is, as of now, primarily concerned with protecting its own by facing the future in a defensive stance of attrition, is of small help in a coalition with the poor. Organized labor will have to change radically if it is to help bring about a radically new society.

Obviously what is needed for change is a redistribution of power. There is no question that eventually a broad-based alliance will be essential, but to act as if it is about to exist now is to act so unrealistically as to slow down any possibilities of basic change.

The kind of power that might begin to lead to structural alteration of the society is going to come first, if it comes at all, from the ghettos. Later there will be allies from labor as unions continue to diminish in membership and as cybernation cuts more and more pitilessly into the lives and aspirations of white workers and *their* children. And later still, those in middle-management and in certain other kinds of doomed white-collar work will also be driven by painful self-interest to become allies.

But right now, the necessity—as SNCC, the Northern Student Movement, sections of CORE, independent urban groups in the ghettos, newly emerging independent political movements such as the Brooklyn Freedom Democratic Party, and similar groups realize—is to start the poor organizing themselves. And in most cases, the initial dynamism—if any—will be among the black poor because their "years of grace" are the smallest.

Admittedly this is an extraordinarily difficult route—beginning first by organizing around inflamed, specific local issues; moving on to other problems as their interconnections become clear; linking up with other "community unions" throughout the country; and thereby amassing power. I mean both political power in the narrow sense and the other kinds of power that can come from an informed, cohesive mass of people.

It is true, as noted earlier in this book, that more and more of the center cities contain growing percentages of blacks. So long as these ghettos continue, that maximization of potential black power can work to begin to end the slums. Bill Strickland, executive director of the Northern Student Movement, makes the corollary point that as the cities grow—and as their needs multiply—it must become clearer that in many of their functions, as related to cities, state legislatures are anachronistic.

"The movement," Strickland says, "has to create new political forms by which those in the city can deal much more directly with the Federal Government—with, let us say, a new Department of Urban Affairs—where the quantities of money are that can help make change in the city." And, Strickland adds, in those cities in which black political power can be amassed in sufficient numbers, the planning and the expenditure of funds must be proportionately controlled by political leaders from—and directly responsible to—the black ghettos.

If this predominantly black leadership were to have sufficiently comprehensive and humanistic programs, they could so radically improve the schools, the mass transit systems, and the way the city looks that many whites would return from increasingly graceless and dehumanized suburbia. By then, moreover, Negroes will have the organized power to be a newly *equal* part of any broad-based coalition resulting from a reaction by more and more whites as well as to the danger of a technological society run by a technological elite.

Admittedly these black movements in the ghettos are infant developments so far and have not yet become even strong enough to deal with a crucial problem as described in the Winter 1965 *Studies on the Left*: "The problem of connecting up these issues with the consciousness of the need for an over-all transformation, in such a way that local power structures will not be able to co-opt the movements by granting parts or all of immediate demands . . ."

I am not certain that this route will work, but I do not see any other in this decade, particularly as Lyndon Johnson's "politics of consensus" (which does not include the underclass among the decision-makers) becomes stronger. What is somewhat encouraging is that most of those working full-time in the ghettos toward a radical change in society are recognizing that they cannot bring in and try to superimpose sectarian ideologies or pre-set tactical glossaries on the poor as the poor find indigenous leaders and reason to move to action. This has to be an existential series of discoveries of what will work to make change.

Arthur Finch of the Boston Action Group (BAG), part of the Northern Student Movement, says, "There is a conflict among civil rights 'theoreticians' as to whether the movement is revolutionary or reformist in character. We, on the other hand, opt for what we can get and take." But implicit in BAG's program is the awareness that, while it is necessary to take whatever can be gotten, meliorism will not fulfill the fundamental needs of those in the ghetto.

And Richard Flacks, an assistant professor at the University of Chicago, writes in the February 1965 issue of the Students for a Democratic Society *Bulletin*, "There ARE times and places where local activists will see the need to work in and with liberal coalitions. One such time and place may be certain Southern areas right now. Or, putting it another way, there are times and places where radicals must absolutely eschew top-down liberal coalition and organize radical constituencies—for example, cities like Chicago or New York right now."

In sum, it is not a question of doctrinaire refusal to work now in particular liberal coalitions for particular goals. It's necessary to take what you can get, but it is also necessary not to be detoured or co-opted in the process. The criteria of any action by any section of the new movement for a new equality beyond civil rights is whether that action—from demonstrations to politics—moves toward real, palpable change in the way the poor live. And, especially in the new age of cybernation, the most important changes cannot come, as Joseph Lyford says, "within the present context of society."

Ultimately, if the movement is to succeed, it must be radical in the denotative sense of that word—getting at the root of problems and of power. Anything less will simply delay the defeat of all the rest of the society as well, except perhaps for the technological elite. And they, as Jacques Ellul has indicated, will themselves be under the control of the technology they have created.

We are at the last exit before the "great society" of 1984.

—N. H.

April 1965